Dear Grandma♡ XOXO —and ~~~~~♡

I know you'll have

time to read this on

your next flight to

somewhere exotic!

love always

Adrienne

LAURELS

Eight Women Poets

∾

We wish to thank Betty Parry for assisting in the interview with Josephine Jacobsen, Marybeth Shea for research on Louise Bogan, Jean Johnson for help in acquiring photographs, Barbara Shaw for typesetting and layout design and Jay Richards for consulting and advising with our printer, McNaughton and Gunn.

LAURELS
Eight Women Poets

Stacy Johnson Tuthill
Editor

SCOP Publications, Inc.
1998

LAURELS: Eight Women Poets
Copyright © by SCOP Publications, Inc. 1998
Library of Congress Catalog number 97-91288
Hard Cover: ISBN 0-930526-23-6
First edition.

Cover and title-page photograph by Joshua A. Bousel is of the front
steps, Jefferson Building, Library of Congress

Photograph of Gwendolyn Brooks by Lee Radziminski

Photograph of Rita Dove by Fred Viebahn

Photograph of Mona Van Duyn by Miriam Berkley, courtesy of the
Library of Congress.

Photographs of Léonie Adams, Elizabeth Bishop, Louise Bogan,
Maxine Kumin, and Josephine Jacobsen appear through courtesy of
the Library of Congress. Photo collections were obtained through
the Library of Congress Photoduplication Service.

Acknowledgments begin on page 183.

Produced, in part, by a mini-grant from the Maryland State Arts
Council.

SCOP Publications, Inc.
Box #9383
Catonsville, MD 21228

CONTENTS

Maxine Kumin ∾   81
interview by Ann B. Knox

Gwendolyn Brooks ∾ 111
essay by Stacy Tuthill, poem selection by Brooks

Mona Van Duyn ∾ 147
essay and poem selection by Jean H. Johnson

Errata
page 11, line 26
30 years, read 20 years

NTRODUCTION

This book is entirely an initiative of Scop Publications, Inc. Board members have chosen to bring together the views and poems of the eight women poets who have served as Consultants or Poets Laureate to the Library of Congress. Thus, while there is no "official" sponsorship of this volume by the Library's Poetry and Literature Program, I am pleased to confirm that these eight poets have enlarged and enriched, not only the nation's store of poetry, but its availability to the nation's readers of all ages and backgrounds.

First-rate poetry speaks to all conditions; Consultants and Laureates have generally interpreted their role as an amplifier of poetry's voice and an attractor of new audiences. I believe that the essays in this volume demonstrate the differing ways in which these eight poets conceived their role at the Library, while sharing common imperatives inherent in the poet's vocation. The Consultant/Laureate position at the Library is deliberately defined in a minimal fashion to allow each poet to channel energy and evocative imagination in ways that seem natural to her.

We are pleased that through their appointments to this position the Library has been able to contribute modestly to public recognition of these poets and their poetry and to enable them in turn to call attention to the significance of poetry for the nation's psyche. To fulfill an emotional need, to provide the sudden slant of a new perspective, poetry has to be within the mind's reach, has to be available within the intellectual pharmacopoeia. As Amherst's Emily put it:

> This was a Poet—It is That
> Distills amazing sense
> From ordinary Meanings—
> And Attar so immense

From the familiar species
That perished by the Door—
We wonder it was not Ourselves
Arrested it-before...

Prosser Gifford, Director
Scholarly Programs
Library of Congress

# EDITOR'S NOTES

This book had its inception as the editors of SCOP Publications, Inc. were searching for a way to celebrate the twenty-first anniversary of the press. We have come of age. Although we have had men on our Board of Directors, all six members are now women. We found our means of celebration by honoring the eight women who have been Consultants in Poetry to the Library of Congress or Poets Laureate.

The title, Consultant in Poetry to the Library of Congress, was established 1936; the first consultant, Joseph Auslander, took office in 1937. In 1963, Senator Spark M. Matsunaga of Hawaii first introduced legislation to designate the position "Poet Laureate Consultant in Poetry." The bill, after repeated introduction, was signed into law twenty-two years later on December 3. 1985 during the term of Gwendolyn Brooks. In his bill, Matsunaga encouraged the government to make use of the Poet Laureate for ceremonial occasions, and added that the work of the individual chosen "should not be impaired."

The first consultants, seeking to find their way, established precedents that have lasted, such as poetry readings, recordings of poets' work, and archival acquisitions. However, the poets chosen have been at liberty to be creative and develop their own programs within limitations of a few prescribed duties. It came to our attention that over the past sixty years, although we have a flood of talented women poets in the United States, only eight have been selected. It came to our attention, also, that after the term of Elizabeth Bishop approximately 30 years elapsed before another woman, Josephine Jacobsen, was offered the position.

This little book is not intended to be an academic treatise on poetry, Laureates or the Consultancy. It was our hope that people interested in poetry might gain some insight into what it might be like to work as Poet Laureate at the Library of Congress and acquire new appreciation for the talent and hard work involved.

We wish to note here the Library of Congress of the United States had no part in the production of this publication. Staff members neither encouraged nor condoned our efforts but were courteous and helpful in finding material. For this we thank Jenny Rutland of the Poetry Office. Prosser Gifford, Director of Scholarly Programs, and Nancy Galbraith, now retired. We are also indebted to the Library of Congress Photoduplication Service for acquiring photographs, and to William McGuire who generously agreed to let us use material from his magnificent book, *Poetry's Catbird Seat*. A special thanks is due Jayne Landis Silva, an original founder of SCOP, and now a retired federal government executive, who for twenty-one years donated her time as treasurer, record keeper, and submitter of state and federal tax-exempt forms. Her quiet, unselfish, and dedicated support has been an inspiration.

LOUISE BOGAN

1945–1946

LOUISE BOGAN

Jean H. Johnson, Stacy Tuthill, Marybeth Shea

Louise Bogan, the first woman poetry consultant, came from New York City to the Library of Congress with honors and a national reputation. She had published four books of poems. Marianne Moore says of her book, *Poems and New Poems*, "She uses a kind of forged rhetoric that nevertheless seems inevitable," and Malcolm Crowley writes, "She has added a dozen or more to our small stock of memorable lyrics. She has added nothing whatever to our inexhaustible store of trash." W.H. Auden praises her by saying that what she has written "is of permanent value" (Frank 319.320).

She began writing in the lyrical tradition of Edna St. Vincent Millay, Elinor Wylie, and Sara Teasdale. Her work changed with the publication of *The Sleeping Fury* after she became acquainted with French Symbolists, the work of Hopkins, Pound, Eliot, Auden, and the English metaphysical movement (Ridgeway 20. 22). Her work grew deeper, richer in subject matter, and more complex in tone. Louis Untermeyer in his anthology, Modern American Poetry, 1932, praises her "mind which is as sensitized as the eye is sharp" (Untermeyer 735). She worked for many years as Poetry Editor of *The New Yorker* where her reviews were influential.

All of her adult life, Bogan was plagued with depression which she believes began when she visited her old childhood neighborhood in Boston. She grew up in an unattractive suburb at the end of the trolley line. Her parents were incompatible, only marginally prosperous, and for a time were separated. Bogan had two unsuccessful marriages. The first, at eighteen, and against her mother's wishes, was to an officer in the United States Army who took her to live in the Panama Canal Zone and then to Nova Scotia. The marriage lasted about two years. The only joy was the birth of her daughter Matilda, called Maidie. Her second marriage to Raymond Holden lasted nine years. According to her notes in *Journey Around My Room*, her marriage to Holden was destroyed when Bogan returned early from a Guggenheim Fellowship in Italy to find her husband's mistress had rearranged the furniture and redecorated her house. She had other losses also. At one time, her house burned destroying all her papers. On another occasion, when evicted from an apartment, she had a "mild illumination" of the importance of money after watching the sheriff stand in her house while the furniture was whisked out the door onto the sidewalk (Limmer xxxix). In 1931 and again in 1933, she admitted herself to a neurological institute for treatment for depression.

From the time her first poem was published in *The Jabberwock*, the magazine of Girls' Latin School in Boston, her first loyalty was to literature. She reports she disliked writing prose, but to support herself, she wrote reviews for *The New Republic, The New Yorker*, and other magazines, eventually becoming proficient. She dropped out of college at Boston University after the first year, but her New England classical education enabled her to continue growing through extensive reading. Among her many loyal friends were Edmund Wilson with whom she read Shakespeare and translated Goethe two nights a week, Morton Dauwin Zabel, who acted as a literary mentor, Rolfe Humphries, and Theodore Roethke. She was a private person, and it was not until she came to Washington that she began to attend social affairs and enjoyed giving readings and teaching seminars.

When Bogan was asked to be the first woman Consultant to the Library of Congress, she was already a Fellow at the Library, was acquainted with the other Fellows, and with the requirements of the position. She subleased an apartment in Georgetown where she developed a lasting friendship with her neighbor, Katie Louchheim. Louchheim later wrote of Bogan, "She laughed a lot, her laughter was deep in her throat and mocking. There was something diabolic about her, this was a woman one could both admire and fear" (McGuire 93).

Her main assignment as Consultant was to compile a bibliography of the little magazines of Great Britain devoted to poetry from the years 1939–1946. Despite difficulties brought on by the war, she collected 978 entries. She also began a reading program in the Coolidge Auditorium for members of the Library's Writers' Club, including primarily poems which had appeared in *The Washington Post*. She continued the project initiated by Archibald MacLeish of poets recording their own poems. Although this first album of records, financed by the Bollingen Foundation, was not completed during her tenure, she persuaded Auden to read, and with the help of Allen Tate, T.S. Eliot agreed to record for her (McGuire 94). She reviewed existing recordings to determine which were most effectively read by the authors. Her own recordings were acknowledged as among the best. William Jay Smith wrote in a tribute after her death in 1970, "With her rich contralto voice, she has the most perfect enunciation that you will encounter among poets today; every consonant, every vowel, every syllable is given its proper value and then there are the pauses around which the poems are constructed, all carefully observed" (McGuire 94).

After a glowing appraisal of her writing, Allen Tate wrote, "...But Miss Bogan is a craftsman in the masculine mode" (Collins 42). This is an especially interesting observation since her Bennington speech, "What the Women Said," September 3, 1962 published in *Journey Around My Room* (Limmer 134-58) is as feminist as anything written today.

Bogan began writing her lecture with the intention of speaking on women poets and poetics, but her inclinations led her to write about women throughout history, selected women writers, and the lack of recognition for accomplished work. Her quotes from both men and women were witty, appropriate, and sometimes profound. In a letter to a friend, October 1, 1962 she writes, "The audience at Bennington laughed in all the right places — and it was a *well-written* lecture."

Bogan is noted for the delicacy of her poetry, the perceptive-

ness of her criticism, and the capable manner in which she ful-
filled her position at the Library of Congress. She is still remem-
bered by people who knew her for her elegance, intelligence, and
competence She writes in her autobiography (Bogan 72) that
the poet represses the narrative of life, absorbs it along with life
itself, and the repressed becomes the poem.

WORKS CITED

Collins, Martha. *Critical Essays on Louise Bogan*. Boston: G.K.
Hall & Co., 1984.
Frank, Elizabeth. *Louise Bogan. A Portrait*. New York: Alfred A.
Knopf. 1985.
Limmer, Ruth. *Journey Around My Room: The Autobiography of
Louise Bogan*, New York: The Viking Press, 1980.
McGuire, William. *Poetry's Catbird Seat*. Washington, D. C.:
Library of Congress, 1988.
Untermeyer, Louis, Editor. *Modern American Poetry*. New York:
Harcourt, Brace & Company, 1930.

OTHER WORKS CONSULTED

Knox, Claire E. *Louise Bogan; A Reference Source*. Metuchen, N.J.,
& London: The Scarecrow Press, Inc., 1990 (Complete list of
works by and about Bogan).
Limmer, Ruth, Editor. *What The Woman Lived: Selected Letters of
Louise Bogan, 1920–1970*. New York: Harcourt Brace
Jovanovich, 1973.
Ridgeway, Jacqueline. *Louise Bogan*. Boston: Twayne Publishers,
1984.

PUBLISHED WORKS AND HONORS

Books
Body of This Death. New York: Robert M. McBride, 1923.
Dark Summer. New York: Charles Scribner's Sons, 1929.

The Sleeping Fury. New York: Charles Scribner's Sons, 1937.
Poems and New Poems. New York: Charles Scribner's Sons, 1941.
Collected Poems, 1923–1953. New York: Noonday Press, 1954.
The Blue Estuaries Poems, 1923–1968. New York: Farrar, Straus & Giroux, 1968.

Criticism
Achievement in American Poetry, 1900–1950. Chicago: Henry Regency, 1951.
Selected Criticism: Poetry and Prose. New York: Noonday Press, 1955.
A Poet's Alphabet: Reflections on the Literary Art and Vocation, Edited by Robert Phelps and Ruth Limmer. New York: McGraw Hill Book Company, 1970 (published posthumously).

Anthologies
Works in the Humanities published in Great Britain 1939–1946: A Selective List. Washington: U.S. Library of Congress, Oct. 1950.
Compiled with William Jay Smith. *The Golden Journey: Poems for Young People.* Chicago: Reilly & Lee, 1965. London: Evans Brothers, 1967.

Honors
John Reed Memorial Prize, 1930
Guggenheim Fellowships, 1933, 1937
Helen Haire Levenson Prize, 1937
Fellow in American Letters, Library of Congress, 1944
Harriet Monroe Award, 1949
Academy of American Poets, 1954
Bollingen Prize, 1955
Senior Creative Arts Award from Brandeis, 1962
National Endowment for the Arts Award, 1967

Ad Castitatem

I make the old sign.
I invoke you,
Chastity
Life moves no more
A breeze of flame.
Alike upon the ground
Struck by the same withering
Lie the fruitful and the barren branch
Alike over them
Closes the mould.
I call upon you,
Who have not known you;
I invoke you,
Stranger though I be.
Against this blackened heart
I hold your offerings—
Water, and a stone.

In this ravaged country,
In this season not yours,
You having no season,
I call upon you without echo.
Hear me, infertile,
Beautiful futility.

Cassandra

To me, one silly task is like another,
I bare the shambling tricks of lust and pride.
This flesh will never give a child its mother,—
Song, like a wing, tears through my breast, my side,
And madness chooses out my voice again,
Again. I am the chosen no hand saves:
The shrieking heaven lifted over men,
Not the dumb earth wherein they set their graves.

From Heine

Der Tod, das ist die kühle Nacht...

Death is the tranquil night.
Life is the sultry day.
It darkens; I will sleep now;
The light has made me weary.

Over my bed rises a tree
Wherein sings the young nightingale.
It sings of constant love.
Even in this dream I hear it.

Men Loved Wholly Beyond Wisdom

Men loved wholly beyond wisdom
Have the staff without the banner.
Like a fire in a dry thicket
Rising within women's eyes
Is the love men must return.
Heart, so subtle now, and trembling,
What a marvel to be wise,
To love never in this manner!
To be quiet in the fern
Like a thing gone dead and still,
Listening to the prisoned cricket
Shake its terrible, dissembling
Music in the granite hill.

Musician

Where have these hands been,
By what delayed,
That so long stayed
Apart from the thin

Strings which they now grace
With their lonely skill?
Music and their cool will
At last interlace,

Now with great ease, and slow,
The thumb, the finger, the strong
Delicate hand plucks the long
String it was born to know.

And, under the palm, the string
Sings as it wished to sing.

Night

The cold remote islands
And the blue estuaries
Where what breathes, breathes
The restless wind of the inlets,
And what drinks, drinks
The incoming tide;

Where shell and weed
Wait upon the salt wash of the sea,
and the clear nights of stars
Swing their lights westward
To set behind the land;

Where the pulse clinging to the rocks
Renews itself forever;
Where, again on cloudless nights,
The water reflects
The firmament's partial setting;

— O remember
In your narrowing dark hours
That more things move
Than blood in the heart.

Poem in Prose

I turned from side to side, from image to image, to put you
    down,
All to no purpose; for you the rhymes would not ring—
Not for you, beautiful and ridiculous, as are always the true
    inheritors of love,
The bearers; their strong hair moulded to their foreheads as
    though by the pressure of hands.
It is you that must sound in me secretly for the little time
    before my mind schooled in desperate esteem, forgets you—
And it is my virtue that I cannot give you out,
That you are absorbed into my strength, my mettle,
That in me you are matched, and that it is silence which comes
    from us.

Single Sonnet

Now, you great stanza, you heroic mould,
Bend to my will, for I must give you love:
The weight in the heart that breathes, but cannot move,
Which to endure flesh only makes so bold.

Take up, take up, as it were lead or gold
The burden; test the dreadful mass thereof.
No stone, slate, metal under or above
Earth, is so ponderous, so dull, so cold.

Too long as ocean bed bears up the ocean,
As earth's core bears the earth, have I borne this;
Too long have lovers, bending for their kiss,
Felt bitter force cohering without motion.

Staunch meter, great song, it is yours, at length,
To prove how stronger you are than my strength.

Sub Contra

Notes on the tuned frame of strings
Plucked or silenced under the hand
Whimper lightly to the ear,
Delicate and involute,
Like the mockery in a shell.
Lest the brain forget the thunder
The roused heart once made it hear,—
Rising as that clamor fell,—
Let there sound from music's root
One note rage can understand,
A fine noise of riven things.
Build there some thick chord of wonder;
Then, for every passion's sake,
Beat upon it till it break.

To Be Sung On the Water

Beautiful, my delight,
Pass, as we pass the wave.
Pass, as the mottled night
Leaves what it cannot save,
Scattering dark and bright.

Beautiful, pass and be
Less than the guiltless shade
To which our vows were said;
Less than the sound of the oar
To which our vows were made,—
Less than the sound of its blade
Dipping the stream once more.

LÉONIE ADAMS
1948–1949

ÉONIE ADAMS

Jean H. Johnson, Stacy Tuthill

Léonie Adams was most prolific as a poet in the 1920's and 1930's. At that time she became part of a New York circle that included Louise Bogan, Edmund Wilson, Ruth Benedict, and Louis and Jean Starr Untermeyer. They published in fashionable magazines of the day, such as *Vanity Fair*, *The New Republic*, *The Nation*, *The New Yorker* and other leading magazines. Adams is known for two books, *Those Not Elect*, (1925), and *High Falcon and Other Poems* (1929) for which she subsequently won prestigious honors and awards. Louis Untermeyer in the introduction of his anthology *Modern American Poetry* says of *Those Not Elect*, "There is not a line in her first book which is without distinction" (Untermeyer 767). Babette Deutsch praises Adams for "her ability…to extract the essence of the temporal and show it involved with what is beyond time" (Deutsch 236).

Adams was seriously considered in 1947-48 for the chair of Consultant in Poetry to the Library of Congress, but Robert Lowell was appointed that year. She was considered again for 1948-49. Allen Tate said, "As to Léonie Adams, we all felt she had prior claim because of age and distinction, but that a man might do this particular job this year better than any woman that could be selected…" (McGuire 98). The following year, 1948-1949, she was appointed. At the completion of her tenure, Luther Evans, Chief Assistant Librarian, thanked Adams for serving "under difficult and surrounding conditions" (McGuire 108).

The Annual Report of the Librarian of Congress for the year ending 1949 provides a picture of Adams' demanding schedule. Her first job was to work with the recording and album collection. This alone would have been a full agenda. Adams was to oversee the preparation of a leaflet to accompany the albums. She had to decide whether to follow the written text or the recorded text, which was sometimes different, and deal with unsettling negotiations with publishers concerning copyright under those conditions. By January, the albums were ready for the public. William Slocum in *Furioso* wrote: "The historical and critical value of these recordings is alone considerable..." (McGuire 108. 109).

During January 1949, Adams with Gertrude Clarke Whittall negotiated to acquire the Louis Ledoux Collection of the manuscripts of Edwin Arlington Robinson which includes about twenty autographed items. When Evans thanked Whittall, who provided money for the purchase, he said the collection was "...perhaps the finest collection of original Robinson materials in any American library." The materials are now a part of the permanent collections at the Library of Congress (McGuire 109).

One of the most trying jobs for Adams was to act as chairman for the Fellows in the selection for the Bollingen Prize. Nominations for the prize included W.C. Williams for *Patterson II*, Randall Jarrell for *Losses*, Muriel Ruckeyser for *The Green Wave*, and Ezra Pound for *Pisan Cantos*. The February 20 vote was in favor of Pound who was an inmate at St. Elizabeth's, a mental hospital near Washington, D.C. This was a sensitive political period in American history. Pound had been tried for treason for fascist sympathies in support of Mussolini and had written and broadcast anti-American propaganda in Italy. Rather than prosecute the aging poet, Pound was declared incompetent and incarcerated in St. Elizabeth's Hospital (McGuire).

The selection for the Bollingen Prize created controversy among poets as well as politicians. Indignant articles and editorials appeared in the press. T.S. Eliot "questioned whether the award would bring Pound undesirable publicity which might be exploited by the wrong elements." Robert Frost considered the selection "an unendurable outrage" (McGuire 111. 115). Francis Biddle, the Attorney General, opposed the award. On June 24, New York Congressman Jacob Javits called for an investigation, and Senator Theodore F. Green, Chairman of the Congressional Joint Committee on the Library of Congress, introduced a reso-

lution on August 19, that the Library abstain from giving prizes
or awards (McGuire 113. 121). Yale University was granted funds
in 1950 to continue giving the Bollingen Award, and these funds
were followed by an Andrew W. Mellon Foundation endowment
in 1973 of one hundred thousand dollars ($100,000.00) to con-
tinue awarding the prize "in perpetuity" (McGuire 124-125).
Louise Bogan, still a Fellow, praised Adams for conducting the
meetings and handling the situation with "great charm and acu-
men and poise." Adams had proved a woman was capable of han-
dling the job, and when she refused the Consultancy for another
year, the Fellows offered the chair to Elizabeth Bishop. (McGuire
110 . 112) Characteristically, Adams stayed on for a while to com-
plete a project and help Bishop become accustomed to the job.

The Annual Report of the Library of Congress for 1949 re-
veals that in addition to the work discussed, Adams answered
300 requests for information, more than 1600 telephone requests,
and received more than 200 visitors. Fifty-five of her requests
came from Congress and 182 from other government agencies,
a statistic that mirrors the original purpose of the Library to serve
Congress. She also gave nine poetry readings or lectures, one
radio and five press interviews. She organized poetry readings
and programs, gave advice on publications and research, com-
piled bibliographies, many of them requiring protracted confer-
ences. She read and gave oral or written comments on twelve
manuscripts and was Secretary of the Fellows of American Let-
ters who chose the poets and the poems for the Library's albums
of recorded poetry.

Adams wrote little after her tenure at the Library of Congress,
but among poets, her contribution to poetry is significant. Adams
herself said, "I sometimes feel that poetry at present, like other
things, is about to undergo the kind of variation that amounts to
the leap to a new genus... I have been silent a long time because
I am now grappling with the limitations of the lyric" (Millet 213).
She had served as a Fellow at the Library of Congress with T.S.
Eliott, Robert Lowell, Randall Jarrell, and others whose poetry

was more in the modern mode. By contrast, Adams writes in traditional forms, rhyme and meter. She admitted being influenced by Elizabethan and Early Romantic poets, and by Yeats and French Symbolist poetry. Tony N. Redd writes that some of the music and irony in her work is reminiscent of the work of John Crowe Ransom, as in, for example, "Here Lies a Lady" and "Antique Harvests" (*Dictionary of Literary Biography*. 4).

Adams never published another book, although she taught as Fulbright Lecturer in France, as visiting professor at the University of Washington in Seattle and at Purdue; won a fellowship from the Academy of American Poets; and won the Brandeis University Creative Arts Award. Only a few more poems came out in journals.

Adams' work is most often described as romantic; she takes refuge in nature as a metaphor to reveal hidden aspects of the human condition. But her poems are not soft. Some of them, such as "Death and the Lady" and "O Grave" contain irony. This trait is also evident as an underlying force or perception in many other poems throughout *Poems: A Selection*.

Although the body of her work is limited in scope, the poems she published and the honors she received are impressive. She mastered the sonnet. Her triple sonnet, "Discourse with the Heart," is considered one of her best, and it is said to contain passages as flawless and beautiful as some of the Shakespeare sonnets. Another splendid sonnet is "Twilight in the Woods." The sonnet begins with the following lines:

Leaf is no more now than corruption's scent
But beautiful are the trees above their dead,
This hour with their summer beauties spent,
When desolate of the thousand sweets they shed,
As to that last and western rite made bare,... (124)

This sonnet contains death and beauty in death as revealed by the seasons. It ends with "Life's self is heard within earth's icy breast," a line suggesting both spring and resurrected life, but there is that underlying touch of irony. A similar idea suggestive

of beauty in the termination of experience (death) is found in how she perceived the setting sun in the ballad, "Sundown":
And rags of shrouding will not muffle the slain.
This is the immortal extinction, the priceless wound
Not to be staunched. The live gold leaks beyond,
And matter's sanctified, dipped in a gold stain. (62)

While the poems above suggest beauty and immortality, the sonnet, "Alas, Kind Element!" also suggests humanity's powerlessness and dependence upon the elements. She writes, "My every leaf leans forth upon the day;/ Alas, kind element! which comes to go."

Most of the poems in *Poems: A Selection* are rich in nature imagery evident in both content and title, such as "Grapes Making," "The Apple in Season," "The Summer Image," "Midsummer," "Winter Solstice," and others. Adams' genius is not so much in what she sees or what surrounds her as in how she processes the language and internalizes experience. Her poems provide us with many landscapes of the mind. Babette Deutsch believes one of Adams' virtues is the awareness of the tenuous loveliness her language portrays. "None of her contemporaries has recorded more subtly the movement of the hours as sky and earth body them forth. She is as no other the poet of light..."

Léonie Adams made her reputation during the 1920's. Today her books are not easily available except in Rare Book Rooms and some university libraries. She was born December 9, 1889 in Brooklyn, New York, as Léonie Fuller Adams, the only daughter of Charles Frederick and Henrietta (Roxier) Adams. On June 3, 1933 she married William E. Troy, a critic, who died in 1961. After his death Adams collected her husband's essays which were published by Rutgers University Press in 1967 and edited by Stanley Edgar Hyman. In 1968, this remarkable book received the National Book Award in Arts and Letters (Redd 9). Adams died of heart failure in the Candlewood Care Center in New Milford, Connecticut at the age of 88. Educated at Bennington College and Columbia University, she was an educator, consultant, editor, and poet. She may be best remembered for her exquisite lyric poetry and her work as Consultant in Poetry to the Library of Congress.

WORKS CITED AND REFERENCE RESOURCES

Annual Report of the Librarian of Congress for the fiscal year ending June 30, 1949. Washington, D.C.: United States Government Printing Office, 1950.

Contemporary Authors—Permanent Series. (alphabetical) Vol. 125. Detroit: Gale Research. Deutsch, Babette. *Poetry in Our Time.* Garden City: Doubleday, 1963.

McGuire, William. *Poetry's Catbird Seat.* Washington, D.C.: Library of Congress, 1988.

Redd, Tony N. *Dictionary of Literary Biography.* Vol. 48. Detroit: Gale Research.

Untermeyer, Louis. *Modern American Poetry: A Critical Anthology.* New York: Harcourt Brace & Company, 1930.

BOOKS

Those Not Elect. New York: Robert M. McBride, 1925.

High Falcon and Other Poems. New York: The John Daly Company, 1929.

This Measure. Number 7 in the Borzoi Chapbook Series. New York: Alfred A. Knopf, 1933 (translator with others and author of introduction).

Poems: A Selection. New York: Funk & Wagnals, 1954.

HONORS AND AWARDS

Guggenheim Fellowship, 1928-30
Consultant in Poetry to the Library of Congress, 1948-49
National Institute of Arts and Letters Grant in Literature, 1949
D. Lit., New Jersey College for Women, 1950
Harriet Monroe Poetry Award, 1954
Shelley Memorial Award, 1954
Bollingen Prize, 1955
Academy of American Poets Fellowship, 1959
National Council of Arts Grant, 1966-67
Brandeis University Creative Arts Award, 1968-69

Sundown

This is the time lean woods shall spend
A steeped-up twilight, and the pale evening drink,
And the perilous roe, the leaper to the west brink,
Trembling and bright to the caverned cloud descend.

Now shall you see pent oak gone gusty and frantic,
Stooped with dry weeping, ruinously unloosing
The sparse disheveled leaf, or reared and tossing
A dreary scarecrow bough in funeral antic.

Then, tatter you and rend,
Oak heart, to your profession mourning; not obscure
The outcome, not crepuscular, on the deep floor
Sable and gold match lustres and contend.

And rags of shrouding will not muffle the slain.
This is the immortal extinction, the priceless wound
Not to be staunched. The live gold leaks beyond,
And matter's sanctified, dipped in a gold stain.

Kennst du das Land

No, I have borne in mind this hill,
For once before I came its way
In hours when summer held her breath
Above her innocents at play;
Knew the leaves deepening the green ground
With their green shadows, there as still
And perfect as leaves stand in air;
The bird who takes delight in sound
Giving his young and watery call,
That is each time as if a fall
Flashed silver and were no more there.
And knew at last, when day was through,
That sky in which the boughs were dipped
More thick with stars than fields with dew;
And in December brought to mind
The laughing child to whom they gave
Among these slopes, upon this grass,
The summer-hearted name of love.
Still can you follow with your eyes,
Where on the green and gilded ground
The dancers will not break the round,
The beechtrunks carved of moonlight rise;
Still at their roots the violets burn
Lamps whose flame is soft as breath.
But turn not so, again, again,
They clap me in their wintry chain;
I know the land whereto you turn,
And know it for a land of death.

Twilit Revelation

This hour was set the time for heaven's descent,
Come drooping toward us on the heavy air,
The sky, that's heaven's seat, above us bent,
Blue faint as violet ash, you near me there
In nether space, so drenched in goblin blue
I could touch Hesperus as soon as you.

Now I perceive you, lapped in singling light,
Washed by that blue which sucks whole planets in,
And hung like those top jewels of the night
A mournful gold too high for love to win.
And you, poor brief, poor melting star, you seem
Half to sink, half to brighten in that stream.

And these rich-bodied hours of our delight
Show like a mothwing's substance when the fall
Of confine-loosing, blue, unending night
Extracts the spirit of this temporal.
So space can pierce the crevice wide between
Fast hearts, skies deep-descended intervene.

Country Summer

Now the rich cherry, whose sleek wood,
And top with silver petals traced
Like a strict box its gems encased,
Has spilt from out that cunning lid,
All in an innocent green round,
Those melting rubies which it hid;
With moss ripe-strawberry-encrusted,
So birds get half, and minds lapse merry
To taste that deep-red, lark's-bite berry,
And blackcap bloom is yellow-dusted.

The wren that thieved it in the eaves
A trailer of the rose could catch
To her poor droopy sloven thatch,
And side by side with the wren's brood-
O lovely time of beggar's luck-
Opens the quaint and hairy bud;
And full and golden is the yield
Of cows that never have to house,
But all night nibble under boughs,
Or cool their sides in the moist field.

Into the rooms flow meadow airs,
The warm farm baking smell's blown round.
Inside and out, and sky and ground
Are much the same; the wishing star,
Hesperus, kind and early born,
Is risen only finger-far;
All stars stand close in summer air,
And tremble, and look mild as amber;
When wicks are lighted in the chamber,
They are like stars which settled there,

Now straightening from the flowery hay,
Down the still light the mowers look,
Or turn, because their dreaming shook,
And they waked half to other days,
When left alone in the yellow stubble
The rusty-coated mare would graze.
Yet thick the lazy dreams are born,
Another thought can come to mind,
But like the shivering of the wind,
Morning and evening in the corn.

Words for the Raker of Leaves

Birds are of passage now,
Else-wending; where —
Songless, soon gone of late —
They night among us,
No tone now upon grass
Downcast from hedge or grove
With goldening day invites.
Cold, wizening, drear
Lies there all shadowing over.
Yet some, then many from
The blanched net flit and call,
Still a time gambolling;
Into, from the numb skein,
Two, a third with least tune;
And one on the sunned end
Of lawn turns and turns,
With rime-bedabbled wing.

Air as of two airs
Through day lifts and plays,
In a day that looks away,
Bloom-dappling in the cleft
Of the stone distances,
And the dimmed forest weft;
And in reddish hues upshed
From about autumnal things
Shines tenderer, afar seen,
Lastingly after-lit,
Out of all seasons spring;
In a day that looks far,
A day that sees plain,
Roseate at feet the fresh
Fall of leaf we rake upon

The fallen mouldered brown;
That infiltrate of light,
Lace then the day pours through,
And the winged seed down-lain.

Clime of two climes
Seems here in time straying,
Its whisperer within sun,
Where in warm musing is stood;
And light to the cheek of flesh
All without sifts cool
Upon the sun-warmed one.
Nearer eared than the heard,
The silences beneath
Of pathos without cry.
In sight fulfilling the eyes,
Vistaed of the beheld
Are its beseechings; wide
Those intimations whence,
Only its offering offering,
Climbs then an eyebeam
To its endless portion;
As it were a vista upon
The suffered and foredone.

ELIZABETH BISHOP
1949–1950

LIZABETH BISHOP

Ann B. Knox

When Elizabeth Bishop began her tenure as Consultant to the Library of Congress in 1948, she was 38 years old and had published one book of poetry, *North & South*. Although not widely recognized, her work was admired by a circle of influential contemporary poets. She was considered a poet's poet. Later works contributed to her growing reputation. *Poems: North & South — A Cold Spring*, published in 1955 by Houghton Mifflin, won her a Pulitzer Prize for poetry and *The Complete Poems*, published by Farrar, Straus and Giroux, received the National Book Award for poetry in 1968. *The Diary of "Helena Morley,"* a translation from the Portuguese, appeared in 1957, *Questions of Travel* in 1965, and *Geography III* in 1976, all published by Farrar, Straus, and Giroux. After her death in 1979 the same publisher brought out *The Complete Poems, The Collected Prose* in 1984; *One Art*, a selection of her letters edited by Robert Giroux, in 1994; and *Exchanging Hats*, a collection of delightful paintings, in 1996.

Elizabeth Bishop's early years were painfully unsettled. She was born in Worcester, Massachusetts in 1911 and before she was a year old her father died. Her mother, deeply disturbed by her husband's death, became emotionally unstable and was in and out of sanitariums for the next few years. When Elizabeth was five they moved to Great Village, Nova Scotia to stay with her mother's family. It was there that her mother permanently entered a mental hospital and Elizabeth Bishop saw her for the last time. She later described the confusion and uncertainty of this period in the prose piece, "In the Village." But her time in Great Village also offered her the warmth of her unassuming grandparents and acceptance by the village community. This period became a rich source for her later poems. When her wealthy paternal grandparents abruptly took her back to Worcester, she found their elegant house cold and the grandparents distant. After her health deteriorated, it became clear she was unhappy, and her mother's sister and her husband brought Elizabeth to live with them in their run-down house in Boston.

Her talent for writing became evident early. Although her primary schooling was interrupted by frequent moves, illness, and allergies, Bishop received a sound education, thanks, in part, to a modest inheritance from her father's family. She went to high school first at the North Shore Country Day School in Swampscott, Massachusetts and later Walnut Hill boarding school. In both places she became involved in editing the schools' literary magazines. A number of her poems appeared in these publications. At Vassar College she was able to shed some of the shyness that haunted her and establish life-long friendships, among them Frani Blough, Louise Crane, and Mary McCarthy. Besides editing the class yearbook, she and several friends inaugurated *Con Spirito*, a literary magazine.

During her senior year a college librarian introduced her to Marianne Moore. They were instantly drawn to each other and Moore became Bishop's literary mentor and close friend. Bishop's facility for friendship gave her a supportive network and a stay against loneliness. Marianne Moore introduced her to many writers, and through residencies at Yaddo she became part of a wide circle of writers and artists that included Loren MacIver, painter and editor, Robert Penn Warren and his wife, Eleanor Clark, who had been a college classmate, Allen Tate and Robert Lowell. Lowell became a close friend and she valued him as critic and reader of her work-in-progress.

From Moore, Bishop honed the art of looking closely at ordinary things and recording them with precision. She also learned the discipline of revision, sometimes taking years to complete a poem. Place was a focus for much of Bishop's poetry. Her early experiences, punctuated by loss and sudden displacement, may have contributed to her intense connection with locale. Except for the nine years during which she had a house in Key West and the period from 1951 to 1966 when she lived in Brazil with her friend Lota de Macedo Soares, Bishop spent much of her time on the move visiting friends, traveling or staying at Yaddo, the artist retreat where she could write without interruption.

Bishop's work is underlaid, as Helen Vendler said, by the "continuing vibration between two frequencies—the domestic and the strange." (*Part of Nature, Part of Us* 97) Her voice is colloquial, her observations precise, but close inspection of the familiar can open up odd connections and raise disturbing questions. Her poems are at the same time reticent and intimate.

The Consultancy at the Library of Congress came at a troubled period. She had recently given up her much-loved house in Key West, and while trying to cope with chronic asthma, depression, and a serious drinking problem, she spent the following year shuttling between hotel rooms, the homes of friends in Maine, Florida, Haiti and Washington DC, and an unhappy residency at Yaddo. When she took up her incumbency at the Library of Congress in Washington she found rooms in a Georgetown boarding house. In a letter Bishop writes with her usual humor and sharp eye, "...the landlady wears a black velvet band around her neck, the place is stuffed with antiques—even things under bell glasses—and for some reason there's no sink in the bathroom..." (*One Art* 194). The Consultancy consumed most of Bishop's time. She wrote to Robert Lowell, "I haven't been able to do any work here at all—I don't know how you ever did—but I have made a few starts..." In another letter to Lowell she wrote: "(Dylan) Thomas's visit was the high point of my incumbency, and he made absolutely beautiful records." Even though she completed no poems during her stay in Washington, she did garner material. Letters from this time are rich with delighted observations of the city and the people. In one she writes: "Washington doesn't seem quite real. All those piles of granite and marble, like an inflated copy of another capital city some place else (the Forum?)." (*One Art* 194) In the poem "View of the Capitol from the Library of Congress," published some years later, she records again that same sense of unreality:

On the east steps the Air Force Band
in uniforms of Air Force blue
is playing hard and loud, but – queer –
the music doesn't quite come through.

The poem "Visits to St. Elizabeth's" clearly reflects the visits she made to see Ezra Pound. She brought a number of poets to meet him during her time in Washington.

Shortly after her Consultancy, she traveled to Brazil, met Lota de Macedo Soares and for fifteen years shared a house with her in the mountains near Petropolis. This proved a settled and productive period. After the death of her friend in 1966 Bishop returned permanently to the United States. Inflation had reduced the value of her inheritance and she often made long visits to friends here and abroad, supporting herself with grants or fellowships and temporary teaching positions such as those at University of Washington in Seattle, Harvard University, New York University, and a visiting professorship at M.I.T. Elizabeth Bishop died of a cerebral aneurysm in Boston, Mass. on October 6, 1979 (Millier 550).

During her lifetime Elizabeth Bishop declined to have her work included in women's anthologies. Her literary executors have honored this decision and we are, therefore, unable to reprint any of her poems. We include, in addition to a biography of her publications, a list of books about Bishop and her work.

WORKS CITED AND REFERENCE RESOURCES

Bishop, Elizabeth. *The Complete Poems, 1927–1978*. New York: Farrar, Straus, and Giroux, 1979.

Bishop, Elizabeth. *The Complete Prose*. New York; Farrar, Straus and Giroux, 1984.

Giroux, Robert. *ONE ART: Letters Selected & Edited*. New York: Farrar, Straus & Giroux, 1994.

McGuire, William. *Poetry's Catbird Seat, the Consultancy in Poetry in the English Language at the Library of Congress, 1937–1987*. Washington, D C: Library of Congress, 1988.

Brett C. Millier. *Elizabeth Bishop, Life and the Memory of It.* Berkeley and Los Angeles California: University of California Press, 1993.

Helen Vendler. *Part of Nature, Part of Us.* Cambridge, Massachusetts and London: Harvard University Press, 1980.

BOOKS

Poems

North & South. Boston: Houghton Mifflin, 1955.

Poems: North & South – A Cold Spring. Boston: Houghton Mifflin, 1955.

Questions of Travel. New York: Farrar, Straus, and Giroux, 1965.

The Ballad of the Burglar of Babylon. New York: Farrar, Straus, and Giroux, 1968. (with woodcuts by Ann Grifalconi).

The Complete Poems, 1927–1979. New York: Farrar, Straus, and Giroux, first edition printed 1969.

Geography III. New York: Farrar, Straus, and Giroux, 1976.

The Complete Poems, 1927-1979. New York: Farrar, Straus, and Giroux, 1983. Copyright © 1979, 1983 by Alice Helen Methfessel.

Prose

The Collected Prose. Edited by Robert Giroux. New York: Straus, and Giroux, 1984. Copyright © Alice Methfessel. Introduction copyright © 1984 by Robert Giroux. Reprinted by permission of Farrar, Straus, & Giroux, Inc.

Translation. *The Diary of "Helena Morley,"* by Alice Brant (translated from the Portuguese) Farrar, Straus, and Giroux, 1957.

Brazil with the authors of *Life.* New York: Life-Times Books, 1962.

One Art. Letters, selected and edited by Robert Giroux. New York: Farrar, Straus, Giroux, 1994.

Exchanging Hats, Paintings by Elizabeth Bishop. New York: Farrar, Straus, and Giroux, 1996.

Anthology
An Anthology of Twentieth Century Brazilian Poetry, edited with
Emanuel Brasil. Introduction by Elizabeth Bishop, Middletown,
Conn.: Wesleyan University Press, 1972.

HONORS
Houghton Mifflin Poetry Award, 1945
Guggenheim Fellowship, 1947
American Academy of Arts and Letters Award, 1950
Consultant in Poetry at the Library of Congress, 1949–50
Lucy Martin Donnelly Fellowship, Bryn Mawr College, 1951
Inducted into National Institute of Arts and Letters, 1954
Pulitzer Prize, 1955
Amy Lowell Traveling Fellowship, 1957
Academy of American Poets Fellowship, 1964
Merrill-Ingram Award, 1968
National Book Award, 1969
Neustadt International Prize, 1976

ACTIVITIES AT THE LIBRARY OF CONGRESS
The following passage is reprinted with permission of William
McGuire author of *Poetry's Catbird Seat: The Consultantship in
Poetry in the English Language at the Library of Congress, 1938–87*,
Library of Congress, Washington, D.C. 1987, copyright © 1988
by William McGuire.

Elizabeth Bishop's report on her term in the Chair of Poetry pic-
tures a calm, uncomplicated, somewhat tedious year, during
which—as she reported apologetically—because of ill health she
didn't accomplish as much work as she "would like to have done
or probably should have done." Poetry she did write. Her dis-
turbing "Visits to St. Elizabeth's," a work seemingly colored by

Ravel's *Bolero* and "The House That Jack Built," gathers force incrementally from its first stanza,

> This is the house of Bedlam.
>
> This is the man
> that lies in the house of Bedlam.
>
> This is the time
> of the tragic man
> that lies in the house of Bedlam.

to its climactic twelfth stanza:

> This is the soldier home from the war.
> These are the years and the walls and the door
> that shut on a boy that pats the floor
> to see if the world is round or flat.
> This is a Jew in a newspaper hat
> that dances carefully down the ward,
> walking the plank of a coffin board
> with the crazy sailor
> that shows his watch
> that tells the time
> of the wretched man
> that lies in the house of Bedlam.

She worked agreeably with Phyllis Armstrong, whose diligence she mentioned in her annual report; she recommended a promotion. They labored at getting the file on the Pound Affair in order. Where was Katherine Anne Porter's eight-page letter to the *S.R.L.*, she asked Tate, which the magazine refused to print and she had mimeographed and distributed on the West Coast? Her recording targets included Kenneth Fearing (didn't record—a pity), Muriel Rukeyser (did), the New Zealand poet Allen Curnow (did), and Dylan Thomas (did). She finally captured the voice of MacLeish, at a Boston studio, as he had become Boylston Professor of Rhetoric and Oratory at Harvard. "I have admired

'You, Andrew Marvell' now for almost twenty years and should
very much like to hear a recording of it, and also of 'The End of
the World.'" She had her wish. The recordings Frost had made
two years before, which were sent him to hear, he found to be
full of mistakes, and he came in December to remake them to
his satisfaction. She gave a tea for Frost in the Poetry Room, the
first function of this sort to take place there, though its refur-
bishment was not completed. The thirty-five guests included Karl
Shapiro and Carl Sandburg. On another occasion she had forty
members of the Library staff up there and gave them a talk about
what she did. "It was interesting to learn how little they knew of
the actual work of the Consultant." She gave the customary read-
ing of her poems in the Coolidge Auditorium. She went through
manuscripts sent in by some twenty-five amateur poets. "I re-
gret to say, however, that I have made no discoveries of new po-
etic talent whatever." She dealt with a swarm of reference inquir-
ies. Armstrong's meticulous statistics: 1,946 general and 1,070
administrative phone calls, 772 letters answered, 445 visitors seen
and talked to, 120 readers assisted. A large part of that, Bishop
reported, "is a serious waste of the time of the Consultant and
the Assistant and should probably be handled elsewhere."

Bishop's view of the recording project, too, was vaguely jaun-
diced. She found the critical response to the first series disap-
pointing and also disappointed. Technical quality was below par,
and the "poet-readers themselves vary greatly and are not usu-
ally subject to improvement. However, as poetry recordings be-
come more popular and widespread… it is possible that more
poets may learn how to read their poetry effectively." In later
years Bishop said she would rather read a poem in peace than
listen to a recording.

OTHER BOOKS ABOUT ELIZABETH BISHOP
for readers who wish to learn more about her life and work.

Doreski C.K. *Elizabeth Bishop: The Restraints of Language*. New York: Oxford University Press, 1993.

Fountain, Gary and Peter Brazeau. *Remembering Elizabeth Bishop: An Oral Biography*. Amherst: University of Massachusetts Press, 1994.

Lombardi, Marilyn May. *THE BODY AND THE SONG: Elizabeth Bishop's Poetics*. Carbondale, and Edwardsville: Southern Illinois University Press, 1995.

McCabe, Susan. *ELIZABETH BISHOP: Her Poetics of Loss*. University Park, Pennsylvania: The Pennsylvania State University Press, 1994.

Stevenson, Ann. *Elizabeth Bishop*. New York: Twayne Publishers, Inc, 1966.

Travisano, Thomas J. *ELIZABETH BISHOP: Her Artistic Development*. Charlottesville: University Press of Virginia, 1951.

JOSEPHINE JACOBSEN
1971–1973

OSEPHINE JACOBSEN

Interview by Marta Knobloch, Betty Parry

M.K. How did you feel when you were approached by the Chief of the Manuscript Division at the Library of Congress, Dr. Roy Basler, to be the consultant in poetry?

J.J. I was surprised and very pleased. There was no job in the world I would rather have had. I thought to promote poetry in America was the best thing anyone could do.

B.P. What was your reaction to being the fourth woman, one of only eight women out of forty to date, to be asked to be the Poetry Consultant?

J.J. I thought it was a great honor, and I was proud to be the first woman since Elizabeth Bishop after a twenty year hiatus. Up to that point, every Consultant named was a prominent figure in American poetry circles, but I found I was not intimidated by the job. I knew this was a job I could do. I love poetry. I know poetry. I felt confident.

M.K. What do you feel you accomplished during your tenure at the Library?

J.J. I was visited by poets from many countries who came to the Library of Congress to talk about poetry all over the world. I had the privilege of bringing some of the finest poets in America to read there. I think James Dickey said that having distinguished poets read at the Library was a tremendous thing. Imagine Keats reading "Ode on a Grecian Urn" and being able to listen to that tape now. Imagine Shakespeare reading his sonnets. It would be a magnificent experience. We invited contemporary poets to read and record. We now have a unique collection of exceptional poets reading their own poems which doesn't exist anywhere else in the world, voices that might otherwise have been lost.

B.P. Who did you invite to read and record their own poetry for the Library?

J.J. I wanted to invite more African-American poets because not many had read there before I was Consultant. We invited Sterling Brown to read Leon Damas' work in translation. We asked Owen Dodson, May Miller, June Jordan, Lucille Clifton and Samuel Allen to read and record. We were necessarily limited by only one reading a month at the Library during the winter. However, we were able to include many more fine poets who had not read there before through the recording program.

B.P. How do you feel about the effects of past discrimination on minorities and women poets?

J.J. I wanted to bring greater participation from groups not previously represented in institutions such as the Library of Congress before that time in the United States. My first lecture at the Library of Congress was "From Anne to Marianne." No one can believe it is a coincidence that earlier there were a large number of exceptional women poets, yet other than Anne Bradstreet, Elinor Wylie and Edna St. Vincent Millay, none were remembered before then, apart from Emily Dickinson, who was the major exception. As long as it was believed that women had no intellectual capacity, there was no place for them in American letters.

M.K. Were you involved in poetry programs in Washington?

J.J. Yes. I gave 40 talks the first year at universities and colleges in Washington and to literary groups. In the second year I cut back because I had to concentrate on other aspects of the job. I spoke about poetry and the Library of

Congress. I was shocked to learn how few people in Washington really knew about the Library's splendid poetry programs. Especially since it was through the generosity and patronage of American women, in this case Gertrude Clarke Whittall, that the fund for poetry and music at the Library of Congress was initiated. Here was this marvelous font of poetry available, and people were not using this great resource.

B.P.   How did being at the Library of Congress affect your own work?

J.J.   My own poetry was exactly the same in quantity. I wrote a rough average of 13 to 16 poems a year. I remember receiving the news that my book *The Shade Seller* had been named a finalist in the National Book Awards of 1974. At that time I was serving as Honorary Consultant and had just completed my tenure as Consultant, but I continued to write poetry all the time I was there.

B.P.   How do you feel about your two terms as Consultant in Poetry to the Library of Congress?

J.J.   I found the second term easier because I knew the staff. Roy Basler and later John Broderick and, of course, Nancy Galbraith and Jenny Rutland in the poetry office were all very supportive and helpful to me. I had a better idea of what I wanted to accomplish and understood the possibilities that the job offered. I think it was the concept of work about the job that was precious to me. I never thought it was a position or a title: "The Consultant in Poetry to the Library of Congress." I thought this is a chance to do something for poetry, and I appreciated being given the opportunity.

This interview with Josephine Jacobsen was conducted in her home, August, 1996 by Marta Knobloch and Betty Parry

PUBLICATIONS

Marble Satyr and Other Poems. Published by Knickerbocker Press, 1928.

Let Each Man Remember. Published by Kaleidograph Press, Dallas, 1940.

For the Unlost. Published by Contemporary Poetry, Baltimore, 1946.

The Human Climate. Published by Contemporary Poetry, 1953.

The Testament of Samuel Beckett, with William R. Mueller. Published by Hill & Wang, 1964 and Faber, London, 1966.

The Animal Inside. Published by Ohio University Press, 1966.

Ionesco & Genet: Playwrights of Silence, with William R. Mueller. Published by Hill & Wang, 1968.

From Anne to Marianne: Some American Women Poets. (Editor) Library of Congress (Washington, DC), 1972.

The Shade Seller, New & Collected Poems. Published by Doubleday, 1974.

The Instant of Knowing. Library of Congress, 1974.

A Walk With Raschid and Other Stories. Published by Jackpine Press, 1978.

The Chinese Insomniacs. Published by University of Pennsylvania Press, 1981.

Adios, Mr. Moxley (short stories). Published by Jackpine Press, 1986.

The Sisters, New & Selected Poems. Published by Bench Press, 1987.

On The Island: New & Selected Stories. Published by Ontario Press, 1989.

Distances. Published by Bucknell University Press, 1991.

In the Crevice of Time: New & Collected Poems. Published by Johns Hopkins University Press, 1995.

What Goes Without Saying. Published by Johns Hopkins University Press, 1996.

The Testament of Samuel Beckett (dramatic criticism), with William R. Mueller. Hill & Wang (New York City), 1964.

Substance of Things Hoped For, Doubleday, 1987.

HONORS AND AWARDS

Doctor of Humane Letters from Towson State University, Goucher College, College of Notre Dame of Maryland, and Johns Hopkins University

Fellowships at Yaddo, the Millay Colony for the Arts, and the McDowell Colony

Literary Lion, New York Public Library, 1985 to the present.

Served Two terms as Poetry Consultant to the Library of Congress. 1971-1973

The Shade Seller: New and Collected Poems nominated for National Book Award, 1974

A Walk with Raschid and Other Stories selected as one of the fifty Distinguished Books of the Year by *Library Journal*, 1978

Shelly Memorial Award for lifetime service to literature, Poetry Society of America for *Three Sisters*, 1992

Inducted into the American Academy of Arts and Letters, 1994

On the Island: Short Stories selected as one of five nominees for the PEN-Faulkner Award

In the Crevice of Time: New and Collected Poems was one of the four nominees for the National Book award, 1995

William Carlos Williams Book Award (Poetry Society of America), for *In the Crevice of Time*, 1966

Won the Lenore-Marshall Award, 1966, for the best book published the previous year

Won the Poets' Prize and the Robert Frost Gold Medal, 1997

Included twelve times in the O. Henry Prize Stories

Represented in *The Nation's* selections from its 125 years, and in *Best Poems*, 1990 and *Best Poems*, 1992

Josephine Jacobsen was born in Canada of parents of United States citizenship and has lived much of her life in Baltimore, Maryland.

Lines to a Poet

Be careful what you say to us now.
The street lamp is smashed, the window is jagged,
There is a man dead in his blood by the base of the fountain.
If you speak
You cannot be delicate or sad or clever.
Some other hour, in a moist April,
We will consider similes for the budding larches.
You can teach our wits and our fancy then;
By a green-lit midnight in your study
We will delve in your sparkling rock.
But now at dreadful high noon
You may speak only to our heart,
Our honor and our need:
Saying such things as, "See, she is alive . . ."
Or "Here is water," or "Look behind you!"

Instances of Communication

Almost nothing concerns me but communication.
How strange: Up the Orinoco, once, far
up the Orinoco after jungle miles, great flowerheads
looping the treecrests, log-crocodiles, crocodile-logs, bob-
    haired
Indians naked in praus; a small, hot, town and in an upper
    dining-room
plashed at by a fountain, cooled by fans, guardian of a menu
    the size of a baby,
speaking six languages, with seven capital cities behind his
    eyes, a headwaiter,
a man, who said without hope, *"And when does your ship sail?"*
    And no one
said to him, *"What are you doing here?"*

In the hall of the inn at Mont Serat I came out of my room and
"Stand back, stand back!" cried the criada in her softest Spanish,
    "the bride—
the bride is coming!" out of her room, down the hall, down to the
    steps
on her way to the church, to the groom. She was pale, and
    dark; she clouded
the carpet with the mist of her train, she moved by me but
    turned and bent and caught
my fingerbones seeing me like fate, watching the three of her,
    the old, tall, childhood girl,
the darkly seen half-a-thing, and the white bride lost on the
    point of love, and *"Buenas,*
o buenas tardes!" she called into my ear, she crushed my fingers
    and laughed with panic
into my widened eyes and went proudly on whispering
over the hall runner.

I drove five madwomen down a roaring redhot turnpike in a July
noon; the one behind me had a fur ragged coat gathered about
    her in that furnace;
she reached in the horrid insides of a purse and offered me a
    chocolate, liquid
and appalling. *"Look! Look! A bird!"* I cried and flung it over the side
and munched my empty jaws as she turned back and cried:
    "How good!"
And while the others hummed and cursed, and watched simply,
    suddenly she put
her lips—behind me—to my ear and soft as liquid chocolate
    came purling
the obscene abuse. *"Hush, hush, Laura, hush,"* said the nurse;
    "the nice
lady likes you!" Laura did not believe so, and went on softly, slowly,
    lovingly,
with O such misery of hate.

In frosty Philadelphia the freighter lay and loaded in the Sunday ice.
The great cranes swung, the huge nets grabbed and everything
    echoed from cold:
docks, warehouses, freightrails, ships' prows; everything clicked
    and echoed;
but it was possible to go down the long cold docks over the strange
    dark street under
the dim sky into a cold great warehouse Sunday still, up still cold
    stairs, along
a dark dim cold thin hall through a brown door into a small square
    room with lit
peaky candles and kneeling take—cool, slick, thin, little larger
    than a quarter—
God's blood and body charged with its speech.

The Wind in the Sunporch

The chinese windchimes
stir
suddenly thin glass rings on thin glass
great leaves
nod
sideways sideways petals stir
to let it pass
clang-cling it plays.

My ribs lift up and
fall
my parted lips could dance a feather
under my palms both
your shoulder-blades fall and
lift
together with that huge light breath.

Deaf-Mutes at the Ballgame

In the hot sun and dazzle of grass
The wind of noise is men's voices:

A torrent of tone, a simmer of roar,
And bats crack, bags break, flags follow themselves.

The hawkers sweat and gleam in the wind of noise,
The tools of ignorance crouch and give the sign.

The deaf-mutes sit in the hurricane's eye,
The shell-shape ear and the useless tongue

Present, but the frantic fingers' pounce-and-bite
Is sound received and uttered.

If they blink their lids—then the whole gaudy circle
With its green heart and ritual figures

Is suddenly not: leaving two animal-quick
Wince-eyed things alone; with masses and masses

And masses of rows of seats of men
Who move their lips and listen.

While secret secret sits inside
Each, his deaf-mute, fingerless.

The Uninvited

Like dew the children beckon to the dry,
Like heat they shimmer to the winter eye;
Limpid and lovely, comfort is their presage:
The glass wall clearly mirrors us, who try
The foolish, hopeful, undeliverable message.

We are not bidden to the birthday meal—
We are distinct from these by blood and steel.
Our tenderest vines have known nocturnal foxes,
The clock's thin hands have crucified our zeal
And we have nailed our dead in wooden boxes.

The Greek Wind

This wind blows still in stone; blows
in still stone: this
stonestill wind lifts

the draped folds, rocks
the wing-tip, combs
back the stonecold curls.

The body breasts it, blown
almost back: the breasts are shaped
by the wind's touch: the breasts' breath

drinks it salt and fresh; in
the instant of centuries that salt
seawind bright

with invisibility, blows back
the fluent tender folds: watch
it tense the instep,

rush the neck's thrust. See:
it plows the stone like fluid wheat
in its passage.

Notes from a Lenten Bar

I know that my redeemer liveth because
the pebble-eyed gent with the briefcase
two tables down has called him by name
3 times in 2 and ¾ minutes;
and because
the guys on my right are liquid with the health
of victorious Immaculate Conception, 46 to 98;
and because
after the last of my supper, I learn once more
as I rise to 1403
there is nothing between the 12th and the 14th floor.

In the Crevice of Time

For Elliott Coleman

The bison, or tiger, or whatever beast
hunting or hunted, and the twiggy hunter
with legs and spear, in the still caves of Spain
wore out the million rains of summer
and the mean mists of winter:
the frightening motion of the hunter-priest

who straight in the instant between blood and breath
saw frozen there not shank or horn or hide
but an arrangement of these by him, and he himself
there with them, watched by himself inside
the terrible functionless whole
in an offering strange as some new kind of death.

The thick gross early form that made a grave
said in one gesture, "neither bird nor leaf."
The news no animal need bear was out:
the knowledge of death, and time the wicked thief,
and the prompt monster of foreseeable grief
it was the tentative gesture that he gave.

Our hulking confrère scraping the wall,
piling the dust over the motionless face:
in the abyss of time how he is close,
his art an act of faith, his grave
an act of art: for all,
for all, a celebration and a burial.

When the Five Prominent Poets

gathered in inter-admiration
in a small hotel room, to listen
to each other, like Mme. Verdurin
made ill by ecstasy,
they dropped the Muse's name.
Who came.

It was awful.
The door in shivers and a path
plowed like a twister through everything.
Eyeballs and fingers littered that room.
When the floor exploded the ceiling
parted
and the Muse went on and up; and not a sound
came from the savage carpet.

Pondicherry Blues

(FOR VOICE AND SNARE-DRUM)

Mrs. Pondicherry was/ fat and mean,
she had four/ pug/ dogs and a limousine
black/ as West Virginia coal;
and she troubled herself about her soul,
yes, she surely was concerned/ about her soul.

Father O'Hare was thin as a steeple,
the poor and the lonely were his passion and his people.
Pondicherry would ask/ that man to come to dinner
and talk/ to him/ about The Sinner.
And Father O'Hare got very/ very/ tired of Mrs. Pondicherry,
he got raw-/ bone/ tired of Pondicherry.

She changed her will like/ she changed her furs
cause she surely did know that they both were hers,
and she drove that man beside himself
with her wills/ and her pelts/ and her pugs/ and her pelf,
she drove him purely beside himself.

One day she was sitting on her velvet seat
her mink/ round her shoulders and footstool for her feet
and a cushion for/ each/ pug;
and her heart gave a leap and she fell on the rug,
she fell/ right/ down/ on her big/ red/ rug.

They put her into/ bed and called Father O'Hare
but he couldn't get there and he couldn't get there
and she lay on her bed for a/ solid/ hour
and she didn't say a word cause she didn't own the power,
didn't own the power to say/ a single word.

Her mind was thin and cold as a hag,
in her eyes was a beggar with a/ bowl and a rag,
and her ears/ heard/ a cold/ wind start
to blow the trash round the alleys of her heart,
to blow/ cold/ trash round the gutters of her heart.

But Father O'Hare he was/ serving the poor,
he never reached the house and he never crossed the door
till she closed her eyes and/ she stopped her breath
in the lonesome/ slum/ of death
that dark/ trashy/ street of/ death.

Lion under Maples

The lion, awake, is out there.
What is a lion doing under maples?
The sun catches him. She knows
the calm ferocious face set

in its monstrance of
chrysanthemum shag. The eye
is golden but too far to see.
Now there is no glimpse at all.

But she has met him before
this. And with fortune,
she will. In a clearing,
in the heat, in a wink.

Then she will be left
without fear. With great power;
everything be still,
the great head lift.

Gentle Reader

Late in the night when I should be asleep
under the city stars in a small room
I read a poet. A poet: not
a versifier. Not a hot-shot
ethic-monger, laying about
him; not a diary of lying
about in cruel cruel beds, crying.
A poet, dangerous and steep.

O God, it peels me, juices me like a press;
this poetry drinks me, eats me, gut and marrow
until I exist in its jester's sorrow,
until my juices feed a savage sight
that runs along the lines, bright
as beasts' eyes. The rubble splays to dust:
city, book, bed, leaving my ear's lust
saying like Molly, yes, yes, yes O yes.

MAXINE KUMIN

1981–1982

Courtesy of the Library of Congress

MAXINE KUMIN

Ann B. Knox

The interview by Ann B. Knox for SCOP Publications, Inc. took place on September 10, 1996 at Maxine Kumin's farm in Warner, New Hampshire.

SCOP When you first knew you had been named as Consultant of Poetry for the Library of Congress, how did you see your job?

MK   I don't think I had a clear notion at all. I understood this was a Consultancy and I would be asked to advise on acquisition of books, set up various programs — who should give readings and so forth. Bill Meredith had pretty much hand picked me. At that time it was the habit for the Consultant to choose his successor and he chose me. However, the formal invitation came so late I couldn't assume the post in September because I had taken on other commitments and so it was agreed I would start in January.

    I remember clearly how Victor and I went down to the announcement luncheon in May or April. The press was there and we all sat around this table and microphones were handed from person to person. When a reporter asked me how I felt about being selected, I said I was particularly flattered because I was only the fifth woman to be invited to be a Consultant since 1935 when the post was created. Daniel Boorstin, the Librarian of Congress, seized the microphone nearest to him and said, "We don't count." I took the microphone near me and said, "We do." Battle lines were joined at that moment. That was quite a day.

SCOP So this was a tender issue for him?

MK Clearly. I think he had acceded to the tradition that one consultant would choose the next and thought he was getting a middle class female intellectual who wasn't going to make waves. I wasn't aware of how many waves I was going to make. It did not occur to me when I accepted the position that I was going to be an embattled feminist while I was there, but that was how my time started.

SCOP What were your living arrangements?

MK Initially I lived on Capitol Hill with Betsy Wright, famous now for her connection with Bill Clinton. Her house wasn't far from the Library and I could walk to and from work. I had a downstairs room and we shared the place; when she was away I took care of her dog and cat. It was a very amicable arrangement. It meant I could leave my truck in her tiny yard. Of course the first thing that happened was that it was broken into and all the tools were stolen. I was so naive about city living.

SCOP Did you go to the Library every day?

MK You know, I brought my horse Boomer down with me and I boarded her in Potomac, Maryland, so what I usually did was drive out there around 6:30, in time to feed her and clean the stall. Then I'd work Boomer for an hour or so, sometimes by myself, sometimes with Jane Wetmore and her horse. I usually showered and changed into working clothes out there. One day I remember driving back in my breeches thinking I don't want to bother to change. I said to myself, "You're a poet, you don't need to." I went to the Library in my breeches.

SCOP What did your work day look like?

MK   The job wasn't defined but I just decided whatever I was asked to do, I would do it, particularly for women's groups. I was involved with a lot of outreach in the schools. I talked with high school teachers about how to present poetry to a class, how to encourage students to write. I also worked directly with students. They were great.

Then letters. I received zillions of letters. A lot of naive people would send me their poems and say, get this published for me, assuming I had the power to command their work in print. I felt I had to answer every letter that came over my desk.

I think if you are going to be Poetry Consultant you need to be a poetry evangelist. I always pretty much saw that as my role: to make poetry accessible. I remember once being on a panel of august poets and educators discussing how to make poetry more accessible. Howard Nemerov was seated beside me and he leaned over and whispered, "Let's not. Let's keep it a secret." Howard was being sardonic because he certainly believed in opening poetry to everyone.

SCOP   I notice your T-shirt says, "Take me to your reader."

MK   Yes, that's Tony Hecht.

SCOP   I've read about your Brown Bag Lunches; how did they begin?

MK   I don't know how the idea evolved, but it did seem to me there was this lovely room in the Library called the Gertrude Whittall Room. It was charming, with Victorian furniture, soft rugs, and a beautiful view of the capitol. The room was hardly ever used, maybe once every few weeks for a half an hour when a foreign poet came through town. I thought, why don't we invite some well known authors in the Washington area and ask each one to bring a disciple or lesser known poet or student and let's just sit around over lunch and read and talk about poetry and literature.

SCOP   What writers took part in them?

MK   Well, Faye Moskowitz, Linda Pastan, Myra Sklarew, May Miller and others. They would bring students. It was a lively group; we'd have wonderful discussions or talk about individual poems. Part of the success was due to the staff. The unfinished bottles of wine, cheese, crackers, etc. from receptions the Library gave the day before would just appear in time for our Brown Bag Lunches. It was great to see the lovely Whittall Room full of people and serving its function.

SCOP   Were there any problems on the job?

MK   One thing I remember. While I was there I was attacked by Denesh D'Sousa, newly of the Heritage Foundation, as a pornographic poet. He based his condemnation on a poem I wrote called "Heaven as Anus"; it had recently been published and created a stir of consternation, a small ripple. The poem is critical of animal experimentation, particularly in the military. We were then housed on the third floor in what is called the Attic. Now, of course, they have self-service elevators, but when I was there, there was always a person running the elevator whom I got to know quite well. I would get out on the third floor and walk down this cavernous hall whistling; my staff began calling me the Whistling Pornographer.

  Then some other things happened. I had arranged for Chris Llewellyn to read at the Renwick from her long poem about the Triangle Shirt Factory Fire in a sweat shop in New York. I was reprimanded for having sent someone who wrote political poetry. There was a very funny right-wing undercurrent in Washington at that time, and I seem to have triggered controversy.

Fortunately, I had settled in my office with the wonderful Nancy Galbraith and wonderful Jenny Rutland to lean on and consult. Nancy once said we all worked together so well we could do brain-surgery. They really made the job; I think if I hadn't had them I wouldn't have lasted the whole time.

SCOP   Did other people at the Library of Congress show an interest in poetry?

MK   I had nothing to do with anyone in the Library except John Broderick, the Assistant Librarian, a really wonderful man in charge of the Consultancy program, and Gillian Anderson, who was a junior member of the Library's music department. Now she's a successful conductor and composer. She told to me, very ardently, how difficult it was for women in the Library to attain any administrative position at all.

SCOP   What about readings?

MK   John Broderick advised me I was expected to give a reading and write a paper. The first year my paper was on the lost women poets of the early twentieth Century — Any Lowell, Mina Loy, Eleanor Wylie, Teasdale, women who had pretty much been passed over. This was before the recent resurgence of interest in Edna St. Vincent Millay. Most of the Consultant's papers were published and widely circulated, but mine apparently was not considered significant enough to be printed as a pamphlet and sent around. I don't know who made the decision, but my guess was it was the subject matter in question.

The following year I hadn't any particular idea for a paper. When I talked it over with John, he asked, "What would you write about if you could choose anything?" "Well," I told him, "I've always been interested in the history of mules." John never turned a hair. He said, "You're in the right place." And so I embarked on an in-depth research of the American mule. It's a fascinating story, reflecting agrarian history of the United States from Thomas Jefferson through World War I. The material that was made available turned up, for example, the list of all of Jefferson's equines, the gifts of potent donkeys from Europe, the great mule nurseries of the early 19th Century in Missouri, and on and on. As I somehow wanted to tie my subject to poetry, I used mule as metaphor for the stubborn perseverance of the poet. When it was time to send out the announcements for the lecture, the copy went to a printer who was sure there was a misprint; he printed the title as, "The Poet and the Muse." All the invitations had to be reprinted. That was my second lecture.

SCOP: What about readings?

MK   I did a reading each of the two years and of course set up readings at the Library.

SCOP   Who did you invite?

MK   I asked Adrienne Rich who had refused all the preceding invitations to read at the Library. The night she read people were lined up around the building. A huge overflow audience had to see her over closed circuit TV.

I tried to find the women writers who had not been invited before — Audre Lorde, Eleanor Ross Taylor. Then there were a few I was told to invite, pretty much a command performance. But that was okay. The readings were interesting and reasonably well attended. A Washington audience is not like a New York audience; that's the most sophisticated poetry audience I have read to.

SCOP Some Consultants traveled a good deal. Did you?

MK   No. Other than visits to Maryland and Virginia, I basically lived in town for the academic year.

SCOP Did you pick your successor?

MK   I am sure I proposed a woman and I'm sure I was shot down. I said, "Oh, god, after me they won't have another woman in years." But then they had Gwendolyn Brooks, probably to show they were not anti-woman and not anti-black.

SCOP Were you able to get your own writing done?

MK   A little. I wrote the poem, "Lines Written in the Library of Congress After the Cleanth Brooks Lecture." In fact I wrote more than I thought I might. I'm able to carry a poem around in my head. I can work on it while I'm driving, riding, or washing dishes and then, when I get back to my desk, I'll write down the first draft.

SCOP When you came away from your two years as Consultant, had your view of the position shifted?

MK   Not really. Basically it's a showcase appointment. Each consultant — or now, Laureate — has to shape the job as he or she sees fit. That's apt and proper and as it should be.

EDUCATION

Radcliffe College, A.B., 1946; A.M. 1948
D. Hum. Lett. (honorary) from: Centre College, Danville, KY,
1976; Davis & Elkins College, Elkins, WV, 1977; Regis Col-
lege, Weston, MA, 1979; New England College, Henniker,
NH, 1982; Claremont Graduate School, Claremont, CA,
1983; University of New Hampshire, 1984; Keene State Col-
lege, 1995

AWARDS AND GRANTS

1996 Centennial Award, Harvard Graduate School of Arts and
Sciences
1995 Aiken Taylor Poetry Prize for *Looking for Luck*
1994 Poets' Prize for *Looking for Luck*
Sarah Josepha Hale Award, Richards Library, Newport, NH,
1992
Levinson Prize, Poetry Magazine, 1986
Fellowship, Academy of American Poets, 1985
Arts America tour, US Information Agency, 1983
American Academy and Institute of Arts & Letters Award, 1980
Radcliffe College Alumnae Recognition Award, 1978
Borestone Mountain Award (first place) Best Poems of 1976
Pulitzer Prize for Poetry, 1973 for *Up County*
Eunice Tietjens Memorial Prize, *Poetry* Magazine, 1972
National Council on the Arts Fellowship, 1967-8
Fellow, Bunting Institute, 1961-3

PUBLICATIONS

Poetry
Selected Poems, 1960-1990. W.W. Norton Co., (May) 1997.
Connecting the Dots. W.W. Norton Co., 1996.
Looking for Luck. W.W. Norton Co., 1992.
Nurture. Viking/ Penguin 1989.
The Long Approach. Viking /Penguin, 1985-6.

Our Ground Time Here Will Be Brief, New and Selected Poems.
Viking/Penguin, 1982.
The Retrieval System. Viking/Penguin, 1978.
House, Bridge, Fountain, Gate. Viking/ Penguin, 1975.
Up Country. Harper & Row, 1972.
The Nightmare Factory. Harper & Row, 1970.
The Privilege. Harper & Row, 1965.
Halfway. Holt, Rinehart & Winston, 1961.

Novels
The Designated Heir. Viking, 1974; Andre Deutsch (England).
The Abduction. Harper & Row, 1971.
The Passions of Uxport. Harper & Row, 1968, Dell paper, 1969.
Through Dooms of Love. Harper & Row, 1965; Hamish Hamilton
& Gollancz (England), Panther paper.

Short Stories
Why Can't We Live Together Like Civilized Human Beings? Viking,
1982.

Essays
Women, Animals, and Vegetables: Essays and Stories. Norton, 1994;
Ontario Review Press, paper, 1996.
In Deep: Country Essays. Viking 1987; Beacon Press 1988.
To Make a Prairie: Essays on Poets, Poetry and Country Living. University of Michigan Press, 1980.

Critique
Telling the Barn Swallow: Poets on the Poetry of Maxine Kumin, ed.
by Emily Grosholz, University Press of New England, 1997.

Lines Written in the Library of Congress
After the Cleanth Brooks Lecture

This morning a new bird is singing
history history
time
personal identity
three
touchstones of the poem
said Mr. Brooks
almost the silver-haired last
of the Fugitives
whose books
The Well-Wrought Urn especially
poured a warm stream of wisdom
on my undergraduate past.

This morning I leave
suburban Maryland
join the warm stream
driving down the George
Washington Memorial Park
past five dead uncurled opossums
past Turkey Run
the Chain Bridge the turn -
off to Arlington's
Unknown Soldier
cross the Potomac and inch
through the bad air
of rush hour
to the identity
of my personal parking space.

Plus ça change plus
c'est la même chose.
To avoid the pestilential
slums of his people
the Sun King had
a scenic route constructed
shrubbed with roses
from Versailles to Paris
I chat while rising
three stories
with the elevator operator
and enter this my office
coming face to face
with the architectural
miracles of
out nation's Capitol.

My door says:
CONSULTANT IN POETRY.
The hand with the arrow points here.
We live
said Mr. Brooks
in the respectable second-best
Silver Age of Literature.
I feel that at my desk.
Across it come
mannerly and rude requests
from Muse and Furies.
My job is metaphor
connotative modes of thought
irony and to introduce
the poets who read in the series.

At home in New Hampshire
the brooks are still frozen.
The barn doors
must be pickaxed loose
each morning from upheaved ground.
Evening grosbeaks cluster
in mobs at noon to devour
a spill of sunflower seed
and are gone.
Sap runs in the sugarbush
plinking from 12 to 3.
My shaggy red cows
meditate lying down
in mud under the pines.
They fatten on hay we hefted
in the sweat of late June.
Though civilization crumble
still their jaws describe
the sweet sideways munch
that works their cuds.

Down here my WATS line
relays news of failed grants
and lost petitions
from New York to California.
Two blocks away
on a gentrified street
heavy with Mercedes and pigeons
glass shatters every night
like a religion.
Thin as an eggshell the wall
crazes between Them and Us.
Newcomers live behind doors

oldtimers can kick in at will.
In a neighboring housing project
spraycan graffiti
—the script is vaguely Arabic—
announce Jesus curse Reagan
pour gall in the cup.

Meanwhile in the East Wing
of the National Gallery
Alexander
is turning into a god.
His eyes
roll up in his head.
His hair
allowed to grow into ringlets
resembles a hippie's.
He has laid waste Persepolis.
He has tramped into India.
Throughout his kingdom
the faces
of leering women look up
from the bottoms of ceremonial cups.

Everywhere lions
are being slaughtered.
Slit open
their hides are hung
on the brows of victors.
In Scythia soft gold
is spun into stalks of wheat
into acorns with pinprick pore holes.
Elaborate coins are struck
and o the horses of antiquity!

Everyman a sculptor
a poet et cetera.

Easy to attain
this cheap nostalgia
for a time as cruel as ours.
All ages are contemporaneous
Pound said
in his Golden One.
This week Pakistan
has reinstituted public floggings
with an electric refinement:
victims wear
microphones around their necks
to amplify their screams.
In an inspired flair
one cut above reading entrails
our government rewards that regime
with military hardware.

This week Lady Bird's
two million spring bulbs
open on Capitol Hill.
My flowerbooks dated 1905
says the yellow tulip
signifies hopeless love.
Magnolias
resisting lead particulates
lift their little beaks
along Pennsylvania Avenue
where triads of the unemployed
squat on the stoops
of vacant brownstones.

Angel dust is dispensed
casually in parking lots
from the front seats of old El Dorados
but to buy a *blanc de blanc*
one must enter a wineshop
barred like an arsenal.

How clumsily
I straddle these two lives!
A house guest in this city
in two weeks I go back
to lilac and apple bloom
to blackflies and caterpillars.
Morels under the apple trees.
Woodchucks. Porcupines.
The grace of mares in new pasture.
The full-time penance of mosquitoes.
Five miles of beans to hoe.
I pay fealty
to the tyranny of weather.

I pay fealty
to the wisdom of the fathers.
When I was eighteen and believed
in infinite perfectibility
I marched at Fore River
organizing the shipyard for the CIO.
Equal pay for equal work
we Cliffies chanted
meaning blacks and women
then took the subway back
to Jolly-Ups and dinners in the dorms
waited on by Irish biddies

in pale green uniforms.
Now I believe in infinite depravity.
Plus ça change....

Mr. Brooks
we live suspended
between apathy and terror.
Decorum has left us.
The Silver Age tarnishes.
While the middle class
dreams of skinny dips
at Truro or the Eastern Shore
Washington slumps
in its opening heat wave.
Today in the *Post*
a respected columnist
fears new riots this summer.
Have we not
named highways and libraries
for Martin Luther King?
Called rocket sites and airports
after either Kennedy?
Weeks apart
a president and pope are shot.
The National Rifle Association
turns up its air conditioners
on Winfield Scott Circle.

Early in May in
suburban Maryland
a new bird is singing
something oracular and bright:
history history

time
running out
the bomb Mr. Brooks
in the furious grip
of the Libyans
the Iraqis Israelis Argentinians
the bomb written large
in the Doomsday Book.

Poetry
makes nothing happen.
It survives
in the valley of its saying.
Auden taught us that.
Next year another
Consultant will sit
under the hand with the arrow
that props the door ajar
for metaphor.
New poets will lie on their backs
listening in the valley
making nothing happen
overhearing history
history time
personal identity
inching toward Armageddon.

Our Ground Time Here Will Be Brief

Blue landing lights make
nail holes in the dark.
A fine snow falls. We sit
on the tarmac taking on
the mail, quick freight,
trays of laboratory mice,
coffee and Danish for
the passengers.

Wherever we're going
is Monday morning.
Wherever we're coming from
is Mother's lap.
On the cloud-pack above, strewn
as loosely as parsnip
or celery seeds, lie
the souls of the unborn:

my children's children's
children and their father.
We gather speed for the last run
and lift off into the weather.

Henry Manley, Living Alone, Keeps Time

Sundowning,
the doctor calls it, the way
he loses words when the light fades.
The way the names of his dear ones
fall out of his eyeglass case.
Even under the face of his father
in an oval on the wall
he cannot say *Catherine, Vera, Paul*
but goes on loving them out of place.
Window, wristwatch, cup, knife
are small prunes that drop from his pockets.
Terror sweeps him from room to room.
Knowing how much he weighed once
he knows how much he has departed his life.
Especially he knows how the soul
can slip out of the body unannounced
like that helium-filled balloon
he opened his fingers on, years back.

Now it is dark. He undresses
and takes himself off to bed
as loose in his skin as a puppy,
afraid the blankets will untuck,
afraid he will flap up, unblessed.
Instead, proper nouns return to his keeping.
The names of faces are put back
in his sleeping mouth. At first light
he gets up, grateful once more
for how coffee smells. Sits stiff
at the bruised porcelain table
saying them over, able
to with only the slightest catch.
Coffee. Coffee cup. Watch.

The Retrieval System

It begins with my dog, now dead, who all his long life
carried about in his head the brown eyes of my father,
keen, loving, accepting, sorrowful, whatever;
they were Daddy's all right, handed on, except
for their phosphorescent gleam tunneling the night
which I have to concede was a separate gift.

Uncannily when I'm alone these features
come up to link my lost people
with the patient domestic beasts of my life. For example,
the wethered goat who runs free in pasture and stable
with his flecked, agate eyes and his minus-sign pupils
blats in the tiny voice of my former piano teacher

whose bones beat time in my dreams and whose terrible breath
soured "Country Gardens," "Humoresque," and unplayable
    Bach.
My elderly aunts, wearing the heads of willful
intelligent ponies, stand at the fence begging apples.
The sister who died at three has my cat's faint chin,
my cat's inscrutable squint, and cried catlike in pain.

I remember the funeral. *The Lord is my shepherd,*
we said. I don't want to brood. Fact: it is people who fade,
it is animals that retrieve them. A boy
I loved once keeps coming back as my yearling colt,
cocksure at the gallop, racing his shadow
for the hell of it. He runs merely to be.
A boy who was lost in the war thirty years ago
and buried at sea.

Here, it's forty degrees and raining. The weatherman
who looks like my resident owl, the one who goes out and in
by the open haymow, appears on the TV screen.
With his heart-shaped face, his is also my late dentists's double,
donnish, bifocaled, kind. Going a little gray,
advising this wisdom tooth will have to come out someday,
meanwhile filling it as a favor. Another save.
It outlasted him. The forecast is nothing but trouble.
It will snow fiercely enough to fill all these open graves.

Connecting the Dots

I think Daddy
just dropped dead
(our son at five)
I'll drive the car
and now they drive
us living, the large

children home
a week at Christmas
ten days in August
posing for
the family snapshot
flanked by dogs.

We're assayed kindly
to see if we're
still competent
to keep house, mind
the calendar
connect the dots.

Well, we're still stack-
ing wood for winter
turning compost
climbing ladders
and they still love us
who overtake us

who want what's best
for us, who sound
(deep reservoirs
of patience) the way
we did, or like
to think we did.

Getting the Message

God, the rabbis tell us, never assigns
exalted office to a man until
He has tested his mettle in small things.
So it is written in the *Midrash*
that when a lamb escaped the flock Moses
overtook it at a brook drinking its fill
and said, I would have taken thee in my arms
and carried thee thither had I known thy thirst
whereupon a Heavenly Voice warmly
resounded, *As thou livest, thou art fit.*

Divine election's scary. The burning bush
might have been brightened by St. Elmo's fire
according to *The Interpretor's One-Volume
Commentary.* The slopes of Exodus,
scrub growth close-cropped by tough horned herds
of Jacob's sheep (now prized as an heirloom breed)
lack treetops, mountain peaks or spires
that might discharge electrical ghost-plumes.
St. Elmo's seems less science than the desire
of modern exegetes to damp the flame.

I like my Bible tales, like Scotch, straight up
incontrovertible as Dante's trip
through seven circles, Milton's map
of Paradise or Homer's wine-dark epic.
On such a stage there falls a scrim between
text and critique where burst of light may crack
and dance as if on masts of sailing ships
and heavenly voices leap from alp to plain.
In Sunday School I shivered at God's command:
Take off thy shoes, thou stand'st on holy ground

and lay awake in the hot clutch of faith
yearning yet fearful that the Lord might speak
to me in my bed or naked in my bath.
I didn't know how little risk I ran
of being asked to set my people free
from fording some metaphorical Red Sea
with a new-sprung Pharaoh raging at my back.
I didn't know the patriarchy that spared me
fame had named me chattel, handmaiden.
God's Angels looked me over but flew by.

I like to think God's talent scouts today
select for covenant without regard
for gender, reinterpreting The Word
so that holy detectives glossing the bush
(most likely wild acacia), scholars of J
E and P deciphering Exodus
will fruitfully research the several ways
divine authentication lights up truth.
Fragments of it, cryptic, fugitive
still spark the synapses that let us live.

from *Tikkun*

The Festung, Salzburg

I shall have to pee out the window, says the translation
in the 1902 pocket phrasebook Alastair's
grandfather gave him. Also, *Call the hostler!*
and *Here are my boots*, meaning polish them
but nothing that helps decipher life in this fortress
four hundred years ago, all cobble and cannon,
all ice storms and armor and horses. How, for example,
did they haul water for livestock and people?
Out of what reservoir make time for
carving twelve marble apostles and a Christ
that are tucked in a chapel chipped from the rock
of the scarp that commands the Salzach?
No idiom to tell us how secure
this Festung was before war took the air.

Down in the candybox town we dawdle
at Tomaselli's over cups of hot chocolate.
I pretend I have come back here for the sake
of my forebears, come back out of exile
to reinvent how it was for them,
seeking among the faces that pass
those as old as I, those few with missing
limbs, or sightless, who endured the Anschluss,
seeking among the dirndls and lederhosen
the unknowable middleaged ones who risked the ovens
and came through stained with a deep understanding.
Bitte, bitte schön. Ropes of rain
fall on a sea of purposeful umbrellas
in calm green homogeneous Austria.

The Envelope

It is true, Martin Heidegger, as you have written,
I fear to cease, even knowing that at the hour
of my death my daughters will absorb me, even
knowing they will carry me about forever
inside them, an arrested fetus, even as I carry
the ghost of my mother under my navel, a nervy
little androgynous person, a miracle
folded in lotus position.

Like those old pear-shaped Russian dolls that open
at the middle to reveal another and another, down
to the pea-sized, irreducible minim,
may we carry our mothers forth in our bellies.
May we, borne onward by our daughters, ride
in the Envelope of Almost-Infinity,
that chain letter good for the next twenty-five
thousand days of their lives.

Heaven as Anus

In the Defense Department there is a shop
where scientists sew the eyelids of rabbits open
lest they blink in the scorch of a nuclear drop

and elsewhere dolphins are being taught to defuse
bombs in the mock-up of a harbor and monkeys
learn to perform the simple tasks of draftees.

It is done with electric shocks. Some mice
who have failed their time tests in the maze
now go to the wire unbidden for their jolts.

Implanting electrodes yields rich results:
alley cats turn from predators into prey,
Show them a sparrow and they cower

while the whitewall labs fill up with the feces of fear
where calves whose hearts have been done away
with walk and bleat on plastic pumps.

And what is any of this to the godhead,
these squeals, whines, writhings, unexpected jumps,
whose children burn alive, booby-trap the dead,
lop ears and testicles, core and disembowel?

It all ends at the hole. No words may enter
the house of excrement. We will meet there
as the sphincter of the good Lord opens wide
and He takes us all inside.

GWENDOLYN BROOKS

1985–1986

Photo by Wayne Lee Radziminski

GWENDOLYN BROOKS

Stacy Tuthill

Gwendolyn Brooks came to the Library of Congress in 1985, the final appointee as *Consultant* in Poetry to the Library of Congress. She was already familiar with the requirements of the office when she accepted the position. Over the years she had participated in various functions on special occasions, had knowledge of work done by her predecessors and was acquainted with the people who would be her associates. She had been offered the position in 1973-74 but had refused for personal and family reasons. She already knew she was expected to enter with a poetry reading and close her term with a lecture. She knew the Consultant was expected to recommend poets to read in the Coolidge Auditorium series of programs. It would be her job to introduce the speakers who read at the Library, some of whom she selected. This was a privilege she said she enjoyed. Other than these expectations, she was left pretty much alone to develop her own programs.

Brooks said she was frequently asked "What does the Consultant in Poetry do?" usually accompanied by a smile, the implication being that the Consultant does nothing. She said many people laugh when they hear the word "poet," imagining someone "akin to a lunatic." People who have little interest in poetry do not know the position is not only intellectually and physically demanding, but also respected and revered.

Brooks lived at the Capitol Hill Hotel across the street from the Library and was readily available to work long hours. She said she never worked so hard in her life and has never been so "gloriously exhausted." On Coolidge Auditorium Reading days, she worked from 9:30 a.m. to 11:00 p.m. She worked in her office on the Third Floor until time for the presentation at 8:00 p.m. followed by a reception from which she and security were among the last to leave. Brooks said she was impressed with the respect afforded the Consultant's office. She described the cooperation she received as "Complete! Super!" and everywhere she went she met people with friendly smiles: "I wanted to hug them all," she notes in her autobiography:

> Semi-saint John Broderick, assistant librarian for research services, has labored mightily and graciously to get the people here whom I wanted to introduce to you. Cheery, expert, cooperative, friendly, self-effacing John "Communications" Sullivan! Poetry associate Nancy Galbraith — not only brilliant and knowledgeable in an assortment of areas, but the magnificent wheel-oiler Upstairs. Because of her mysteriously expert influence, achievements seem seamless. She has coordinated my matters — appointments, rearrangements, visitor reception, general clarification — with what seems to me a special genius. Jenny Rutland — our second poetry associate — new-penny bright, reliable, hard-working, genial and generous (Brooks, Part II).

Brooks opened her season with the traditional poetry reading. The Coolidge Auditorium was packed with a long line waiting outside. She was the first African-American woman and the second African-American (Robert Hayden was the first) to be Consultant in Poetry to the Library of Congress. At the end of her reading, her daughter, Nora, who sat in a front seat, stood up and said, "Oh, Mama, it's The Day of the Gwendolyn," a title she chose for her closing lecture. William McGuire notes how she stayed almost two hours after her final lecture to talk with friends and acquaintances, to sign books, and to sign her name on slips of paper, envelopes or napkins.

Gwendolyn Brooks was one of the best loved and most active and accessible of the Consultants in Poetry to the Library of Congress. Although her term began and ended with a flurry of activity, she said she still found time to write. In addition to inviting nationally-known poets to read, she also held noontime readings for local poets and regional poets. She usually paid an honorarium from her own funds, and afterwards took as many as twenty poets to a luncheon for which she also paid. She held three "brown-bag" noontime sessions for local poets, a practice initiated by Maxine Kumin. A number of foreign visitors came to her office. Some came only to meet her and engage in conversation, but she was able to arrange readings and receptions for others. Writers and critics came with interpreters from places like Poland, Jordan, Costa Rica, Bolivia, El Salvador, Columbia, Argentina, and other places in the world where her poetry is known. She also recommended some of these poets for recordings.

In addition to being taped, interviewed, and televised, she visited many area educational institutions — Georgetown University, George Washington University, University of Virginia, Community College of Baltimore, the Enoch Pratt Free Library, and the University of Virginia as well as distant educational institutions in Atlanta, Seattle, and the University of Vermont. During that year she gave commencement addresses and was awarded four of her more than seventy honorary doctorate degrees.

Brooks visited elementary and high schools in Washington D.C., Maryland, and Virginia. She answered mail from Monday to Wednesday afternoons from people nationwide asking for advice or help with poetry. According to McGuire, she "answered each letter warmly and constructively" (430). When work permitted, she traveled by train to her home in Chicago.

Her list of activities reveals she took her mission into the community. Understanding the healing power of poetry, she visited a senior wellness center, the Maryland Correctional Facility in Jessup. Lorton Prison in Virginia, and the Comprehensive Alcohol and Drug Abuse Center. She also read and spoke at churches as well as schools. She writes in her autobiography:

> "I have managed to excite many area youngsters toward a realization that poetry can be nourishing and enhancing and, again, extending. I have not told these youngsters that handling paper and pencil will guarantee a Pulitzer Price. I tell them, chiefly, that poetry, written or read, can enrich and strengthen their lives. I tell that to other sizes of people too" (Brooks, Part II).

The Washington poetry community was saddened that Gwendolyn Brooks did not stay on for a second year. John Sullivan and Nancy Galbraith were eager for her to stay. The re-naming of the position to "Poet Laureate" was made *after* she had announced her decision to leave. She indicated in correspondence that she liked everything about the job. Then as now, she travels steadily for readings all over the country but might have been able to adjust her schedule if asked to continue as the *first* Poet Laureate. She wrote in a letter saying "Spark Matsunaga was quoted in the *Washington Post* at that time, that he had "naturally" expected me to inherit the title, to go *on* with the job." (see Editors' Notes) The position was subsequently awarded to Robert Penn Warren.

Brooks indicated in correspondence that she likes the continued practice of allowing candidates to develop their own programs. She is also pleased the Library of Congress continues to select a different poet every year or two, which stills the fears of some that the title "Poet Laureate" might mean a lifetime position as it has in some countries.

There was sadness because Brooks is a rare mold among people, especially poets. She exudes warmth, love, generosity, modesty, compassion, has a great sense of humor and a willingness to give encouragement to anyone, especially poets. She attributes much of her success to the love and encouragement of her parents. She wrote in her autobiography that she has met two queens and three presidents, but she has never seen better role models than her mother and father. Her parents, religious and nourishing, not only praised her writing from an early age, but they made her feel "good" to be Black. She also indicates in her autobiography (Brooks, Part II) that it was not until the Civil Rights Movement of the 1960's that she developed an active African-American awareness. She notes the effect of the movement on her writing is reflected in *The Mecca* and *Winnie*. Although her work was already accepted by a large publisher (Harper & Brothers) and she had a national reputation, she chose to support small presses operated by African-Americans, such as Dudley Randall's Broadside Press and Haki R. Madhubuti's Third World Press.

Mrs. Gwendolyn Brooks-Blakely (as she is called in private life) gives much credit for her success to her husband, Henry L. Blakely II, also a writer, who died July 3, 1996. He told her she must never sacrifice her writing for sweeping, cooking, or washing dishes. He always supported her efforts and expressed delight at her many honors. Perhaps it was these positive influences that led Gwendolyn Brooks to be friendly, loving, and generous with herself and her time as she fulfilled her demanding duties as Poetry Consultant to the Library of Congress.

SOURCES CITED

Brooks, Gwendolyn: correspondence and written interview questions.

Brooks-Blakely, Gwendolyn, *Report From PART TWO*. autobiography. Chicago: Third World Press, 1966.

McGuire, William. *Poetry 's Catbird Seat*. Library of Congress, Washington, D.C. 1995.

The Contemporary Forum, 2528 W. Jerome Street, Chicago, Ill. 60645-1507 provided information on honors, books, and schedules).

PUBLICATIONS

A Street in Bronzeville (poems), 1945
Annie Allen (poems), 1949 (Received Pulitzer Prize, 1950)
Maud Martha (novel), 1953
Bronzeville Boys & Girls (poems), 1956
The Bean Eaters (poems), 1960
Selected Poems, 1963
In the Mecca (poems), 1968
Riot (poems), 1969
Family Pictures (poems), 1970

The Tiger Who Wore White Gloves (poems), 1970
Aloneness (poems), 1971
World of Gwendolyn Brooks (poems), 1971
Jump Bad: A New Chicago Anthology, 1971
Report from Part One (autobiography), 1972
Capsule Course in Black Poetry Writing, 1975
Beckonings (poems), 1975
Primer for Blacks (poems/essays), 1980
To Disembark (poems), 1981
Young Poet's Primer (poems/lessons), 1981
Very Young Poets (poems/lessons), 1983
The Near-Johannesburg Boy (poems), 1986
Blacks (formerly The World of Gwendolyn Brooks), 1987
Gottschalk and the Grande Tarantelle (poems), 1988
Winnie (poems), 1988
Children Coming Home (poems), 1991
Report from Part Two (second part of autobiogrpahy), 1996

The following publishing companies can be contacted for books by Gwendolyn Brooks:
Third World Press, 7822 South Dobson, Chicago, IL 60619. Phone: 312-651-0700. Fax 312-651-7286.
Broadside Press, 4734 Sturtevant, Detroit, MI 48204. Phone: 313-934-1231.
For *Gwendolyn Brooks: Poetry and the Heroic Voice* by Dr. D. H. Melhem and *Gwendolyn Brooks, a Life* by Dr. George Kent, contact the University Press of Kentucky, 102 Lafferty hall, Uniersity of Kentucky, Lexington, KY 40506-0024.

HONORS

Gwendolyn Brooks' honors are too numerous to list in entirety, but we will name here those most recent and/or notable:
Guggenheim Fellowships, 1946 and 1947
Shelley Memorial Award and Anisfield-Wolf Award, 1940s
Pulitzer Prize for *Annie Allen*, 1950

Poet Laureate of Illinois since 1968, following Carl Sandburg
Kuumba Liberation Award, 1969
Named a member of the Academy and Institute of Arts and Letters, 1985
Named Consultant in Poetry to the Library of Congress, 1985
Inducted into the National Women's Hall of Fame, 1988
Frost Medal from the Poetry Society of America, 1989
Lifetime Achievement Award, National Endowment for the Arts, 1989
Society of Literature Award, University of Thessalonike, Athens, Greece, 1990 (only American to receive this award)
Dedication of The Gwendolyn Brooks Center for Literature and Culture, Chicago State University (where Brooks is writer in residence), 1993
Named Jefferson Lecturer, for Distinguished Intellectual Achievement in the Humanities by The National Endowment for the Humanities, 1994
Medal for Distinguished Contribution to American Letters (for *In the Mecca*), National Book Foundation, 1994
National Medal of Arts presented by President and Mrs. Clinton, 1994
Bronze bust of Ms. Brooks placed in Chicago's Harold Washington Library and in main Chicago Library, 1994
Chicago Pioneer Award from The Before Columbus Foundation presented at American Book Award Conference, 1995
Copy of bronze bust commissioned by National Portrait Gallery, Washington, DC, 1995
Invested as a Laureate of the Lincoln Academy of Illinois (the highest honor bestowed on residents of Illinois), April 26, 1997
Ms. Brooks has received over 70 honorary degrees

Gwendolyn Brooks was born in 1917 to David and Keziah Wims Brooks in Topeka, Kansas. She has lived in Chicago since she was six weeks old. There she met and married Henry L. Blakely in September, 1939. He was also a writer. She has two grown children, Nora Brooks Blakely and Henry Blakely, III.

In the Mecca

Sit where the light corrupts your face.
Mies Van der Rohe retires from grace.
And the fair fables fall.

S. Smith is Mrs. Sallie. Mrs. Sallie
hies home to Mecca, hies to marvelous rest;
ascends the sick and influential stair.
The eye unrinsed, the mouth absurd
with the last sourings of the master's Feast.
She plans
to set severity apart,
to unclench the heavy folly of the fist.
Infirm booms
and suns that have not spoken die behind this
low-brown butterball. Our prudent partridge.
A fragmentary attar and armed coma.
A fugitive attar and a district hymn.

Sees old St. Julia Jones, who has had prayer,
and who is rising from amenable knees
inside the wide-flung door of 215.
"Isn't He wonderfulwonderful!" cries St. Julia.
"Isn't our Lord the greatest to the brim?
The light of my life. And I lie late
past the still pastures. And meadows. He's the comfort
and wine and piccalilli for my soul.
He hunts me up the coffee for my cup.
Oh how I love that Lord."
                              And Mrs. Sallie,
all innocent of saints and signatures,
nods and consents, content to endorse
Lord as an incense and a vintage. Speaks
to Prophet Williams, young beyond St. Julia,

and rich with Bible, pimples, pout: who reeks
with lust for his disciple, is an engine
of candid steel hugging combustibles.
His wife she was a skeleton.
His wife she was a bone.
Ida died in self-defense.
(Kinswomen!
Kinswomen!)
Ida died alone.

Out of her dusty threshold bursts Hyena.
The striking debutante. A fancier of firsts.
One of the first, and to the tune of hate,
in all the Mecca to paint her hair sun-gold.
        And Mrs.
Sallie sees Alfred. Ah, his God!—
To create! To create! To bend with the tight intentness
over the neat detail, come to
a terrified standstill of the heart, then shiver,
then rush—successfully—
at that rebuking thing, that obstinate and
recalcitrant little beast, the phrase!
To have the joy of deciding—successfully—
how stuffs can be compounded or sifted out
and emphasized; what the importances are;
what coats in which to wrap things. Alfred is un-
talented. Knows. Marks time and themes at Phillips,
stares, glares, of mornings, at a smear
which does not care what he may claim or doubt
or probe or clear or want, or what he might have been.
He "fails" no one; at faculty lunch hour
allows the zoology teacher, who has great legs,
to fondle him and curse his pretty hair. He

reads Shakespeare in the evenings or reads Joyce
or James or Horace, Huxley, Hemingway.
Later, he goes to bed with Telly Bell
in 309, or with that golden girl,
or thinks, or drinks until the Everything
is vaguely a part of One thing and the One thing
delightfully anonymous
and undiscoverable. So he is weak,
is weak, is no good. Never mind.
It is a decent enough no-goodness. And it is
a talkative, curly, charitable, spiced weakness
which makes a woman in charge of zoology
dream furiously at night.
When there were all those gods
administering to panthers,
jumping over mountains,
and lighting stars and comets and a moon,
what was their one Belief?
what was their joining thing?

A boy breaks glass and Mrs. Sallie
rises to the final and fourth floor.

Children, what she has brought you is hock of ham.
She puts the pieces to boil in white enamel, right
already with water of many seasonings, at the back
of the cruel stove. And mustard mesmerized by
eldest daughter, the Undaunted (she who once
pushed her thumbs in the eyes of a Thief), awaits
the clever hand. Six ruddy yams abide, and
cornbread made with water.

Now Mrs. Sallie
confers her bird-hat to her kitchen table,
and sees her kitchen. It is bad, is bad,
her eyes say, and My soft antagonist,
her eyes say, and My headlong tax and mote,
her eyes say, and My maniac default,
my least light.
"But all my lights are little!"
Her denunciation
slaps savagely not only this sick kitchen but
her Lord's annulment of the main event.
"I want to decorate!" But what is that? A
pomade atop a sewage. An offense.
First comes correctness, *then* embellishment!
And music, mode, and mixed philosophy
may follow fitly on propriety
to tame the whiskey of our discontent!
"What can I do?"
          But World (a sheep)
wants to be Told.
If you ask a question, you
can't stop there.
You must keep going.
You can't stop there: World will
waive; will be
facetious, angry. You can't stop there.
You have to keep on going.

Doublemint as a protective device. Yvonne
prepares for her lover.
Gum is something he can certify.
Gum is something he can understand.
A tough girl gets it. A rough

Ruthie or Sue. It is unembarrassable,
and will seem likely. It is very bad,
but in its badness it is nearly grand,
and is a crown that tops bald innocence
and gentle fright.
It is not necessary, says Yvonne,
to have every day him whom
to the end thereof you will love.
Because it is tasty to remember
he is alive, and laughs
in somebody else's room,
or is slicing a cold cucumber,
or is buttoning his cuffs,
or is signing with his pen
and will plan
to touch you again.

Melodie Mary hates everything pretty and plump.
And Melodie, Cap and Casey
and Thomas Earl, Tennessee, Emmett and Briggs
hate sewn suburbs;
hate everything combed and strong; hate people who
have balls, dolls, mittens and dimity frocks and trains
and boxing gloves, picture books, bonnets for Easter.
Lace handkerchief owners are enemies of Smithkind.

Melodie Mary likes roaches,
and pities the gray rat.
To delicate Melodie Mary
headlines are secondary.
It is interesting that in China
the children blanch and scream,
and that blood runs like a ragged wound

through the ancient flesh of the land.
It matters, mildly,
that the Chinese girls are grim,
and that hurried are the seizures
of yellow hand on hand....
What if they drop like the tumbling tears
of the old and intelligent sky?
Where are the frantic bulletins
when other importances die?
Trapped in his privacy of pain
the worried rat expires,
and smashed in the grind of a rapid heel
last night's roaches lie.

Briggs is adult as a stone
(who if he cries cries alone).
The gangs are out, but he must go
to and fro,
appease what reticences move
across the intemperate range.
Immunity is forfeit, love
is luggage, hope is heresy.
Gang
is health and mange.
Gang
is a bunch of ones and a singlicity.
Please pity Briggs. But there is a central height in pity
past which man's hand and sympathy cannot go;
past which the little hurt dog
descends to mass—no longer Joe,
not Bucky, not Cap'n, not Rex,
not Briggs—and is all self-employed,
concerned with Other,

not with Us.
Briggs, how "easy," finally, to accept (after the shriek and
          repulsion)
the unacceptable evil. To proceed with some éclat;
some salvation of the face;
awake! to choke the chickens, file their blood.

One reason cats are happier than people
is that they have no newspapers... I must be,
culls Tennessee,
like my cat, content to gaze
at men and women spurting here and there.
I must sit, let
them stroke me as and when they will;
must drink their milk and cry
for meat. At other times I must be still.
Who tingles in
and mixes with affairs and others met
comes out with scratches and is very thin
and rides the red possession of regret.

      In the midst
of hells and gruels and little halloweens
tense Thomas Earl loves Johnny Appleseed.
"I, Johnny Appleseed."
It is hard to be Johnny Appleseed.
The ground shudders.
The ground springs up;
hits you with gnarls and rust,
derangement and fever, or blare and clerical treasons.

Emmett and Cap and Casey
are skin wiped over bones

for lack of chub and chocolate
and ice cream cones,
for lack of English muffins
and boysenberry jam.
What shall their redeemer be?
Greens and hock of ham.
For each his greens and hock of ham
and a spoon of sweet potato.

Alfred says:
The faithless world!
betraying yet again
trinities!
My chaste displeasure
is not enough;
the brilliant British of the new command
is not enough;
the counsels of division, the hot counsels,
the scuffle and short pout
are not enough, are only
a pressure of clankings and affinities
against
the durable fictions of a Charming Trash.
Mrs. Sallie
evokes and loves and loathes a pink-lit image
of the toy-child. Her Lady's.
Her Lady's pink convulsion, toy-child dances
in stiff wide pink through Mrs. Sallie. Stiff pink is
on toy-child's poverty of cream
under a shiny tended warp of gold.
What shiny tended gold is an aubade
for toy-child's head! Has ribbons too!
Ribbons. Not Woolworth cotton comedy,

not rubber band, not string....
"And that would be my baby be my baby....
And I would be my lady I my lady...."

What else is there to say but everything?

SUDDENLY, COUNTING NOSES, MRS. SALLIE
SEES NO PEPITA. "WHERE PEPITA BE?"

...Cap, where Pepita? Casey, where Pepita?
Emmett and Melodie Mary, where Pepita?
Briggs, Tennessee, Yvonne, and Thomas Earl,
where may our Pepita be?—
our Woman with her terrible eye,
with iron and feathers in her feet,
with all her songs so lemon-sweet,
with lightning and a candle too
and junk and jewels too?
My heart begins to race.
I fear the end of Peace.

Ain seen er I ain seen er I ain seen er
Ain seen er I ain seen er I ain seen er

Yvonne up-ends her iron. And is constrained.
Cannot now conjure love-within-the-park.
Cannot now conjure spice and soft explosion
mixing with miffed mosquitoes where the dark
defines and re-defines.

And Melodie Mary
and Thomas Earl and Tennessee and Briggs
yield cat-contentment gangs rats Appleseed.

Emmett and Cap and Casey
yield visions of vice and veal,
dimes and windy carnival,
candied orange peel,
peppermint in a pickle;
and where the ladybug
glistens in her leaf-hammock; *light*
lasses to hiss and hug.

And they are constrained. All are constrained.
    And there is no thinking of grapes or gold
    or of any wicked sweetness and they ride
    upon fright and remorse and their stomachs
    are rags or grit.
In twos!
In threes! Knock-knocking down the martyred halls
at doors behind whose yelling oak or pine
    many flowers start, choke, reach up,
    want help, get it, do not get it,
    rally, bloom, or die on the wasting vine.

"One of my children is missing. One of my children is gone."

Great-great Gram hobbles, fumbles at the knob,
mumbles, "I ain seen no Pepita. But
I remember our cabin. The floor was dirt.
And something crawled in it. That is the thought
stays in my mind. I do not recollect
what 'twas. But something. Something creebled in that dirt
for we wee ones to pop. Kept popping at it.
Something that squishied. *Then* your heel come down!
I hear them squishies now.... *Pop*, Pernie May!
That's sister Pernie. That's my sister Pernie.

Squish.... Out would jump her little heel.
And that was the end of Something. Sister Pernie
was our best popper. Pern and me and all,
we had no beds. Some slaves had beds of hay
or straw, with cover-cloth. We six-uns curled
in corners of the dirt, and closed our eyes,
and went to sleep—or listened to the rain
fall inside, felt the drops
big on our noses, bummies and tum-tums...."

Although he has not seen Pepita, Loam
Norton considers Belsen and Dachau,
regrets all old unkindnesses and harms.
...The Lord was their shepherd.
Yet did they want.
Joyfully would they have lain in jungles or pastures,
walked beside waters. Their gaunt
souls were not restored, their souls were banished.
In the shadow valley
they feared the evil, whether with or without God.
They were comforted by no Rod,
no Staff, but flayed by, O besieged by, shot a-plenty.
The prepared table was the rot or curd of the day.
Anointings were of lice. Blood was the spillage of cups.
Goodness and mercy should follow them
        all the days of their death.
They should dwell in the house of the Lord forever
and, dwelling, save a place for me.
I am not remote,
not unconcerned....

Boontsie De Broe has
not seen Pepita Smith: but is

a Lady
among Last Ladies.
Erect. Direct.
An engraving on the crowd, the blurred crowd.
She is away and fond.
Her clear voice tells you life may be controlled.
Her clear mind is the extract
of massive literatures, of lores,
transactions of old ocean; suffrages.

Yvonne
recovers to aver
despite the stomp of the stupor.
          She will not go
in Hudson's hashhouse. And the Tivoli
is a muffler of Love.
In the blasé park,
that winks and mocks but is at all times
tolerant of the virtuous defect, of audit,
          and of mangle and of wile, he
may permit perusal of their ground,
its rubble-over-rose: may look to rainbow:
may sanction bridal tulle, white flowers,
may allow a mention of a minister and twins....

          But *other* Smiths are twitching. They recall
vain vagrants, recall old peddlers, young fine bumlets,
The Man Who Sells The Peaches Plums Bananas.
They recall the Fuller Brush Man,
oblique and delicate, who tries on
the very fit and feature of despair.
"Pepita's smart," says Sallie; her stretched eyes
reject the exact despatches of a mind turned boiler,

epithet, foiler, guillotine. *What*
of the Bad Old Man? the lover-like young man? the
half-mad boy who put his hand across Pepita's knee?
"Pepita's smart," says Sallie.
Knowing the ham hocks are burning at the bottom of the pan.

S. and eight of her children reach their door. The
door says, "What are you doing here? and where
is Pepita the puny—the halted, glad-sad child?"
They pet themselves, subdue
the legislation of their yoke and devils.
        Has just wandered!
        Has just blundered
        away
        from her own.
        And there's no worry
        that's necessary.
        She
        comes soon alone.
Comes soon alone or will be brought by neighbor.
Kind neighbor.

"Kind neighbor." They consider.
Suddenly
every one in the world is Mean.
Could that old woman, passively passing, mash a child?
Has she a tot's head in that shiny bag?
And that lank fellow looking furtive.
What
cold poison could he spew, what stench commit
upon a little girl, a little lost girl,
lone and languid in the world, wanting
her ma, her glad-sad, her Yvonne?

Emmett runs down the hall.
Emmett seizes John Tom's telephone.
(Despite the terror and the derivation,
despite the not avuncular frontier,
John Tom, twice forty in 420, claims
Life sits or blazes in this Mecca.
  And thereby—tenable.
  And thereby beautiful.)

Provoking calm and dalliance of the Law.
How shall the Law allow for littleness!
How shall the Law enchief the chapters of
wee brown-black chime, wee brown-black chastity?

The Law arrives—and does not quickly go
to fetch a Female of the Negro Race.
A lariat of questions.
The mother screams and wants her baby. Wants her baby,
and wants her baby wants her baby.

Law leaves, with likeness of a "southern" belle. Sheriffs,
South State Street is a Postulate!
Until you look. You look—and you discover
the paper dolls are terrible. You touch.
You look and touch.
The paper dolls are terrible and cold.

Aunt Dill arrives to help them. "Little gal got
raped and choked to death last week. Her gingham
was tied around her neck and it was red
but had been green before with pearls and dots
of rhinestone on the collar, and her tongue
was hanging out (a little to the side);

her eye was all a-pop, one was; was one
all gone. Part of her little nose was gone
(bit off, the Officer said). The Officer said
that something not quite right been done that girl.
Lived Langley: 'round the corner from my house."
Aunt Dill extends
sinister pianissimos and apples,
and at that moment of the Thousand Souls is
a Christ-like creature, Doing Good.

The Law returns. It trots about the Mecca.
It pounds a dozen doors.

No, Alfred has not seen Pepita Smith.
But he (who might have been an architect)
can speak of Mecca: firm arms surround
disorders, bruising ruses and small hells,
small semiheavens: hug barbarous rhetoric
built of buzz, coma and petite pell-mells.
No, Alfred has not seen Pepita Smith.
But he (who might have been a poet-king)
can speak superbly of the line of Leopold.
The line of Leopold is thick with blackness
        and Scriptural drops and rises.
The line of Leopold is busy with betrothals of royal rage
        and conditional pardon and with
refusal of mothballs for outmoded love.
Senghor will not shred
love,
gargantuan gardens careful in the sun,
fairy story gold, thrones, feasts, the three princesses,
summer sailboats
like cartoon ghosts or Klansmen, pointing up

white questions, in blue air....
No.
Believes in beauty.
But believes that blackness is among the fit filters.
Old cobra
coughs and curdles in his lungs,
spits spite, spits exquisite spite, and cries, "Ignoble!"
Needs "negritude."
Senghor (in Europe rootless and lonely) sings in art-lines
of Black Woman.
Senghor sighs and, "negritude" needing,
speaks for others, for brothers. Alfred can tell of
Poet, and muller, and President of Senegal, who
in voice and body
loves sun,
listens
to the rich pound in and beneath the black feet of Africa.

Hyena, the striking debutante, is back;
bathed, used by special oils and fumes, will be
off to the Ball tonight. She has not seen
Pepita— "a puny and a putrid little child."

Death is easy.
It may come quickly.
It may come when nobody is ready.
Death may come at any time. Mazola
has never known Pepita S. but knows
the strangest thing is when the stretcher goes!—
the elegant hucksters bearing the body when the body
leaves its late lair the last time leaves.
With no plans for return.

Don Lee wants
not a various America.
Don Lee wants
a new nation
under nothing;
a physical light that waxes; he does not want to
be exorcised, adjoining and revered;
he does not like a local garniture
nor any impish onus in the vogue;
is not candlelit
but stands out in the auspices of fire
and rock and jungle-flail;
wants
new art and anthem; will
want a new music screaming in the sun.

Says Alfred:
To be a red bush!
In the West Virginia autumn.
To flame out red.
"Crimson" is not word enough,
although close to what I mean.
How proud.
How proud.
(But the bush does not know it flames.)

"Takes time," grated the gradualist.
"Starting from when?" asked Amos.
Amos (not Alfred) says,
"Shall we sit on ourselves; shall we wait behind roses and veils
for monsters to maul us,
        for bulls to come butt us forever and ever,
shall we scratch in our blood,

point air-powered hands at our wounds,
reflect on the aim of our bulls?" And Amos
(not Alfred) prays, for America prays:
"Bathe her in her beautiful blood.
A long blood bath will wash her pure.
Her skin needs special care.
Let this good rage continue out beyond
her power to believe or to surmise.
Slap the false sweetness from that face.
Great-nailed boots
must kick her prostrate, heel-grind that soft breast,
outrage her saucy pride,
remove her fair fine mask.
Let her lie there, panting and wild, her pain
red, running roughly through the illustrious ruin—
with nothing to do but think, think
of how she was so long grand,
flogging her dark one with her own hand,
watching in meek amusement while he bled.
Then shall she rise, recover.
Never to forget."

The ballad of Edie Barrow:
        I fell in love with a Gentile boy.
All creamy-and-golden fair.
He looked deep and long in my long black eyes.
And he played with my long black hair.
He took me away to his summertime house.
He was wondrous wealthy, was he.
And there in the hot black drapes of night
he whispered, "Good lovers are we."
Close was our flesh through the winking hours,
closely and sweetly entwined.

Love did not guess in the tight-packed dark
it was flesh of varying kind.
Scarletly back when the hateful sun
came bragging across the town.
And I could have killed the gentle Gentile
who waited to strap him down.
He will wed her come fall, come falling of fall.
And she will be queen of his rest.
I shall be queen of his summerhouse storm.
A hungry tooth in my breast.

"Pepita who?" And Prophet Williams yawns.
Prophet Williams' office in the Mecca
has a soiled window and a torn front sign.
His suit is shabby and slick.
He is not poor (clothes do *not* make the man).
He has a lawyer named Enrico Jason,
who talks. The Prophet advertises
in every Colored journal in the world....
An old woman wants
from the most reverend Prophet of all prophets
a piece of cloth, licked by his Second Tongue,
to wrap around her paralytic leg.
Men with malicious sweethearts, evil sweethearts—
bringers of bad, bringers of tedium—
want Holy Thunderbolts, and Love Balls too.
And all want lucky numbers all the time.
Mallie (the Superintendent of six secretaries)
types. Mallie alone may know
the Combinations:
14-l 5-16
and l 3-14-15...
(magic is Cut-out Number Forty-three).

Prophet will help you hold your Job, solve problems,
and, like a Sister Stella in Blue Island,
"can call your friends and enemies by name
without a single clue."
There is no need to visit in Blue Island.
Prophet will give you trading stamps and kisses,
or a cigar.
One visit will convince you.
Lucky days
and Lucky Hands. Lifts you
from Sorrow and the Shadows. Heals the body.
A Sister Marlo on east Sixty-third
announces One
Visit Can Keep You Out of the Insane Asylum,
but
she stocks no Special Holiday Blessings for
Columbus Day and Christmas, nor keeps off
green devils and orange witches with striped fangs.
Prophet
has Drawing and Holding Powder, Attraction Powder, Black
Cat Powder, Powerful Serum,
"Marvelous Potency Number Ninety-one"
(which stoppeth husbands and lovers from dastardy),
Pay-check Fluid, Running-around Elixir,
Policy Number Compeller, Voodoo Potion.
Enrico Jason, a glossy circular blackness, who
sees Lawmen and enhances Lawmen, soon
will lie beside his Prophet in bright blood,
a rhythm of stillness
above the nuances.

How many care, Pepita?—
Staley and Lara,

the victim grasped, the harlot had and gone?
Eunie, the intimate tornado?
Simpson, the peasant king, Bixby and June,
the hollowed, the scant, the
played-out deformities? the margins?
Not those.
Not these three Maries
with warm unwary mouths and asking eyes
wide open, full of vagueness and surprise;
the limp ladies
(two in awful combat now:
a terrible battle of the Old:
speechless and physical: oh horrible

the obscene gruntings
the dull outwittings
the flabby semi-rhythmic shufflings
the blear starings
the small spittings).
Not Great-uncle Beer, white-headed twinkly man!—
laugher joker gambler killer too.
Great-uncle Beer says, "Casey Jones.
Yes, Casey Jones is still alive,
a chicken on his head."
Not Wezlyn, the wandering woman, the woman who wanders
the halls of the Mecca at night, in search
of Lawrence and Love.
            Not Insane Sophie! If
you scream, you're marked "insane."
But silence is a *place* in which to scream!
Hush.
An agitation in the bush.
Occluded trees.

Mad life heralding the blue heat of God
snickers in a corner of the west windowsill.
"What have I done, and to the world,
         and to the love I promised Mother?"
An agitation in occluded trees.
The fires run up. Things slant.
The pillow's wet.
The fires run down and flatten.
(The grilles will dance over glass!)
You're marked "insane."
You cower.
Suddenly you're no longer
well-dressed. You're not
pretty in halls.

Like the others you want love, but
a cage is imminent.
Your doll is near. And will go with you.
Your doll, whom none will stun.

… How many care, Pepita?
Does Darkara?
Darkara looks at *Vogue*. Darkara sees
a mischievous impromptu and a sheen.
(In Palm Beach, Florida, Laddie Sanford says:
"I call it My Ocean. Of course, it's the Atlantic.")
The painter, butcher, stockyards man, the Typist,
Aunt Tippie, Zombie Bell,
Mr. Kelly with long gray hair who begs
subtly from door to door, Gas Cady
the man who robbed J. Harrison's grave of mums
and left the peony bush only because
it was too big (said Mama), the janitor

who is a Political Person, Queenie King who
is an old poem silvering the noise,
and Wallace Williams who knows the
Way the Thing Is Supposed To Be Done—
these little care, Pepita, what befalls a
nullified saint or forfeiture (or child).

Alfred's Impression—his Apologie—
his Invocation—and his Ecstasie:
"Not Baudelaire, Bob Browning, not Neruda.
Giants over Steeples
are wanted in this Crazy-eyes, this Scar.
A violent reverse.
We part from all we thought we knew of love
and of dismay-with-flags-on. What we know
is that there are confusion and conclusion.
Rending.
Even the hardest parting is a contribution…
What shall we say?
Farewell. And Hail! Until Farewell again."

Officers!—
do you nearly wish you had not come into this room?
The sixtyish sisters, the twins with the floured faces,
who dress in long stiff blackness,
who exit stiffly together and enter together
stiffly,
muffle their Mahler, finish their tea,
stare at the lips of the Law—
but have not seen Pepita anywhere.
They pull on their long white gloves,
they flour their floured faces,
and stiffly leave Law and the Mecca.

Way-out Morgan is collecting guns
in a tiny fourth-floor room.
He is not hungry, ever, though sinfully lean.
He flourishes, ever, on porridge or pat of bean
pudding or wiener soup—fills fearsomely
on visions of Death-to-the-Hordes-of-the-White-Men!
Death!
(This is the Maxim painted in big black
above a bed bought at a Champlain rummage sale.)
Remembering three local-and-legal beatings, he
rubs his hands in glee,
does Way-out Morgan. Remembering his Sister
mob-raped in Mississippi, Way-out Morgan
smacks sweet his lips and adds another gun
and listens to Blackness stern and blunt and beautiful,
organ-rich Blackness telling a terrible story.
Way-out Morgan
predicts the Day of Debt-pay shall begin,
the Day of Demon-diamond,
of blood in mouths and body-mouths,
of flesh-rip in the Forum of Justice at last!
Remembering mates in the Mississippi River,
mates with black bodies once majestic, Way-out
postpones a yellow woman in his bed, postpones
wetnesses and little cries and stomachings—
to consider Ruin.

"Pepita? No."
Marian is mixing.
Take Marian mixing. Gumbo File or roux.
At iron: at ire with faucet, husband, young.
Knows no
gold hour.

Sings
but sparsely, and subscribes to axioms
atop her gargoyles and tamed foam. Good axioms.
Craves crime: her murder, her deep wounding, or
a leprosy so lovely as to pop
the slights and sleep of her community,
her Mecca.
A Thing. To make the people heel and stop
and See her.
Never strides
about, up!
Never alters earth or air!
Her children cannot quake, be proud.
Her husband never Saw her, never said
her single silver certain Self aloud.

Pops Pinkham, forgetting Pepita,
is somewhat doubtful of a specific right
to inherit the earth or to partake of it now....

Old women should not seek to be perfumed, said Plutarch.
But Dill, the kind of woman you
peek at in passing and thank your God or zodiac you
may never have to know, puts on *Tabu*.
Aunt Dill is happy. Nine years Little Papa
has been completely at rest in Lincoln Cemetery.
Children were stillbirths all. Aunt Dill
has bits of brass and marble, and Franciscan
china; has crocheted doilies; has old mahogany,
polished till it burns with a smothered glow; has
antimacassars, spreads, silk draperies,
her silver creamer and her iron lamp,
her piece of porcelain, her seventeen

Really Nice handkerchiefs pressed in cedar. Dill
is woman-in-love-with-God.
Is not
true-child-of-God—for are we ever to
be children?—are we never to mature,
be lovely lovely? be soft Woman
rounded and darling... almost caressable...
and certainly wearing *Tabu* in the name of the Lord.
Dill straightens—tries to forget the hand of God
(...which would be skillful ... would be flattering...)

    I hate it.
    Yet, murmurs Alfred—
who is lean at the balcony, leaning—
something, something in Mecca
continues to call! Substanceless; yet like mountains,
like rivers and oceans too; and like trees
with wind whistling through them. And steadily
an essential sanity, black and electric,
builds to a reportage and redemption.
    A hot estrangement.
    A material collapse
that is Construction.

Hateful things sometimes befall the hateful
but the hateful are not rendered lovable thereby.
The murderer of Pepita
looks at the Law unlovably. Jamaican
Edward denies and thrice denies a dealing
of any dimension with Mrs. Sallie's daughter.
    Beneath his cot
a little woman lies in dust with roaches.
She never went to kindergarten.

She never learned that black is not beloved.
Was royalty when poised,
sly, at the A and P's fly-open door.
Will be royalty no more.
"I touch"—she said once— "petals of a rose.
A silky feeling through me goes!"
Her mother will try for roses.

She whose little stomach fought the world had
wriggled, like a robin!
Odd were the little wrigglings
and the chopped chirpings oddly rising.

MONA VAN DUYN

1992–1993

Photo by Miriam Berkley, courtesy of the Library of Congress

ONA VAN DUYN

Jean H Johnson

Mona Van Duyn came to the Library of Congress in 1992 as an honored and widely published poet. Dana Gioia characterized her work as "very much in the mainstream of a kind of Nemerov-Wilbur, Hecht generation" (Streitfeld, *W. Post* C1). By this he implies that her work tends to be formal, closely reasoned, often rhymed, and clearly stated.

Van Duyn's excellent final lecture, *Matters of Poetry*, delivered at the Library of Congress, May 7, 1993 drew a distinction between the amateur poet and the professional. She said, "Expression of the self in amateur poetry is an attempt to validate the self and its perceptions, its inmost feelings and thoughts." She went on to say that a few professional poets who have developed a strong inner sense of self, "are happy to be indistinguishable in public, lead quiet, domestic lives" and write. In light of this distinction, one must recognize that Van Duyn is a consummate professional. Her first book, *Valentines to The Wide World*, came out in 1959 and was followed by eight further volumes published over a span of 35 years. From 1947 to 1969, she and her husband edited a literary magazine, *Perspective: A Quarterly of Literature*.

One amusing paradox to her long and presumably quiet writing life with her husband, Jarvis Thurston, is the regularity with which reviewers and others praised her work as a "celebration of married love and daily life" (Streitfeld, *W. Post* C1.15). These people are ignoring the brilliance with which Van Duyn has used her daily life to illuminate profound insights into the human condition. Many of her poems, often long and basically narrative, are about married people, but they are really about the power of love and art to give meaning to life. A central theme in her work is that love and the creation of a poem are ways of harmonizing a discordant universe.

In her acceptance speech for the National Book Award for Poetry in 1971, Van Duyn said, "Poetry honors the formed use of language particularly, being concerned with both its sound and its meaning, and a poet spends his life's best effort in shaping these into a patterned experience... (CLC vol. 63. 434). "The patterned experience" of her work is skillful indeed. Most poems are in formal verse with strongly marked rhythm and lavish use of off-and slant rhyme. She is a master of the extended metaphor as in "A Time of Bees," a narrative of a married couple getting rid of a hive of bees which becomes a metaphor for the relationship between husband and wife. The wife cannot touch the dying bees; she says "The men did it." Characteristically, Van Duyn's tone incorporates wry humor and irony. Van Duyn quotes Yeats in an epigraph to her poem "Leda"; Yeats makes him a god, but Van Duyn makes him an ordinary self-centered man.

Van Duyn delivers a trenchant analysis in her final lecture, *Matters of Poetry*, later published by the Library of Congress, of the changes she has noted on the poetry scene in the last few decades. She describes the astonishing increase in the numbers of people of all ages and backgrounds flocking to campuses and summer programs to write poetry. Her estimate is that one in every twelve or thirteen persons in the country writes poetry. The number of poetry readings in YMCAs, coffee houses, churches, poetry festivals and workshops, and the establishment of Poets' Houses and Writer's Places, had exploded.

Nonetheless, while more people are giving and attending more readings, fewer books are sold. While twenty years ago there were twenty of so successful published poets, now there are hundreds. There is also a veritable flood of ethnic poetry and translations. Despite the explosion in the number of people writing poetry, in the number of magazines publishing poetry, and in the increased size of prizes, the number of books sold has dropped. There is a dearth of honest, discriminating reviews in newspapers and magazines (Van Duyn 1-8). The public, she says, needs help in the confusion of the contemporary poetry scene.

One thing Van Duyn says has not changed is the continuing discrimination against women. She gathered statistics from ten anthologies published from 1962 to 1990 to show a stunning discrepancy between the number of men and the number of women chosen. Even in 1990 there were 48 men to 16 women (Van Duyn 9). The numbers are significant because anthologies imply that the editors are selecting the best. Van Duyn suggests that the reviews of women's books are often prejudiced. This discrimination as well as the general decline in the number of newspapers and magazines that review poetry prevent the public from being aware of what is published and how poetry is evaluated.

Van Duyn recommends that instead of awarding big grants, the NEA and State Arts Councils might support reviews of books by poets and subsidize shelves of poetry in bookstores (Van Duyn 14). She hopes such a move would help poetry regain the excitement it held during the 1920's.

When the Poet Laureateship was offered to Van Duyn. she had already committed herself to reading and teaching trips all over the United States. As she said, this "is the way poets make their living. It's certainly not by selling books" (Streitfeld, *W. Post* C11). Before assuming the role, Van Duyn indicated that since she was already heavily committed, she would concentrate on choosing poets to read at the Library of Congress. She could not be in Washington, D.C. much more than one week of each month. Although she was the first woman to be named Poet Laureate, she said, "I'm so used to there being so few women in anthologies and places of power in the poetry world that I didn't find it odd that the Library of Congress should wait seven years to get a woman."

SOURCES CITED:

Greiner, Donald J. editor. *American Poets Since World War II, Dictionary of Literary Biography*. Vol. 5, part 2, 334-340. Detroit: Gale Research Company, Inc. 1982.

Matuz, Roger, editor. *Contemporary Literary Criticism*. vol. 63, 434-445. Gale Research Company, Inc. 1991 (not to be confused with *Contemporary Literary Criticism* by Gale Research Company, Inc. containing literary movements rather than biographies).

Streitfeld, David. "Van Duyn Named New Poet Laureate." *The Washington Post* C1 (1 and 11) June 15, 1992.

Van Duyn, Mona. *Matters of Poetry*. Final lecture at the Library of Congress, Washington: Superintendent of Documents, U.S. Government Printing Office 20402, 1993.

PUBLICATIONS

Valentines to the Wide World: Poems. 1958
A Time of Bees. 1964
To See, To Take: Poems. 1970
Bedtime Stories. 1972
Merciful Disguises: Published and Unpublished Poems. 1973
Letters from a Father, and Other Poems. 1982
Near Changes. 1990
If It Be Not I: Collected Poems. 1958–1982
Firefall. 1993

HONORS AND AWARDS

Eunice Tietjens Memorial Prize from *Poetry* magazine, 1956
Harriet Monroe Award from *Poetry* magazine, 1968
Two Helen Bullis Prizes from *Poetry Northwest*, 1964 and 1976
National Endowment for the Arts grant, 1966
Hart Crane Award, 1968
National Book Award, 1971
The Bollingen Prize, 1970

Loines Prize, National Institute of Arts & Letters, 1976
Elected Member of Institutes of Arts & Letters, 1976
Chancellor of the Academy of Arts & Letters, 1985
Guggenheim Fellowship, 1972–73
National book Award for *To See, To Take*, 1971
Shelly Memorial Prize from Poetry Society of America, 1987
Ruth Lilly Prize, 1989
Honorary Doctor of Letters, Washington University, 1971
Honorary Doctor of Letters, Cornell College, 1972

Late Flight of the Love God

In one late dart,
exhausted, blind,
he missed a heart
and lit in a mind,

a huge, open shelf
full of rustling things.
He lost himself
among other wings.

When he opened his eyes
his wings had grown
for undreamed-of-skies.
He had never known

so rich a rest,
an aim so blest.

The Challenger

"Perhaps a great love is never returned. Had it been given warmth
and shelter by its counterpart in the Other, perhaps it would have
been hindered from ever growing to maturity." Dag Hammarskjold

Old liar, death, do you think I don't see you?
There is not one of your masks I don't know,
even this one, soft and winning—the half-truth.

When the fruit in its bowl turns green I see you, death.
When a sleep-walker hears the clock hands unwind,
when a hand jerks back from a reaching hand.

Even in the motion of rest I touch your face.
I know its shape in love, and in the wit of madness.
I will face up to you, my sleepy lover.

I will fight you with nuance and with cleverness,
with the making and breaking of form and measure,
with a greedy face and with an immaculate.

I will lie with clocks, which are always a little late,
I will lie with madness, with the fact that you love me,
and for a long time you will believe me.

Ringling Brothers, Barnum and Bailey

Thirty striped rumps in a circle with tails dangling.
One rump lifts and begins to dump, then spray.
At the crack of the cue, still pissing, she leaps to the ring
with the others and they all stand on their hind legs pawing
the air for balance. The dwarf on ten foot stilts
keeps stalking around the show, his little hands
waving, and we all wave every time round, and he tilts
to one side and staggers but now everybody is watching
the pony walk on his hind legs round and round
the kneeling camels while the whip flicks his strained belly.
Then, hanging by one wrist only, the aerialist spins
her whole body over... fifty times "That's easy,
I could do that," the child behind me whines.
Directly overhead the tight rope walkers
work in a hush. (Three days from now one will smash
to her death in another town.) Absent watchers
are my two friends, one in the last months
of cancer, one in depression so deep she'll crash.
One leaps over the other. The rope holds. No one killed
today. "Anybody could do that. So what?"
the child whines, and I'd like to throw the child
and all brutal innocence under the elephant's foot.

Open Letter From A Constant Reader

To all who carve their love on a picnic table
or scratch it on smoked glass panes of a public toilet,
I send my thanks for each plain and perfect fable
of how the three pains of the body, surfeit,

hunger, and chill (or loneliness), create
a furniture and art of their own easing.
And I bless two public sites and, like Yeats,
two private sites where the body receives its blessing.

Nothing is banal or lowly that tells us how well
the world, whose highways proffer table and toilet
as signs and occasions of comfort for belly and bowel,
can comfort the heart too, somewhere in secret.

Where so much constant news of good has been put,
both fleeting and lasting lines compel belief.
Not by talent or riches or beauty, but
by the world's grace, people have found relief

from the worst pain of the body, loneliness,
and say so with a simple heart as they sit
being relieved of one of the others. I bless
all knowledge of love, all ways of publishing it.

RITA DOVE

1993–1995

Photo by Fred Viebahn

# ITA DOVE

Carolyn Kreiter-Foronda

When selected a Presidential Scholar in 1970, Rita Dove described herself as "dreamy, sensitive, and mild," adjectives that fit this young woman who in high school had never sought center stage (*The Poet's World* 99). The limelight continued to single her out, and in 1987 Dove was honored with a Pulitzer Prize for the lyrical collection of narrative poems, *Thomas and Beulah*, based loosely on the lives of her maternal grandparents. Although she appreciated the immensity of this award, a part of her realized that her writing space—that inner sanctum she deeply treasured and needed— would never again be a place she could easily retreat to for hours at a time.

In May 1993 when Dove was named the seventh Poet Laureate, she was again called upon to balance personal writing needs with a public duty to promote poetry in a country that she felt had never sufficiently supported its poets, nor adequately recognized the voice of black writers. With dignity and characteristic grace, she welcomed this new challenge, which Librarian of Congress James H. Billington observed had been given to her "to explore and enrich contemporary American poetry" ("Librarian of Congress Appoints" 1). *The Washington Post* called the selection "a surprise move" to invigorate the post. After all, the 40-year-old Dove was "energetic, female and black, and thus a good candidate to do more than draw the usual 200 hardy souls to the Library of Congress readings" (Streitfeld, "Laureate," A1).

As the youngest writer to hold this position, Dove sought to increase poetry's popularity and make it a part of everyday life. She hoped to use her energy in classrooms, interviews, and projects to "keep poetry and the cause of literature in the national eye" (Streitfeld, "Laureate" A14). Simultaneously, she strove to serve as a positive role model, perhaps one who would inspire young people in her audiences to want to be poets, just as a writer years earlier had instilled in her this same desire (Flanagan 1).

To give herself the time needed to accomplish her goals, Dove took leave from her position at the University of Virginia as Commonwealth Professor of English, focusing her attention on a range of activities. In October of 1993, as the restored statue Freedom was hoisted back onto the Capitol dome in Washington, DC, Dove read her celebrated poem, "Lady Freedom Among Us," a work which became the four-millionth volume added to the University of Virginia Libraries' collection ("A Few Words," Internet 1 -2). As laureate, Dove also communicated with students via a telecommunications classroom. She read and talked about poetry to the staff of MTV. She participated in *The United States of Poetry*, aired nationally, and worked as well with a film company that put poetry Public Service Announcements on Lifetime cable, animated poems that she viewed as "beautiful collages of images and sound" ("Rita Dove," *The Plum Review* 37-391). She even denounced "gangsta rap," telling *The Washington Post*; "I feel distressed by its lack of tolerance and [by its] violence" (Knight-Ridder, D1). Quick to point out the positive elements of rap music, Dove remained true to her commitment to speak for the most fitting possibilities of the English language.

At a time when Congress was approving a budget that would reduce funding for the arts, Dove's voice supporting poetry m everyday life remained strong. Recognizing from the start the difficulties that confronted any poet laureate in a city devoted largely to politics, she seemingly ignored the problems her predecessors talked about, instead working tirelessly with the Library's staff to attain her goals. Even after organizing numerous programs, including a much lauded reading by Crow Indian children from Montana and an annual poetry and jazz series (Schmidt, *NY Times* 39), Dove accepted the offer of a second term, for she felt that the initial eight-month stint had not been adequate to accomplish all within her reach

By this time Dove was often receiving as many as 600 letters a month, far more than she could answer to her satisfaction. "There's an incredible hunger out there. I feel it. There's a hunger for poetry," she told journalist Elizabeth Kastor (*W. Post* C1). Prosser Gifford, director of scholarly programs at the Library of Congress, applauded Dove "for making the laureate, in Teddy Roosevelt's words, a bully pulpit" (Kastor, *W. Post* C1). To satisfy the requests for her time, she worked with a fevered pitch. Even her husband, German novelist and accomplished photographer Fred Viebahn, joined a volunteer support staff to assist his wife with the continuing demands of her job.

Dove spent her second year as poet laureate fulfilling the mounting number of speaking and reading engagements, but the activity that especially peaked her interest was a two-day symposium, "The Black Diaspora," organized to address the common roots of blacks in the Americas, Africa, Europe and the Caribbean. Held at the Library of Congress, this gathering brought together a large group of eminent writers, including Gerald Early and Walter Mosley. Dove enjoyed the occasion so much that she displayed her ever-engaging exuberance by dancing during a reception (Streitfeld, "Continental Drift," *W. Post* D1).

What she did not welcome about her years as poet laureate was the time it detracted from reading and writing. In an interview with *The Plum Review*, she remarked that even though she had found time to write in the summer between stints, while serving as laureate there was "simply no way to create the kind of space necessary for poetry" (35). She felt that the position forced her into being a public person. "Talk—this constant chat," she said, "kills the poetry more than anything else" (35). Yet in the same interview, she acknowledged that she couldn't refuse the laureateship since it was a chance to quit complaining about poetry's unpopular stance and to "actually do something" (36).

That Dove contributed significantly to a growing appreciation of poetry is undeniable. That she sacrificed her own privacy and writing time is apparent, but to a cause she deemed worthy. Perhaps it is through her lectures delivered at the Library of Congress that we best see her mind distilling the implications of the two-year stint.

The lectures, collected in *The Poet's World*, include ruminations that reveal the conflict Dove felt in leaving her private arena behind for the less comfortable public stage. Appropriately, she calls her first lecture "Stepping Out: the Poet in the World." Here, she explores "the dynamics of inside versus outside in some contemporary American poetry—or to put it in the more provocative form of a question: Do we, as poets, peer through a window at the world or do we step out to meet it?" (Dove, *The Poet's World* 19). Central to this discussion is the notion of place, viewed first in the context of her own poems and then in the larger realm of poetry. As she sees it, the backyard of her poems opens metaphorically on the world beyond. Ironically, at Dove's home her own writing space is a cabin in the backyard, overlooking a private pond that mirrors the rolling hills near Charlottesville Virginia, where she lives with her husband and daughter Aviva. A photograph taken by her husband and displayed in *The Poet's World* (14) captures Dove in reverie gazing out of her window at the timelessness beyond as if waiting for the magic of language.

Later in this essay, Dove examines the space her office occupies at the Library of Congress, a room that looks out on the grandeur of Capitol Hill. Dove views this office not as a lofty perch from which to distance herself from the people below, but as a place that ultimately enables her to reach large audiences with her message. She concludes this discussion by observing a possible solution to poetry's current dilemma that poets need to be more involved in matters of the world, perhaps as "the unacknowledged legislators of the race," to use Percy Bysssche Shelley's words (42). True to her convictions, Dove devoted her tenure to stepping out and acting on her vow to promote the genre largely ignored by the masses.

In the second lecture from *The Poet 's World*, titled "A Handful of Inwardness: the World in the Poet," delivered at the beginning of her second term, Dove introduces the theme: "the need for the intimate and private in poetry, and the ways in which poetry reaches out while turning inward" (46). Between stints, Dove and her husband had rented a home in an isolated section of France, where they could both turn inward from the outward thrust of the previous year. In her lecture, she expresses a need to "wonder, and the desire to communicate that wonder" (67). That summer in France nourished the inner self that she would call upon the subsequent year in order to continue what she believed was a moral duty to the arts.

In an address, *To Make a Prairie*, delivered to Phi Beta Kappa initiates at the University of Virginia, Dove extols the power of daydreaming to lead us into imagined landscapes, into places that often surprise us with their uniqueness and importance. She said that "poets do not have a monopoly on imagination: each of us makes our most vital and exciting contributions via a felicitous combination of scholarly inquiry, intellectual acumen, grit and imagination" (7). In a sense, this is a message to us all to look to our inner selves for the power that can lead to greatness.

One of the lasting gifts that Rita Dove gave to our country during her term as poet laureate was to our children. May these young people who heard her speak during visits to their schools or via television broadcasts act on her words and reverently carry her vision further.

WORKS CITED

Dove, Rita. *To Make a Prairie*. Washington, DC: Library of Congress, 1993.

Dove, Rita. *The Poet 's World*. Washington, DC: Library of Congress, 1995.

"A Few Words from Karin Wittenborg, University Librarian." Internet (http://www.lib.virginia.edu/etext/ fourmill.html).

Flanagan, Anna. "Poet Laureate Has a Message for Youngsters." *The Council Chronicle*. September 1993, pp. 1, 3.

Kastor, Elizabeth. "Rita Dove: The People's Poet." *The Washington Post.* 22 April 1994, C1-2.

Knight-Ridder. "Poet Laureate Decries Gangsta Rap." *The Washington Post.* 18 March 1994, D1.

"Librarian of Congress Appoints Rita Dove Poet Laureate." *The Library of Congress News.* Public Affairs Office. 19 May 1993.

"Rita Dove." Interview conducted by Mike Hammer and Christina Daub. *The Plum Review.* No. 9. 1996, pp. 27-41.

Schmidt, Elizabeth. "Ill Paid, Ill Defined and Nearly Irresistible." *New York Times Book Review.* 17 December 1995, p. 39.

Streitfeld, David. "Continental Drift: At the Library of Congress, Deconstructing the African Diaspora." *The Washington Post.* 21 April 1995, D1, D4.

Streitfeld, David. "Laureate for a New Age." *The Washington Post.* 19 May 1993, A1, A14.

HONORS

Phi Beta Kappa Senator, 1994–2000

U.S. Poet Laureate/Consultant in Poetry, Library of Congress (1993–1995)

Commonwealth Professor of Poetry, University of Virginia, 1989–

D. Litt. (Hon.): Miami U.-1988, Knox-1989, Tuskegee U., U. of Miami, Washington U., Case Western Reserve U.-1994, U. of Akron, Arizona State, Boston College, Dartmouth College, Spelman College, U of Pennsylvania.

Renaissance Forum Award, Folger Shakespeare Library, 1994.

Distinguished Achievement Medal, Miami University Alumni Association, 1994

Golden Plate Award, American Academy of Achievement, 1994

Carl Sandburg Award, International Platform Association, 1994

NAACP Great American Artist Award, 1993

Woman of the Year Award, *Glamour* Magazine, 1993

Virginia College Stores Association Book Award, 1993

Literary Lion, New York Public Library, 1991

Phi Beta Kappa poet, Harvard University, 1993

Ohioana Award, 1990, 1994
Fellow, Center for Advanced Studies, U. of Virginia, 1989-92
Mellon Fellow, National Humanities Center, 1988-89
Bellagio Residency, The Rockefeller Foundation, 1988
Ohio Governor's Award, 1988
General Electric Foundation Award, 1987
Pulitzer Prize in Poetry, 1987
President, Associate Writing Programs, 1986/87
Lavan Younger Poet Award, The Academy of American Poets, 1986
Callaloo Award, 1986
Chair, poetry grants panel, National Endowment for the Arts, 1985
Guggenheim Fellow, 1983-84
Portia Pittman Fellow, National Endowment for the Humanities, Tuskegee Institute, 1982
International Working Period for Authors Fellow, North-Rhine-Westphalia Ministry of Culture and Universität Bielefeld, 1980
Ohio Arts Council Grant, 1979
National Endowment for the Arts Creative Writing Fellow, 1978, 1989
Fulbright Scholar, Universität Tübingen, 1974-75

PUBLICATIONS

Books

Mother Love (poems). W. W. Norton, 1995.
The Poet's World (essays). Library of Congress, 1995.
The Darker Face of the Earth (verse drama). Story Line Press, 1994 and 1996.
Selected Poems. Pantheon/Vintage, 1993.
Selected Poems (audio book). Random House, 1993.
Through the Ivory Gate (novel). Pantheon Books, 1992.
Grace Notes (poems). W.W. Norton, 1989.
Die gläserne Stirn der Gegenwart (selected poems in German translation) Heiderhoff Verlag, 1989.

Die morgenlandische Tänzerin (selected poems in German translation). Rowholt Verlag, 1988.
Thomas and Beulah (poems). Carnegie-Mellon, 1986.
Fifth Sunday (short stories). Callaloo Fiction Series, 1985.
Museum (poems). Carnegie-Mellon, 1983.
The Yellow House on the Corner (poems). Carnegie-Mellon, 1980.

Plays
The Darker Face of the Earth, Premiered at Oregon Shakespeare Festival, July, 1996.

Lady Freedom Among Us

don't lower your eyes
or stare straight ahead to where
you think you ought to be going

don't mutter *oh no*
not another one
get a job fly a kite
go bury a bone

with her oldfashioned sandals
with her leaden skirts
with her stained cheeks and whiskers and heaped up trinkets
she has risen among us in blunt reproach

she has fitted her hair under a hand-me-down cap
and spruced it up with feathers and stars

slung over one shoulder she bears
the rainbowed layers of charity and murmurs
all of you even the least of you

don't cross to the other side of the square
don't think *another item to fit on a tourist's agenda*

consider her drenched gaze   her shining brow
she who has brought mercy back into the streets
and will not retire politely to the potter's field

having assumed the thick skin of this town
its gritted exhaust its sunscorch and blear
she rests in her weathered plumage
bigboned   resolute

don't think you can ever forget her
don't even try
she's not going to budge
no choice but to grant her space
crown her with sky
for she is one of the many
and she is each of us

Pamela

"...the hour was come when the man must act, or forever be a slave."

At two, the barnyard settled
into fierce silence—anvil,
water pump glinted
as though everything waited
for the first step.
She stepped
into the open. The wind
lifted—behind her,
fields spread their sails.

There really is a star up there and moss on the trees. She
discovered if she kept a steady pace, she could walk forever.
The idea pleased her, and she hummed a hymn to herself—
Peach Point, Silk Hope, Beaver Bend. It seemed that the
    further
north she went, the freer she became. The stars were plates
for good meat; if she reached, they flashed and became coins.

White quiet. Night pushed over the hill.
The woods hiss with cockleburs,
each a small woolly head.
She feels old, older
than these friendly shadows
who, like the squirrels, don't come too near.
Knee-deep in muscadine, she watched them coming,
snapping the brush. They are
smiling, rifles crossed on their chests.

Dusting

Every day a wilderness—no
shade in sight. Beulah
patient among knickknacks,
the solarium a rage
of light, a grainstorm
as her gray cloth brings
dark wood to life.

Under her hand scrolls
and crests gleam
darker still. What
was his name, that
silly boy at the fair with
the rifle booth? And his kiss and
the clear bowl with one bright
fish rippling
wound!

Not Michael—
something finer. Each dust
stroke a deep breath and
the canary in bloom.
Wavery memory: home
from a dance, the front door
blown open and the parlor
in snow, she rushed
the bowl to the stove, watched
as the locket of ice
dissolved and he
swam free.

That was years before
Father gave her up
with her name, years before
her name grew to mean
Promise, then
Desert-in-Peace.
Long before the shadow and
sun's accomplice, the tree.

Maurice.

The Oriental Ballerina

twirls on the tips of a carnation
while the radio scratches out a morning hymn.
Daylight has not ventured as far

as the windows—the walls are still dark
shadowed with the ghosts
of oversized gardenias. The ballerina

pirouettes to the wheeze of the old
rugged cross, she lifts
her shoulders past the edge

of the jewelbox lid. Two pink slippers
touch the ragged petals, no one
should have feet that small! In China

they do everything upside down:
this ballerina has not risen but drilled
a tunnel straight to America

where the bedrooms of the poor
are papered in vulgar flowers
on a background the color of grease, of

teabags, of cracked imitation walnut veneer.
On the other side of the world
they are shedding robes sprigged with

roses, roses drifting with a hiss
to the floor by the bed
as, here, the sun finally strikes the windows

the rest is shadow.
The head on the pillow sees nothing
else, though it feels the sun warming

its cheeks. *There is no China*;
no cross, just the papery kiss
of a kleenex above the stink of camphor,

the walls exploding with shabby tutus...

The Island Women of Paris

skim from curb to curb like regatta,
from Pont Neuf to the Quai de la Rappe
in cool negotiation with traffic,
each a country to herself
transposed to this city
by a fluke called "imperial courtesy."

The island women glide past held aloft
by a wire running straight to heaven.
Who can ignore their ornamental bearing,
turbans haughty as parrots,
or deft braids carved into airy cages
transfixed on their manifest brows?

The island women move through Paris
as if they had just finished inventing
their destinations. It's better
not to get in their way. And better
not look an island woman in the eye—
unless you like feeling unnecessary.

Parsley

1. The Cane Fields

There is a parrot imitating spring
in the palace, its feathers parsley green.
Out of the swamp the cane appears

to haunt us, and we cut it down. El General
searches for a word; he is all the world
there is. Like a parrot imitating spring,

we lie down screaming as rain punches through
and we come up green. We cannot speak an R—
out of the swamp, the cane appears

and then the mountain we call in whispers *Katalina.*
The children gnaw their teeth to arrowheads.
There is a parrot imitating spring.

El General has found his word: *perejil.*
Who says it, lives. He laughs, teeth shining
out of the swamp. The cane appears

in our dreams, lashed by wind and streaming.
And we lie down. For a drop of blood
there is a parrot imitating spring.
Out of the swamp the cane appears.

2. The Palace

The word the general's chosen is parsley.
It is fall, when thoughts turn
to love and death; the general thinks
of his mother, how she died in the fall
and he planted her walking cane at the grave
and it flowered, each spring stolidly forming
four-star blossoms. The general

pulls on his boots, he stomps to
her room in the palace, the one without
curtains, the one with a parrot
in a brass ring. As he paces he wonders
Who can I kill today. And for a moment
the little knot of screams
is still. The parrot, who has traveled

all the way from Australia in an ivory
cage, is, coy as a widow, practising
spring. Ever since the morning
his mother collapsed in the kitchen
while baking skull-shaped candies
for the Day of the Dead, the general
has hated sweets. He orders pastries
brought up for the bird; they arrive

dusted with sugar on a bed of lace.
The knot in his throat starts to twitch;
he sees his boots the first day in battle
splashed with mud and urine
as a soldier falls at his feet amazed—
how stupid he looked!—at the sound

of artillery. *I never thought it would sing*
the soldier said, and died. Now

the general sees the fields of sugar
cane, lashed by rain and streaming.
He sees his mother's smile, the teeth
gnawed to arrowheads. He hears
the Haitians sing without R's
as they swing the great machetes:
Katalina, they sing, *Katalina,*

mi madle, mi amol en muelte. God knows
his mother was no stupid woman: she
could roll an R like a queen. Even
a parrot can roll an R! In the bare room
the bright feathers arch in a parody
of greenery, as the last pale crumbs
disappear under the blackened tongue. Someone

calls out his name in a voice
so like his mother's, a startled tear
splashes the tip of his right boot.
My mother, my love in death.
The general remembers the tiny green sprigs
men of his village wore in their capes
to honor the birth of a son. He will
order many, this time, to be killed

for a single, beautiful word.

Mother Love

Who can forget the attitude of mothering?
        Toss me a baby and without bothering
to blink I'll catch her, sling him on a hip.
        Any woman knows the remedy for grief
is being needed: duty bugles and we'll
        climb out of exhaustion every time,
bare the nipple or tuck in the sheet,
        heat milk and hum at bedside until
they can dress themselves and rise, primed
        for Love or Glory—those one-way mirrors
girls peer into as their fledgling heroes slip
        through, storming the smoky battlefield.

So when this kind woman approached at the urging
        of her bouquet of daughters,
(one for each of the world's corners,
        one for each of the winds to scatter!)
and offered up her only male child for nursing
        (a smattering of flesh, noisy and ordinary),
I put aside the lavish trousseau of the mourner
        for the daintier comfort of pity:
I decided to save him. Each night
        I laid him on the smoldering embers,
sealing his juices in slowly so he might
        be cured to perfection. Oh, I know it
looked damning: at the hearth a muttering crone
        bent over a baby sizzling on a spit
as neat as a Virginia ham. Poor human—
        to scream like that, to make me remember.

Teotihuacán

The Indian guide explains to the group of poets
how the Aztec slaves found parasites in cocoons
spun like snowdrifts around the spinules
of a cactus pad (his aide scrapes some free with a stick)
and ground them to a fine red paste.
Next, an unassuming stalk which, chewed,
produced a showy green (a younger stalk
made yellow) and these they used
to decorate the Temple of the Sun.
Plumed serpent who reared his head in the east,
his watery body everywhere: Quetzalcoatl
was a white man, blond hair and tall.
It took millions of these bugs to stain a single wall.
The poets scribble in assorted notebooks. The guide moves on.

ACKNOWLEDGMENTS

LOUISE BOGAN: (Consultant, 1945-1946) "Ad Castitatem," "Cassandra," "From Heine," "Men Loved Wholly Beyond Wisdom," "Musician," "Night," "Poem in Prose," "Single Sonnet," "Sub Contra," and "To Be Sung on the Water" from *The Blue Estuaries* by Louise Bogan. Copyright renewed © 1996 by Ruth Limmer by permission of Farrar, Straus & Giroux, Inc.

LÉONIE ADAMS: (Consultant, 1948-49) The editor and members of the board of directors of Scop Publications, Inc. have done everything possible to locate the estate and get permission for right to publish Léonie Adams' poems. We paid for a Library of Congress search, contacted the nursing home where she spent her last days, called probate courts in the area, and contacted publishing companies that were rumored to have bought rights to her books. We were also unable to trace the person whose name was given to us as a contact and have documented our efforts. Her first book is *Those Not Elect*, copyright © 1925 and 1953, by Léonie Adams, Robert M. McBride and Company, New York. Her second book is *High Falcon*, copyright © 1929, by Léonie Adams. Selections from both books were published in *Poems: A Selection* by Funk & Wagnalls Company, New York, copyright © 1954 by Léonie Adams. All publishing companies which published her books are no longer in existence. Books-in-Print lists her two books for sale by Reprint Services Corporation of California. A call to the Sales and Service department on October 29, 1997 indicates the corporation does not own the copyright as they publish books that are in the public domain.

ELIZABETH BISHOP (Consultant, 1949-50) It was not possible to negotiate rights to publish a selection of Elizabeth Bishop's poems from Farrar, Straus and Giroux because of "a promise made to her before her death." Information about her tenure as Consultant in Poetry at the Library of Congress was included with permission of William McGuire, *Poetry 's Catbird Seat: The Consultantship in Poetry in the English Language at the Library of Congress, 1938-1987*, Library of Congress, Washington, D.C., 1987, copyright © 1988 by William McGuire. Comments which are common knowledge and published in many books were added by Ann Knox.

RITA DOVE: (Laureate, 1993-1995) "Lady Freedom Among Us" from *The Poet's World* (essays), Library of Congress, copyright © 1995; "Parsley," (poems) reprinted from Carnegie-Mellon, copyright © 1983; "The Oriental Ballerina" reprinted from *Thomas and Beulah* (poems), Carnegie-Mellon, copyright © 1986; "Dusting" reprinted from *Thomas and Beulah*, Carnegie-Mellon, copyright © 1986; "Pamela," *The Yellow House on the Corner* (poems), reprinted from Carnegie-Mellon, copyright © 1980. All reprinted with the permission of the author. "The Island Women of Paris," reprinted from *Grace Notes*, W.W. Norton, copyright © 1989; "Mother Love" and "Teotihuacán" reprinted from *Mother Love*, W. W. Norton, copyright © 1995. The last three poems are reprinted with permission of the author and W.W. Norton.

ABOUT THE AUTHORS

Carolyn Kreiter-Foronda is a poet, painter, sculptor and teacher. She holds two Master's degrees and a Ph.D. from George Mason University, where she received the first doctorate presented by the school. Her many awards include three Artist-in-Education grants, an Arts-on-the-Road grant from the Virginia Commission for the Arts, a Council for Basic Education fellowship award, a Meritorious Educator Award from the Springfield Rotary Club, and a National Scholastic Teacher Portfolio Award. In 1992, she was named a Virginia Cultural Laureate for her contributions to American Literature. Her poems and writings appear in over 150 magazines and journals, including *Hispanic Culture Review*, *Prairie Schooner*, *Poet Lore*, *Mid-American Review*, and *Antioch Review*. She has published two books of poetry, *Contrary Visions* (under the name Carolyn Kreiter-Kurylo) and *Gathering Light*.

Jean H. Johnson published her first book of poems, *Forgotten Alphabet*, with SCOP Publications, Inc. in 1994. She has been a scholar at the Jenny McKean Moore seminar at George Washington University and a Fellow at the Virginia Center for the Creative Arts. Her work has appeared in *New Poets Anthology*, Heatherstone Press, in *Free State*, *Poet Lore* and other publications. She has read at the Library of Congress, the Corcoran, The Writer's Center, the Martin Luther King Library and many other places. She lives and teaches in Bethesda, Maryland.

Marta Knobloch's collection of poems, *The Room of Months*, was published in a bilingual edition in Italy and was the first international recipient of Ferrar's *Premio Donna*. She received the Artscape Literary Arts Award of Baltimore in 1988 for a chapbook, The Song of What was Lost. Her second book of poems, *Sky Pond*, was co-winner of the Columbia Book Award in 1993. Marta Knobloch's poetry has been published in numerous literary journals in the United States, Italy, Australia, Ireland, and England.

Ann B. Knox published her first book of poetry, *Stonecrop*, with Washington Writers' Publishing House in 1988 and *Late Summer Break*, a collection of stories, with Papier Mache Press in 1995. *Staying is No-*

where, poetry, was the first in a series of co-published titles with small presses and the Writers' Center, Bethesda, Maryland and was published by SCOP Publications, Inc. She received her MFA in writing from Warren Wilson College. For the past twelve years she has edited *Antietam Review* and teaches at the Writers' Center. She grew up in Massachusetts and New York, graduated from Vassar College, and lived for fifteen years in Europe and Asia.

Marybeth Shea has been Poet in Residence in elementary schools in both Prince George's County and Montgomery County, was scientific editor and writer for *Global Change* Magazine, is the mother of three children and lives in College Park, Maryland.

Jayne Landis Silva has won the Shapiro Award for poetry, an American Pen Women's Contest and placed in the *Baltimore Sun* short story contest. Her poems and short stories have been included in various anthologies. She majored in English and creative writing at the University of Maryland. She has co-edited anthologies and has a novel in progress. She was a federal government executive at the International Trade Commission until her retirement. She was a founding member of SCOP Publications, and has been treasurer and business manager for twenty-one years. She presently lives in Laurel, Maryland.

Stacy Johnson Tuthill is the author of three books, *Pennyroyal* (poetry), *House of Change* (poetry), and *The Taste of Smoke: Stories about Africa* (fiction). She was the winner of the first *Permafrost* chapbook contest with *Necessary Madness*, and won a chapbook contest sponsored by the Ministry of Culture in Zambia with *Postcards*. She was awarded fellowships from the Maryland State Arts Council, and has consistently won contests from magazines and the NLAPW for poetry, prose, and short stories. She was also a PEN Syndicated Fiction winner and has been published in numerous literary magazines and newspapers. She founded SCOP Publications, Inc. in 1977, has edited anthologies through SCOP and has served as president.

I want people to look back and remember me as a key person who coached them through a difficult moment in their career, or helped them make significant improvements in their technical and teaming skills — large enough impacts that it changed the course of their careers.

I want to be viewed as a technical leader who drove new ideas to reality, and who changed and improved how groups and teams can operate together and how programs can be operated.

I want to influence positive changes in how our programs are run by developing long term strategies and influencing management to make the changes.

- Build a team that builts a positive culture of improvement — P29
- What does success look like? P.33
- EQ: Know how to respond to others P42
- What is your vision for yourself? How do you achieve it? P.43
- Need business plan, objectives, strategies P.53
- Keep a clear vision in front of the team P. 78
- The mission connects to a larger purpose P87

If you look over people in your business life, you are a coach. Face it. You may hide behind a title like manager, VP, or director—but in the end, if you aren't a coach, no one will follow you. This book will help you embrace your potential coach and flex it to the benefit of your people. Daniel's advice is crisp and actionable. Give him a few hours to change your leadership life.

TIM SANDERS,
former Chief Solutions Officer at Yahoo!
and author of *Love Is the Killer App*

In theory, all leaders should be coaching leaders, but in practice, that often isn't the case. If you want to be a coaching leader, develop others, and show them the path to greatness, this book is for you. Daniel Harkavy's new book goes beyond the "what" and the "why" to provide the much needed "how" of coaching leadership.

MARK SANBORN, CSP, CPAE
President, Sanborn & Associates
and author of *The Fred Factor*

Daniel Harkavy is a great coach and a great coaching leader. Nobody knows more about coaching than Daniel. This new book is invaluable, a great addition to the library of anyone who wants to have a positive impact on the lives of their team. I recommend it highly.

BILL ARMSTRONG

U.S. Senator (ret) and
President, Colorado Christian University,
Chairman, Cherry Creek Mortgage
Company

The best way to tap the potential of people is to lead them to that unique place where their talent, their calling, and their passion match the description of what you want them to do. Daniel Harkavy powerfully demonstrates how to do this in an empowering, effective, and energizing way."

TODD DUNCAN,
New York Times best-selling author of
Time Traps: Proven Strategies for Swamped Business Professionals

Becoming a Coaching Leader is a must read for the person who has the courage to journey down the path of becoming the leader you could not become on your own. In a clear and concise manner, Daniel Harkavy shares his system which fills our own leadership gaps, and when followed, leads to tremendous improvement, significance, and abundance in all aspects of life.

JAMES O. WHITE, CPA
DeLap White Caldwell & Croy, LLP

Five years ago some of our key managers were being coached by Daniel Harkavy through his Building Champions program. The sales people and managers coached performed significantly better than those not in the program. Over several years comparisons between all levels of sales professionals and managers clearly showed that the Building Champions program helped even top-tier sales people excel. . . . The program has made a profound difference in my professional and personal life, too. I am grateful for the experience and would recommend the Building Champions program to anyone wanting to improve in everything important to them.

GERALD (JERRY) L. BAKER, CEO
First Horizon National Corporation
First Tennessee Bank

It's easy to get caught up in the day to day details of the work world and even easier for a leader to lose sight of his vision while managing a team. . . . If you are a leader who is seeking to develop a team of significance, Becoming a Coaching Leader is a must read. Daniel has given us the vision of the promised land and an easy-to-follow road map to get there. If you choose to accept his challenge the quality of your leadership and your team will be transformed as will the lives of those you lead. I encourage you to make this book a priority and to join the ranks of "Coaching Leaders" today.

JIM MCQUAIG
Founder
Nations Home Funding, Inc.

Everyone talks about leadership. Few people talk about coaching. Yet, this is the missing paradigm that makes good leaders great. In this fascinating book, Daniel Harkavy offers a new model, practical advice, and the motivation to take your entire team to the next level. If you're ready to turn on the after-burners in your organization, this is all the fuel you need!

MICHAEL S. HYATT
President & Chief Executive Officer
Thomas Nelson Publishers

BECOMING
A COACHING
LEADER

BECOMING A COACHING LEADER

The Proven Strategy for Building a Team of Champions

DANIEL HARKAVY

WITH STEVE HALLIDAY

Published by
THOMAS NELSON
Since 1798

www.thomasnelson.com

Published in Nashville, Tennessee, by Thomas Nelson, Inc.

Published in association with Yates & Yates, LLP, Attorneys and Counselors, Orange, California.

All scripture quotations are taken from The Holy Bible, New International Version. Copyright
© 1973, 1978, 1984, International Bible Society. Used by permission of Zondervan.

Thomas Nelson, Inc., titles may be purchased in bulk for educational, business, fundraising, or
sales promotional use. For information, please e-mail SpecialMarkets@ThomasNelson.com.

Library of Congress Cataloging-in-Publication Data

Harkavy, Daniel.
    Becoming a coaching leader : the proven strategy for building a team of champions /
Daniel Harkavy.
      p. cm.
    ISBN-13: 978-0-7852-1982-8 (hardcover)
    ISBN-10: 0-7852-1982-X
    1. Leadership. 2. Employees—Coaching of. I. Title.
HD57.7.H366 2006
658.4'092—dc22   2006032845

Printed in the United States of America

4 5 6 QW 08 07

CONTENTS

FOREWORD

I'll get right to the point. Coaching, the kind that Daniel Harkavy does and writes about in this book, is not what you think it is.

Coaching is not management consulting. It is not psychological counseling. It's not personal training. It is nothing short of a new way to think about managing and leading and living with and for others. It is as practical and tangible as it is conceptual and comprehensive.

Whether you are a CEO, a manager, a minister, a teacher, or a basketball coach, this book is about to change the way you look at your work and your life. But, before you read this, it's worthwhile to get to know its author.

Daniel Harkavy is, first and foremost, a coach. In his job, in his home, in his church—in every aspect of his life, he is a coach. Coaching isn't merely something he does for short bursts of time during a phone call or a meeting with a client. It's how he sees life. It gives meaning and purpose to virtually everything he does. He is a fanatic, a surfer, a father, a husband, and a nut. He is completely authentic and cannot help but bring out the best in everyone he meets. And luckily for us, the lengths he goes to and the energy he puts into others has been translated into a powerful coaching methodology that has convinced me that coaching is both real and ridiculously powerful.

Becoming a Coaching Leader is a how-to guide for anyone who wants to transform their lives and those of the people they lead and serve. It is a reservoir of concepts, ideas, and tools that will help so many readers be the people they are meant to be and help others do the same. I know these concepts are helping me—through my coach, Daniel—become a better leader and a better person. If you have never read a book on coaching, or are skeptical about whether it is real, use this book to transform your people, your organization, and your life. Really.

PATRICK LENCIONI,
author of *The Five
Dysfunctions of a Team*

A Superior Way to Lead

*You want to make a greater difference in the lives of those you lead
and experience more success and significance as you do so.*

The statement above is the foundation of *Becoming a Coaching Leader*. You are a student of leadership. You desire to create a culture of champions and to trade in your working hours for something that makes a real difference. Becoming a coaching leader is the next step in your leadership journey.

This book is a result of the countless insights my team and I have gleaned from spending the last ten years coaching thousands of leaders just like you. These leaders hold various positions in a multitude of industries. We took the lessons we learned and created an effective methodology to train leaders to become coaching leaders fully able to build their own teams of champions.

In the past few decades, leadership has become a fiery topic. Executive coaching has recently claimed viable space in the business world. For many business leaders, the concept of "coaching" is still ambiguous; no one method or defined set of guaranteed outcomes exists.

Nevertheless, today's business leaders commonly seek out guidance from a professional coach to assist them with reaching personal and professional goals. The business and life coaching industry today includes more than forty thousand coaches worldwide. Coaching has been featured in just about every mainstream business publication, from the *Harvard Business Review* to *Fast Company* to *Fortune*. Look up "executive coaching" on Amazon.com, and hundreds of books pop up.

Becoming a Coaching Leader takes the phenomenon of coaching to the next level. As you work your way through our proven coaching strategy, you will learn to use the effective coaching tools and systems we have designed to help you improve your ability to develop your people. You will find supporting insights from some of our coaches at Building Champions throughout the book in what I call the "Coach's Corner." As coaches, we find ourselves continually recapping key points from our meetings or conversations as we draw them to a close. I attempt to do the same, calling out some of the they key benefits for your team members, your company, and you, the leader, at many of the chapter endings.

Whether you are the owner of a small to midsize company, an executive within a larger corporation, or in middle management, becoming a coaching leader will help *you* to leave behind those discouraging days when your job felt either overwhelming or underwhelming. If you seek fulfillment, exhilaration on the job, and improved results then you can do no better than to become a coaching leader.

PART ONE

Why Change Your Title to Coaching Leader?

ONE

Living Out
Your Purpose at Work

In business we live and breathe numbers. Every year we set new goals; every month we accomplish one-twelfth of those goals, then wipe the slate clean. Every week in production we celebrate those running ahead and lament over those lagging behind. Every day we crack the quota whip.

No matter what we're talking about—leads needed, prospects converted, Units sold, deals closed, income generated—it all focuses around numbers. We measure performance by teammember, profitability by product, and keep careful track of return on investment, gross margin, and net worth requirements. You know the indicators on which you need to focus most intently to reach your annual targets.

This is what business is all about, right?

I say, yes and no.

On the one hand, you can't succeed in business without paying careful attention to numbers. That's obvious. Neglect the numbers, and you fail.

But don't forget that other hand!

The frightening truth is, you can come up with all the right numbers *and still fail.* You can meet your quotas, improve your profitability, expand your market share, keep the shareholders happy, increase efficiency . . . and still get out of bed every day wondering, *Do I really have to do this again?*

I've met too many less-than-happy, stressed out, unfulfilled, bitter leaders—who were all good at their jobs—to believe that making your numbers alone will solve all your problems. These men and women would be the first to tell you that there *has* to be more to business than numbers.

But if that's so, then what could it be? If producing good numbers doesn't make for success in business, what does?

I believe the answer revolves around discovering your *vocational purpose.*

HELPING YOUR PEOPLE TO DEVELOP

What is *your* vocational purpose? Your business card or title may say this or that, but what is your *vocational purpose*?

Is it more than "to build great systems"?

Is it more than "to create accurate and efficient processes"?

Is it more than "to build a furniture company" or "to sell a lawn-care product"?

You may be very good at what you do, but if at the end of the day you leave the office feeling professionally empty, spiritually hollow, and bored or weighed down, then most likely you need to reinfuse your task with a healthy dose of job significance. You need to reconnect the purpose of your heart to your actions. You need to start asking yourself not just "How can I lead better?" but "Why do I lead in the first place?"

It may feel easier to skip such a big question, but doing so will almost certainly saddle you with a host of unwelcome passengers: boredom, fatigue, discouragement, even despair. Many who refuse to ask themselves about their

> *Your purpose as a coaching leader is to add the most value to the people you lead and to help them improve.*

vocational purpose wind up meandering from job to job, always searching (always unsuccessfully) for that "something else" that will finally give real meaning and significance to their workdays.

What a waste!

Why a waste? Because you can find all the meaning and significance and purpose you need *right where you are now.* You don't have to be constantly looking for greener grass. You needn't be always on the hunt for a shining kingdom somewhere over the rainbow. The job you have *right now* has the potential to supply you with all the purpose you need to feel fulfilled and satisfied in your role as leader—you just need to change the way you think about your job. Based on my work with thousands of leaders over the past two decades, I believe it comes down to this: The key is to see yourself as more than a mere manager. Begin to perceive your role as that of a career and life improver for the people you lead! When you take on *that* challenge, you'll find your job overflowing with purpose.

Coach's Corner

Leaders are called to develop people. Their passion for people drives everything—and few things in life feel sweeter than investing in the lives of others and then watching them grow and succeed as a result of your efforts.

Can you imagine leaving your people a legacy that will far outlast your hours spent working alongside them? This is what excites me most about coaching. I know I can have a lasting impact on others that only those most passionate about their calling at work can enjoy. Coaching your people gives you all the structure you need to achieve that lasting impact.

Greg Harkavy
Coach
Building Champions, Inc.

Do you want to become an even more effective leader than you already are? Effective leadership is all about taking followers on a journey that enables them to experience and accomplish more as a result of the coaching and vision you bring to them. Truly great leaders walk alongside their followers and help them to become *more* on this journey. That's what these leaders see as their main purpose: to help their people develop professionally, personally, relationally and even spiritually. The journey could last one year, three years, five years, thirty years—however long their teammates remain with them. But regardless of the time frame involved, *people development* is a top priority. *That's* how they find real and satisfying purpose in their jobs.

And there's no reason the same thing can't become true for you.

GOOD OR GREAT?

Over the past two decades of coaching leaders, I have observed many good leaders and a few really great leaders. At first, it's not easy to tell the difference. But as you spend time with these men and women and observe their teams, the subtle differences begin to stand out.

Both good and great leaders are numbers driven. They know what needs to be measured, and they have systems and reports that provide essential data to help them manage their operations effectively. Both good and great leaders remain very clear on their team's convictions, purpose, and vision. They look the same, dress the same, and have similar backgrounds. So what's the difference?

They communicate in very different ways and tell very different stories.

Good leaders tell you about their successes. They describe how they have surrounded themselves with good talent. They report how their teams meet quotas and exceed goals. They show you wonderful systems and clever tools that help them in their pursuit of efficiency. But you probably won't hear much about how they develop their people, and that's where great leaders stand apart from the good.

> *A commitment to people development is what separates good leaders from great leaders.*

Great leaders tell you about their successes, too. They describe the superb talent around them and show you wonderful systems and clever tools for efficiency. But they take special and obvious delight in developing their people. *That's* the crucial difference.

6

Quick Leadership Quiz

1. Have I demonstrated a high level of competency in my role as manager or leader?

2. Do my personal and professional behaviors line up with my convictions?

3. Have I put corporate convictions, purpose, and vision in writing, and do I share these things strategically and consistently to everyone on my team?

4. Do my team members know—that is, can they clearly articulate—our convictions, purpose, and vision?

5. Do I commonly talk more about my team's success than my own?

6. Do I derive greater satisfaction out of what my team has created or what I have created?

7. Do I methodically and intentionally develop my people?

8. Do I have preset, scheduled coaching sessions with each of my key teammates?

9. Do I have a method for coaching my teammates?

10. Do I have a system for following up with my teammates when their action plans are due?

11. Do I know my teammates' dreams?

12. Do I know my teammates' greatest fears?

13. Do I know what truly motivates each of my teammates?

14. Am I most fulfilled by helping others reach new heights in business and in life?

If you answer "yes" to the majority of the questions above, this book will affirm your efforts and sharpen some of the skills you already possess. If you answered "no" more often than "yes," don't worry; you'll find help in the pages that follow.

All leaders, both good and great, fall into one of five camps when it comes to people development. Into which group do you think you fall?

1. *The "Self-Made" Leader.* The self-made leader buys into the philosophy that each individual is responsible for his or her own professional and personal development. After all, this leader never had anyone really develop *him*, so why should anyone else need such hocus-pocus? Besides, he succeeded in an independent role and later won a management position, or he ventured out on his own because he knew he could do it better. He did it all on his own—and that's how it should be for everyone.

   This type of leader will usually plateau early and never reach his full potential.

2. *The "Perk-and-Pray" Leader.* The perk-and-pray leader invests in occasional training and by doing so thinks she is hitting the mark. When a "superstar" seminar comes to town, the leader sends a few of her key people to the event. Yet very rarely does this leader do any real follow-up to assess what was learned and how the information will enhance her teammates' careers or lives. Because the leader has no real plan, she coughs up the $295, treats it like a perk, and prays that it will improve the life of her employees (and perhaps spark some appreciation).

3. *The "Mentor" Leader.* This leader has climbed through the ranks and has mastered the various positions now occupied by those who report to him. He is respected for his knowledge and the success he has attained. This leader invites his people to come to him with problems and opportunities and will tell them how he successfully handled a very similar situation. People will work for the mentor leader because of the draft effect; success comes their way as a result of what they learn by drafting off their mentor.

4. *The "Outsourcing" Leader.* This leader partners with an industry-specific training firm and contracts them to train her teammates on specific

skill sets. She understands the return on investment in her people and has created a plan and budget to develop her people with the help of an outside expert. This is a great strategy for the leader whose organization benefits more from her focusing on other priorities. It frees her up to focus on executing her vision, working with larger clients, setting direction, and working with key partners and board members.

5. *The "Coaching" Leader.* This leader has embraced the idea of building a "coaching culture" and follows a proactive coaching plan for his direct reports. This leader sees his purpose and responsibility as investing in his people so that they grow professionally and personally.

This type of leader spends a large percentage of his week coaching others to higher levels of performance and effectiveness. He usually feels very fulfilled and enjoys a good amount of success. People actually line up at the door of his department or company to sign on. The coaching leader uses this strength as a unique leadership proposition.

Do you see yourself in any of these five leader types? Each of them can earn the title of "good" leader; but if you want to move from being a "good" leader to becoming a "great" one, work at becoming a coaching leader. That's just what most great leaders tend to do. And in this book, I want to give you a proven model that will enable you to truly become an excellent coaching leader.

COACHING:
THE BEST ROUTE TO YOUR PURPOSE

Most leaders know they must devote time and resources to develop their people and teams. Unfortunately, however, few have a plan capable of bringing about measurable change in the careers and lives of their teammates. In most organizations, in fact, team member development reaches its peak before that organization reaches any notable level of success. Why? It's really very simple.

Before orders start pouring in, members of a new team have lots of time on their hands. That means leaders have the time to train and observe their young and energized employees. But then "it" happens. Success! Orders start pouring in and the organization's team, systems, and infrastructure get maxed out. They simply cannot take on any more business, and almost overnight the life cycle of the team changes from *sowers and growers* to *managers and maintainers.*

As the company or department continues to make money, the leader must deal with all the challenges that go along with running a growing business. That means the old training disciplines quickly get replaced with crisis management conversations. People development screeches to a halt—and soon the leader starts wondering whether it makes any difference if he makes 50, 500, or 50 gazillion widgets an hour.

This all-too-common scenario rarely takes place in a coaching culture. Leaders who become skilled coaches, who have made coaching one of their highest payoff activities, are some of the most fulfilled and passionate leaders in business. They have to deal with crises and quotas, too, just like everyone else, but the coaching culture they have developed spares them headaches that tend to crush other managers.

No matter what product your company makes or what service your organization provides, you have the opportunity to master a skill that can forever change how the people who call you "leader" live and work. By mastering your one-on-one coaching skills and by following a proven coaching model, you can truly help your teammates build more "switched on" careers and balanced lives than they ever dreamed possible. That helps your company—which, of course, helps you.

AN INTENTIONAL COACHING LEADER: MICHAEL'S STORY

Supremely confident and polished, yet humble, Michael Van Skaik was an incredibly successful division president in a national banking firm. He had no problem with goal setting and execution. He was a gifted planner and team builder. Michael had built and sold one company and was working on his second career, leading a multibillion dollar division for this national firm.

When Michael came to me, his team consisted of strong leaders and mega producers. The environment he had created attracted highly energized and talented people. Michael knew he had a lot to learn about balancing his personal life with his career. He understood that his job was not merely about making a lot of money, but he didn't know what else to strive for.

Through our coaching sessions, we discovered Michael's real passions. He was a builder. He loved building structures with his hands and with his mind. He knew how to find, attract, and hire the smartest and hardest working people, and then get them meshing with others to build a winning team. But he had never given much thought about how to go beyond that.

This much he did know: every time he returned from a vacation or business trip, Michael always worried about which of his teammates had been recruited away from him. To better retain the talent he had amassed, he realized he needed a way to add value to their lives. He also suspected that by doing so, he would find real fulfillment in his own career.

More than halfway through our first year of coaching, I asked Michael a simple question: "What is your plan to develop your team?" He had a one-word answer.

"Huh?"

The question dumbfounded him. He had never thought of *intentionally* developing his people. He planned to hire the right people and provide them with an environment where they could operate as effectively and autonomously as possible—and it had worked, to an extent. He was a "self-made" leader. But he quickly realized his strategy lacked the power to help him make a significant difference in the lives of his teammates.

BUILDING A TEAM DEVELOPMENT PLAN

I challenged Michael to create a team development plan. First, I encouraged him to identify as many strategies as possible to add value to the careers and lives of those who called him leader. I didn't give him much specific direction. And in his next coaching session, he shared his plan.

"I want to do for my people what you've done for me," he declared. "I want to coach them."

Michael just *had* to become a coach! His job was about to change; his purpose was about helping his people to succeed. He felt energized about helping his teammates to build businesses that would enable them to enjoy even more success at work and at home. In fact, Michael was so convinced of this, he said that if he couldn't positively impact his people at these levels, he didn't want his job anymore. He felt sure the change would enable him to take his own life and his region to new levels.

To make a long story short, Michael requested that we give him a proposal that would enable him to coach up to twenty of his teammates. He shared the details of the proposal with the CEO of his firm and assured his boss that the plan would produce significant benefits for the company, a firm with about six thousand employees.

The CEO not only agreed to his request, but he offered to fund the coaching initiative and suggested beta testing it with more than a single coach. Within the first year, a total of forty-five employees went through our coaching process. The benefits that ensued, both in terms of retention and increased production, were so great that the company agreed to underwrite coaching for a second year.

Next we certified twelve branch managers to become coaches so they could coach their own team members. The coaching culture quickly spread, with more than 150 team members receiving coaching. The company charted production numbers for the regions receiving coaching and compared them to the regions that were not. They found that among the employees with a top performance history, those who received the coaching out-performed their non-coached peers by 22 percent. But that wasn't all: among employees who tended to underperform, those who received coaching grew as much as 60 percent over their noncoached peers.

Results like these led to our current five-year agreement with this company to train and certify up to three hundred coaching leaders, who will coach up to three thousand of their team members in the years ahead.

This investment in coaching continues to produce amazing benefits. Teams in the program are seeing a unity they have never before witnessed. Team members' loyalty to the company, as well as overall morale, has noticeably improved. When team members from other regions or from the corporate office spend time in the regions previously led by Michael, they all comment on the amazing culture they find there.

Truly, Michael and this company are building a company of coaching leaders. It's making a huge difference in thousands of lives, both professionally and personally. And that gives me a great deal of satisfaction, because Michael's experience tends to echo the journey I began about two decades ago.

MY OWN STORY

For many years I was a coach and didn't know it.

Almost twenty years ago I was promoted into my first formal management position while working at a mortgage banking firm. At twenty-three years old, I had no management experience or training when I moved out of my cubical into the corner office. I sat down at the desk where my last two managers had worked and struggled with one question swirling in my head: *Now what do I do?*

I had no clue, no plan, and no experience. Somehow I needed to transfer my passion, experiences, and success as a solo producer into others.

At the end of my first day as leader, I called for my first all-staff team meeting. All three employees showed up. I told them there was a "new sheriff" in town, and we were going to take this branch from its fifth-place ranking (out of eight) and move us up to number one. I did not tell them how; I just told them we were really going to kick it up.

On day two, my only salesperson resigned, leaving just my receptionist and my processor remaining. Not the impressive results I was hoping for in my first twenty-four hours of leadership.

Recruiting became my new game. But since I also had P&L responsibilities, I could not allow my own production to drop. I had watched corporate close branch offices before, and I refused to let that become my destiny. So I created a simple but specific plan that focused on finding, recruiting, and retaining quality people. I believed that if I could add more value to their lives than they were receiving from their current employers, my team would grow.

A bright UCLA grad with a great work ethic became my first loan officer and my first "player" (employee I coached). I pledged to help him map out a plan for his business and then help him make the necessary improvements to build it. From this foundation, we would work on the goals, skills, knowledge, and disciplines necessary to make it all happen.

In time, he grew to become our company's top loan officer. The story of his success—both business and personal—repeated itself many times between 1987 and 1993. Our branch did take the number one position in the company, even as the organization grew to seventeen branches. And still today, I am privileged to be coaching him as a client.

Nothing excited me more than walking side by side with an individual who wanted to grow and who would allow me to be part of the process. And while my teammates made more money than their peers, the stories that really got my heart pumping revolved around how they were getting married, developing healthy habits, learning and growing and reaching new goals, and contributing in their homes and communities. Eventually our business successes led to the expansion of territory—and to promotions for my teammates and me.

Of those I coached in the early days, today the majority of them are owners or top producers/managers of great companies. They're very successful, becoming more successful than I ever was in those positions. Their success made me realize that I needed to market my commitment to coaching; that was a unique selling proposition for me: "If you join my team, I'm going to coach you. This is more than leadership; it's more than management. You want to join this team because you want to become *more*. And I promise to take on that project, to help you."

I spent the last two years of my mortgage career as the vice president of production, responsible for seventeen offices and roughly two hundred producers and leaders in offices throughout California, Oregon, Washington, and Nevada. I filled my days with coaching the leaders of these offices and with helping them to coach their teams. I planned to replicate the coaching culture I had created in my branch.

Then it all got a bit rocky.

By that time I had ten years with this company and this wonderful team. The founder and CEO had become a mentor and friend who said he was grooming me to take his seat in the years ahead. Our company had gone public the previous year, and the future looked incredible. I was far exceeding my financial goals, and I couldn't imagine a better plan for my career.

As I became more successful with our company, my definition of success began to change. What previously motivated me lost its attraction. It was no longer about my W-2, possessions, or title. I wanted more, but I was not sure what I wanted more of.

While attending a men's conference, I decided to trade my proven career for the unknown. Even though I worked for a great company, had a substantial income, had huge upside potential, and was surrounded by a magnificent team, I felt that I needed to change my course. So in 1995, I took a one-year sabbatical to think it all over. What was I really good at? What did I love to do? And how could I make a career out of that and still support my family?

In that year off, I realized, *I loved developing leaders! I love helping people. If I could do anything, I would invest myself in those who could invest themselves in others.* I've always liked the leverage effect.

So in 1996 I launched Building Champions. Today our company employs twenty full-time coaches in seven states, more than forty corporate coaches trained and licensed in the Building Champions curriculum, and another twenty supporting team members. We also founded Ministry Coaching International, a not-for-profit coaching organization that employs ten coaches. To date we have coached more than 2,500 individuals through our one-on-one coaching models. It has been an amazing journey so far. And the adventure ahead looks even more exciting.

Why do I tell you about my own journey? Because I want you to see that coaching is not merely "another thing" for me; it's the chosen focus of my life. I love adding value to leaders and showing them how they can do the same for the members of their own teams. Coaching is the best way I know to increase company profits, raise employee morale, and give you, the leader, the kind of deep purpose that gets you out of bed every morning, excited to meet the new challenges ahead.

Lessons Learned

In ten years of coaching others I've learned . . .

- Coaching others positively impacts the coach. Focusing on others improves my own game.

- Coaching others intentionally is one of a leader's highest payoff activities.

- Following our model will make you a focused and intentional manager as well as a more effective leader.

- When you coach your own team, everybody wins: you, your teammates, and your company.

- Everybody can teach you something.

- Lifelong learning enables you to add more value to those around you—and that is very rewarding.

- Everybody can improve, including you.

- Spending a day with a team of champions is much more fun than being surrounded by complacency.

- Making your career fit into your overall plan for life is more than smart; it is wise.

- Knowing your purpose in life and living it out in your vocation equals a life well lived.

GO FOR MORE

There really is a lot more to business than numbers. In this book, you will discover all that coaching can do for your company, for your employees, and for you.

I have done my best to fill the following pages with practical instruction, personal inspiration, and powerful motivation. I know you need to become the kind of coaching leader who can bring a whole new level of satisfaction, fulfillment, and purpose to those in your sphere of influence. And that, of course, includes you.

"But I don't manage a division of six thousand employees," you reply. "I lead a very small company. What can coaching do for me?"

Let me introduce you to another client.

This young leader learned of Building Champions at a convention and promptly decided he could learn to coach without our services. But before he makes any major decision, he always checks with his friend and mentor, who has been financially independent for many years.

"If it's worth anything at all," the friend told him, "it's worth that amount."

So about a year ago he signed up with us. At the time, he said, "I was a producing owner, manager, compliance specialist, sales trainer, operations manager, processing manager, president, CEO, and janitor. I worked a legitimate seventy-hour work week that included at least half a day every Saturday and resulted in me getting home after midnight at least three to five times per month."

This summer he extended his coaching contract for an additional two years. He also invested additional funds for his coach to make an on-site visit with his team. Why?:

- He is on pace to have year-over-year growth of 177 percent.

- Company production is on pace to exceed its record 2004 year, despite having 20 percent fewer salespeople (having dismissed their third and eighth greatest producers the year before).

- He has reduced his workweek from seventy hours to near forty.

- He has worked two Saturdays in the past 120 days.

- His golf handicap has improved by more than five shots. "We live on a course, and I take my boys with me," he says.

Oh, and one last thing. He reports he has taken a stress-free vacation with very limited interruptions, he is much easier to get along with, and—well, I have to let him say it—"My wife is about ten weeks pregnant. Had to find something to do with the free time."

I can't guarantee you'll have identical results if you decide to take the challenge to become a coaching leader. Maybe you don't want the same results anyway! However, I can promise that life will be very different. That's true no matter how large your business is, or how small.

Or how many extra mouths you want to feed.

TWO

The Fuel
of Great Leaders

Have you ever been to a NASCAR or Indy-style race? Thousands of fans crowd the stands to watch expert drivers push their high-performance vehicles to the limit, every daring competitor trying to outmaneuver all rivals to the checkered flag. Every year these high-stakes spectacles of speed, danger, and power draw increasing numbers of rabid spectators.

But what if the cars had no fuel?

How many fans would show up weekend after weekend to watch sleek racing machines, armed with muscle-bound engines, high-performance tires, and state-of-the-art aerodynamics just sit there? No movement. No speed. No danger. How many spectators would come out to pay good money for *that*? Without fuel, the most advanced race cars in the world are nothing more than expensive statues—suitable for a museum, perhaps, but not for winning the Daytona 500 or the Nextel Cup.

In many ways, great leaders are just like great race cars. They need high-performance fuel to keep them charging around the track. They can have all the high-tech gadgets and brilliant systems and superb "pit crews" available, but unless they fill their tank with the right fuel, they're not going anywhere.

So what fuels great leaders? I believe *convictions* and *courage* are the oxygen and octane that power up winning leaders. And any leader who neglects to fill up on the right stuff winds up, almost by default, in the local pinewood derby.

A Stunning Discovery

For over a decade we have coached hundreds of leaders at some of America's most successful companies. And I've noticed a startling trend: while a high percentage of these professionals get publicly recognized as the best of the best—every year receiving glowing accolades at Presidents Clubs and Chairman's Circle events for their professional accomplishments—they themselves feel less than fulfilled in their lives.

When we invite them to rate the quality of their lives on a scale from 0 (dreadful) to 10 (couldn't be better), too many reply with numbers in the lower end of the range. And that begs the question: Why do these business powerhouses rarely rate their lives with 9s and 10s?

I believe the answer can be found in coaching and direction. While these executives are built for speed and have all the resources to make them into champions, they've forgotten the fuel. And when your gauge reads "empty," you not only *feel* like you're going nowhere in a hurry, you really *are*.

And so are most of those following you.

A Society of Beat-up People

To understand why convictions and courage are so essential to success, you must recognize that many beat-up and beaten-down people walk through your office doors every morning. These frazzled men and women are stumbling through many seasons of life: pregnancy concerns, teenage conflicts, empty-nest issues, menopause, divorce, messy financial challenges, you name it.

Don't indulge the fantasy that your organization or industry is somehow different from every other organization or industry in America with regard to the available talent pool. The fact is our people today *are* beat up. Just consider a few of the societal facts that shape the lives of those who work with and around and for you:

- We are seeing record numbers of bankruptcies in America.[1]

- Unwed pregnancies continue to soar. Unwed mothers recently accounted for more than four in five births among teens, more than half of births among women in their early twenties, and for three in ten births among women ages twenty-five to twenty-nine.[2]

- Divorce rates continue to plague our country and wreak havoc on today's families and workforce.[3]

- According to the U.S. Department of Labor's *Occupational Outlook Handbook,* the number of clinical counselors and psychologists will continue to rise. "Overall employment of psychologists is expected to grow *faster than average* for all occupations through 2012 due to increased demand for psychological services. . . . [Employment for] clinical, counseling, and school psychologists will grow [at a] *faster than the average* [rate], while industrial-organizational psychologists will have average growth."[4]

Our companies are filled with people suffering from broken or breaking lives. Even though they may appear to be doing well, they struggle with failing relationships at home, with serious health issues, with addictions, and with directionless lives, and this hurts our companies in countless ways.

Today's team members bring a lot more hurt to work than did those of just a few years ago. Your people simply don't leave their "stuff" at the door—and if you think they do, or if you try to insist that they do, you're headed for serious trouble. Realize that this is *life* in this century. This is what we have to deal with. This is the nature of our workforce.

For twenty years, I have watched this reality unfold in my own offices. I have watched my people bring in domestic challenges, financial hardships, and relationship breakdowns, and if I try to tell them, "Just work harder!" my counsel flops. I can tell them to work harder until they walk right out the door. And beyond that, many days *I* struggle with the same issues facing my team. Of course, I don't need to compromise on what I need from my teammates. But I do need, at the very least, to acknowledge where they are. I need the kind of convictions that challenge them to take responsibility for what they can control. And I need the courage to say, "Okay, this is still what's required. Can you do it? And how can I help you to succeed?"

No team can achieve long-term success with players who continually battle, all alone, the kind of destructive issues just mentioned. Challenges like these severely limit a teammates' ability to sustain champion levels of work performance. Failure to acknowledge and deal with these issues can result in high turnover, poor morale, mediocre performance, and a culture filled with men and women who are not experiencing all the good things they could be.

If you understand the current workforce landscape, however, and have decided to coach them—if you have the conviction to help people improve and the courage to enter into their world—then you'll become a student in many of these areas so that you can offer helpful, empathetic advice. Your people will know they don't have to hide their problems from you. They won't live in fear that you'll terminate them if you discover their struggle. And even if you don't have the competency to help them effectively, as a coach you know someone who *can* help them, and you will immediately send them there for relief.

When we risk diving into our people's lives with the kind of convictions and courage that can truly help them, we partner with them in a way that enables them (and us) to make better life decisions. By choosing to become a coaching leader, you tell your people that you really care about them. You show them that they are important, that they are valuable, and that they matter to you. You show them that you care about them not just for what they can produce; you care about them as people.

When this happens, they'll see that you have what I call *heart*. And when they see that, they'll follow you just about anywhere.

HEART: THE GREAT DIFFERENCE MAKER

Heart is the difference maker in great leaders. You cannot be a great coach without heart. If you don't genuinely care about people—if you are coldly tactical and distantly technical and efficiently process oriented and you leave your heart out of it—then your people will follow you only part of the way. They need to believe that by following you, they will go places they would not even see without you at the helm. Heart is the home to both convictions and courage; it is the fuel of all exceptional leaders. Your beliefs about your people and their potential inevitably impact your success or failure as a leader.

Are you having a problem with turnover? It may be a heart issue.

Are you having a problem with employee performance? Could be a heart issue.

Are you having a problem with people lying, stealing, and cheating? Perhaps it's a heart issue.

Are you having a problem with people showing up only to collect a paycheck? Probably it's a heart issue.

Are you having a problem with people not wanting to grow? Check your own heart; the issue could lie there.

In all these cases, *your heart may be the problem*. Your head may be engaged, and you may have great systems in place. You may have all the best processes and technology. You may have great marketing. You may have an outstanding product. But today's generation, especially, wants to belong to something special. If your teammates don't sense "something special" in you, they will leave even for less money. They want to trade their life for something that matters, and the specific product or service makes little difference.

Our late coach, Michelle Feenstra had a rich passion for those new to the workforce. She shared the following with me. "Many of the young men and women who entered the workforce in their twenties and who are now in their thirties—the Millennials, Gen Xers, or 'Echo Boomers,' as some still refer to them—are about much more than money. They are looking for more than a paycheck. They want to work with a group of people who care about each other, who care about winning, and who care about what their careers enable them to accomplish in life. Today's employees know they have choices and options, and they'll exercise them to find what they're looking for."

If you want to succeed as a leader in today's business world, you have to understand both the mind-set of the Millennial generation and the differing perspective of our own generation. In her book *Connecting Generations*, Claire Raines offers one such example.

[handwritten annotation: USA centric?]

23

Dear Claire,

I always have to tell my teenagers and twenty-something employees to do a task—they don't take the initiative to get the work done. They just don't seem to have the work ethic that my older workers do. What's the secret to motivating them?

ERIC

Dear Eric,

This is a challenge that lots of managers and supervisors face. The work ethic of older generations was different. Typically, the oldest generation was intrinsically motivated—they worked for work's sake, and considered it an honor just to have a job. Baby Boomers characteristically have worked hard because their self-image was based on their careers. Teenagers and twenty-something employees often have a different work ethic. Most are in the "no fear" category, not motivated by threats of punishment or firing.

The key is to get to know each as an individual: Find out what is important to them, why they're working, what they want to get out of their jobs. Get them to teach you how to motivate them. Then ask them to do the task and sell them on the benefit to them of doing the task. It may also help to set goals with each of them for the next sixty days, with a reward at the end, so that when you assign tasks, they can see where accomplishing that task will take them. I know it sounds complicated, but it's all based on getting to know each person as an individual, something I'll bet you're already good at.

CLAIRE[5]

The bottom line is that today's workforce wants to grow and succeed in all aspects of life. Its members respond amazingly well to leaders who care and who have the ability to help them succeed in all aspects of their lives. I do not believe this truth is limited to any demographic. I know this to be true with those who are nearing their retirement years as well.

You know what that means, don't you? Our teammates, regardless of age, want coaching leaders. And all coaching leaders need the fuel of both *convictions* and *courage*.

THE OXYGEN OF CONVICTIONS

In my years of coaching, I have observed that extraordinary leaders all have one trait in common: deep convictions about helping others to improve. *This* is their heartbeat. They have mastered the skills and disciplines needed to help others reach peak levels of performance. This is one of their primary areas of focus.

Everything they do flows out from a deep conviction that people are worth developing. They see their job as an opportunity, and maybe even a responsibility, to help others discover and fully experience what is possible for them.

Do you have this conviction? I'm not asking merely if it sounds like a great idea, or if you value the concept. A conviction goes deeper than a mere value (even a "core value"). A conviction is nonnegotiable. You may commit to a value, but you'll sacrifice for a conviction. When problems arise, you may ponder the cost of a value, but you'll ante up for a conviction no matter what the cost.

So . . . do you believe that you have something of significant value to offer your key team members? That because of your choice to become a coaching leader, your teammates will grow both professionally and personally? That you really try to walk your talk and are qualified to coach others in a proactive and holistic way? If you don't believe these things, then I doubt whether many will feel inspired to follow your leadership. Few will work hard to make your professional dreams come true. But if you do, then you and your teammates can experience exciting new heights.

This primary conviction, the commitment to help others improve, usually gets strengthened by a few other important convictions.

1. Tell the truth. Many great leaders share this conviction. It's called many things: doing the right thing, integrity, honesty, etc. To them, it's never a mere saying trotted out for the media at the appropriate time. Even at the risk of losing short-term income or seeing stock prices drop, they tell the truth.

2. Serve others. Great leaders are also committed to *serving others*. The leaders who bring this conviction to their organizations and customers have a deep belief that they can grow personally, as well as professionally, by continually looking for ways to best serve others. The coaching leader is all about servant-leadership; she devotes a great percentage of her time and energy to helping others to become *more*.

3. Be aware of time. Many great leaders are profoundly aware of the brevity of life and the uncertainty of tomorrow. This conviction brings them to a more intense level of focus and urgency. It also impacts how they prioritize their activities and how they go about making decisions. They have an uncommon ability to keep one eye focused on their vision while the other remains focused on the now, the immediate.

Let me introduce you to the CEO of a midsized service firm in Texas with roughly six hundred employees. You can see his passion for his people throughout his organization. His awareness of time and of the reality of storms that hit people at different times in life has caused him to set up extraordinary benefits for his team. One such benefit is a family hardship fund that he set up with his employees, who contribute a portion of their paychecks to sustain the fund. This fund helps members of his team when they encounter certain hardships. He has countless thank-you notes from very grateful team members.

Why does he do this, and how has it impacted his team? He says he values his teammates as if they were family. He wants to make sure he is doing all he can to help them succeed in life, knowing that all of us will encounter unforeseen hardships in life.

4. Appreciate talent. Great leaders have a conviction about filling their organization with talent. They know what talent (and talent in the making) looks like for their company, and so they spend a good percentage of their time with those who possess such talent, both outside the organization for recruiting purposes and inside the organization for coaching and retention purposes. As Jim Collins states in his best-selling book, *Good to Great*, great companies have the right people in the bus and in the right seats on the bus.

THE OCTANE OF COURAGE

Early in my sales career, I gauged the caliber of a prospect I was calling on by how I felt. If I felt too relaxed and not at all nervous, I knew I was calling on the wrong prospect. Why? Chances were, the person represented only a small opportunity.

On the other hand, I knew I had enjoyed a good day when I finished my meetings with sweaty palms. That meant I had placed myself in situations definitely out of my comfort zone—and probably had been calling on prospects that represented much larger opportunities.

That same kind of gauge works well for leaders who choose to coach their people in life. Such coaching requires that we stretch beyond our comfort zone, and that takes real courage. Why? Some of these conversations will make your palms sweat. Some will take a long time, and you must make sure you have the time and the courage to go there. You don't need to have all the answers, of course, but you do have to be willing to work through the situation, to follow up, to confront behaviors that do not line up with stated convictions, and to encourage at all times.

The fact is, helping people to succeed after 5:00 p.m. is risky. To become a coaching leader who goes beyond work performance, you must have the courage to risk entering the uncomfortable.

This is where many begin to hear ugly voices: "You can't help him! You are blowing it here in your own life, you hypocrite. *You're* not living up to your own standard, so who are you to ask him to do it?" I recognize those voices; I have heard them all in the past twenty years.

When your palms begin to sweat, you have two options. The first is to sneak back to the comfortable, to return to what is easy—namely, your skills or knowledge. The second option is to dive in and to risk helping. Sure, it may feel deeply uncomfortable for you. Certainly, there is a chance that your own actions will come into question. But is that a bad thing?

One of the greatest benefits of being a coaching leader is that it forces me to improve my own disciplines and actions. Leadership requires us to maintain higher standards. The old saying "More is caught than taught" is true. Every day, it seems, we read headlines filled with examples of leaders who have not grasped this truth.

With leadership comes responsibility. Our team members will allow us to be a part of who they are only to the extent that we have earned their trust and respect. The level of character, care, and discipline they see in us will determine the level of coaching they will invite and accept from us.

I believe our businesses (and our lives) would improve greatly if we leaders would make our palms sweat more when it comes to coaching our team members. Coaching a team member to improve how he makes his sales calls is not too risky, nor is coaching that same person to define what success looks like to him or her.

SOLD OUT AND PASSIONATE

Helping their employees to perform at peak levels from 8:00 to 5:00 was not enough for two leaders of a national mortgage-banking firm headquartered in Colorado. They set out to build a coaching culture and have already created a company of a few hundred teammates who are sold out and passionate about what they do.

These coaching leaders offer life planning to every employee (see chapter 5) and have committed to walking every member of their team through the process personally. They do this fully realizing that helping teammates grow in areas outside of work can be both risky and messy.

For example, they will spend a couple of hours helping an employee to write out his own epitaph as an exercise in self-assessment. "If you were to die today," they ask, "what would be said about you? What accounts in your life are most important to you? What vision do you have for each one of those accounts? Who do you want to become? What do you want to experience? What are the three to five things you need to do in each one of those areas so that you can accumulate net worth in all areas of your life?"

After that's done, these leaders follow up from time to time to see how the teammate is doing, understanding that as the employer, they have direct impact over the teammate's professional and financial accounts.

Do you see how unique this is? How countercultural? Most businesses don't generally do this—yet it's precisely how this company has built an incredibly attractive culture. Year after year, this company gets very high scores on employee satisfaction surveys.

They have grown as coaching leaders as a result of their deep desire to be surrounded with high-energy, balanced professionals who work and live at masterful levels. Since 1998, when our relationship began, we have been coaching multiple members of their team and have watched these leaders build a thriving coaching culture.

I have had the honor of speaking at their company's last four annual leadership retreats, and I simply can't deny the improvements I have observed. They want to help their team members succeed in all of life, including after 5:00 p.m. That is why they have placed life planning at the very core of their company's purpose, which is:

> To build and become a great company. In this process we aspire to positively impact the lives of those individuals who come into contact with our organization and to honor God in all that we do.

You can see that they are building something much greater than a home loan company. This company is building a life-changing environment for all team members and having a positive impact on all who come in contact with the organization. Convictions and courage are fueling this highly successful ride.

PLAYING WITH CHAMPIONS

It's a heck of a lot more fun to surround yourself with a team of champions than to spend your days swimming in a cauldron of dysfunction. When everyone in your organization or group speaks the same lingo, with everybody trying to build a culture of improvement in all aspects of life, you find yourself in the most switched-on, energetic culture imaginable. People *feel* it when they walk through your doors. They get different greetings, see different looks on teammates' faces, and hear different stories.

Take a look at your own team. What do you see? Are you surrounded by wonderfully gifted and skillful individuals who are able to perform at peak levels? Coaching leaders feel driven to help team members perform at peak levels in both their positions and their lives, something that may not be achievable without the leader's input. They see a team of champions (or champions in the making) long before its members come to see and believe that's who they really are.

I have both observed and experienced the significant fulfillment that results from really investing in a team member's life. I agree with John Maxwell, who insists, "It is *not* lonely at the top."

Think about your personal history. Who has made the most significant impact in your life? Why? What did this person teach you or share with you? Chances are, you are thinking of an individual who really cared for you, someone willing to take a risk and invest in you.

Do you want to know something? Your offices are filled with people who would love for *you* to be just that person.

I know hundreds of leaders who began to enjoy greater levels of success after they came to understand the crucial role they play in building a coaching culture. Whether your teammates say life is great or miserable, you need to own the role that your leadership has played in creating that reality. If it's good, then keep looking for ways to add even more value to their lives. If it's average or below average, then you must immediately assess how to start creating an environment that causes people to flourish.

One caution, though. Whatever you do, don't forget the fuel. Don't neglect either the necessary convictions or the courage.

Why hang out at the pinewood derby when you can be master of Daytona?

LEADERSHIP ASSESSMENT TOOL

Use the tool on page 31–32 to rank each of your teammates in ways we will further explain in the chapters ahead. This tool can be used to see where your team is strong or where they could be strengthened. It is easy to complete and will help you develop each of your direct reports. More talk in the chapters ahead will help you apply what you learn through the Leadership Assessment tool.

Leadership Team Assessment and Developmental Tool

Team Members' Names				
Heart	1 2 3 4 5 Comments:	1 2 3 4 5 Comments:	1 2 3 4 5 Comments:	1 2 3 4 5 Comments:
Vision	1 2 3 4 5 Comments:	1 2 3 4 5 Comments:	1 2 3 4 5 Comments:	1 2 3 4 5 Comments:
Emotional IQ	1 2 3 4 5 Comments:	1 2 3 4 5 Comments:	1 2 3 4 5 Comments:	1 2 3 4 5 Comments:
Key Strengths	1 2 3 4 5 Comments:	1 2 3 4 5 Comments:	1 2 3 4 5 Comments:	1 2 3 4 5 Comments:
Obvious Gaps	1 2 3 4 5 Comments:	1 2 3 4 5 Comments:	1 2 3 4 5 Comments:	1 2 3 4 5 Comments:
Blind Spots	1 2 3 4 5 Comments:	1 2 3 4 5 Comments:	1 2 3 4 5 Comments:	1 2 3 4 5 Comments:
Communication	1 2 3 4 5 Comments:	1 2 3 4 5 Comments:	1 2 3 4 5 Comments:	1 2 3 4 5 Comments:
Planning	1 2 3 4 5 Comments:	1 2 3 4 5 Comments:	1 2 3 4 5 Comments:	1 2 3 4 5 Comments:
Follow-up	1 2 3 4 5 Comments:	1 2 3 4 5 Comments:	1 2 3 4 5 Comments:	1 2 3 4 5 Comments:
Cultural Fit	1 2 3 4 5 Comments:	1 2 3 4 5 Comments:	1 2 3 4 5 Comments:	1 2 3 4 5 Comments:
Self-Development	1 2 3 4 5 Comments:	1 2 3 4 5 Comments:	1 2 3 4 5 Comments:	1 2 3 4 5 Comments:

Life Balance	1 2 3 4 5 Comments:	1 2 3 4 5 Comments:	1 2 3 4 5 Comments:	1 2 3 4 5 Comments:
Greatest Value to the Company	1 2 3 4 5 Comments:	1 2 3 4 5 Comments:	1 2 3 4 5 Comments:	1 2 3 4 5 Comments:
Greatest Risk to the Company	1 2 3 4 5 Comments:	1 2 3 4 5 Comments:	1 2 3 4 5 Comments:	1 2 3 4 5 Comments:
Their Life Goals or Dreams	1 2 3 4 5 Comments:	1 2 3 4 5 Comments:	1 2 3 4 5 Comments:	1 2 3 4 5 Comments:
Time Efficiencies	1 2 3 4 5 Comments:	1 2 3 4 5 Comments:	1 2 3 4 5 Comments:	1 2 3 4 5 Comments:
Organization	1 2 3 4 5 Comments:	1 2 3 4 5 Comments:	1 2 3 4 5 Comments:	1 2 3 4 5 Comments:
Self-Assuredness	1 2 3 4 5 Comments:	1 2 3 4 5 Comments:	1 2 3 4 5 Comments:	1 2 3 4 5 Comments:
My Actions to Recognize Their Contributions				
My Key Areas to Focus on for Their Development				
What I See for Their Future				

THREE

What Is a Coach?

Our next client leads a small yet dynamic company based in Los Angeles. He is the firm's top salesperson, the controller, and the head of marketing. He's also an athlete. So when he considered signing up for business coaching, he assumed that our coaching relationship would look a lot like the ones he remembered from his athletic career. Since his coaches had helped him to focus on all aspects of a single sport, he hired me to coach him for the same reason—only this time, to improve on all aspects of his business performance.

It surprised him when in our first session we did little more than a high-level, brief review of his business vitals. We spent the majority of our two-hour coaching session helping him to discover his own definition of success. As we do with all of our clients, I coached him through our life planning process, explaining that before we can help clients to succeed, we must first help them to clearly and succinctly define what success looks like for them.

To begin that process, I asked about his personal desires, the things he liked to do and wished he had more time for. He never imagined that we would discuss the "nonbusiness" parts of his life. Throughout his very successful career, no manager had ever assumed the role of coach with him. Some had been great leaders and had provided terrific role models, but none had asked him about how his business impacted his personal life. They never crossed the line between his life inside and outside of the office.

It didn't take him long to realize that *this* was the piece he had been missing. Over the years he had attended many goal-setting seminars and worked with many managers, but until we started our coaching relationship, he had never seen how closely his personal desires shadowed his professional ones and how the success of one relied so heavily on the status of the other.

The "big picture" view that a coaching relationship offers has given him the chance to create and to live a plan for a well-balanced and fulfilling life. He is now able to give the same gift to those on his team as he has become their coaching leader.

> *We ask all leaders to develop a Life Plan to help them define who they want to become in the various aspects of their lives that they consider most important.*

He places a huge value on the opportunity to discuss *anything* with our coaches, from an important business decision to a struggle he's having at home. He trusts our advice and expertise because he knows that we have no predetermined agenda other than his ultimate success. We won't steer him toward one decision or another for our own benefit, because we believe that a coach's ultimate purpose is helping others to succeed.

The success we've enjoyed together has prompted him to start coaching his own employees. He has created an environment within his company that encourages life and business planning, mentorship, and forward thinking. Each teammate has a mentor and a personalized plan for development. Most important, he acts as a caring sounding board for each team member—and the marked improvements that these measures have produced in his already successful company have convinced him that he's on exactly the right track.

BUT WHAT *IS* IT?

Like many others, at first he did not fully understand what business coaching involves. He took the plunge because he saw how others had gained such big benefits from it. However, when he began, he still didn't have a clear idea about what a business coach is and does. So let's start with a succinct definition:

A coach helps others win by helping them to discover the knowledge, strategies, Action Plans, inspiration, and accountability they need to excel and to reach even greater levels of success.

Like a *stagecoach*, coaching leaders *move people along*. How? They . . .

- Help teammates to identify gaps in their businesses and in their personal lives;
- Recognize and affirm the gifts of teammates;
- Discover their teammates' convictions and encourage them to create a vision consistent with those convictions;
- Assist with creating plans necessary for further levels of success;
- Keep teammates focused, passionate, and on track in regard to their plans;
- Pinpoint and assess their team's resources
- Provide the fresh perspective their teammates may need to complete their goals and actions; and
- Hold teammates accountable to their commitments.

A good coaching leader . . .

- is always moving and improving,
- sees who his people can become,
- is an improver,
- helps his players move from point A to point B,
- never accepts the status quo,
- is succinct, and truthful,
- identifies gaps and gifts,
- inspires, and
- sees the big picture and clarifies the steps necessary for success.

The mission of a coaching leader is to meet his teammates where they are in order to move them forward by helping them to improve the skills, disciplines, and knowledge they need to succeed. He does this by helping his teammates to clearly see the right action steps to take, and then by holding them accountable as they complete each step.

No coach needs to have an entire game plan for every team member. When you coach people one on one, each person develops his or her own plan. A good coach becomes skillful in asking questions that will enable the teammate to gain more clarity on how he or she wants to improve the various aspects of his or her professional and personal life. *Your purpose is to help your people improve.*

The late Tom Landry, celebrated coach of the Dallas Cowboys, once said, "A coach is someone who tells you what you don't want to hear and has you see what you don't want to see, so that you can be who you've always known you could be."

The way to enjoy success yourself is to focus on the success of those around you, by making *their* success *your* mission. Help them to figure out how to win both in their career and in life, and you will enjoy both success and significance.

Coach's Corner

As a coach, I help my clients to . . .

1. Make sure they have defined their reality, to stop, think, and truly assess their current situation.

2. Clarify their vision and define their goals; most people constantly react to events, people, and things . . . and therefore are not driven by purpose.

3. Understand and address roadblocks to their vision; we are most blinded to the things that are most comfortable or familiar to us.

4. Test their thinking, opinions, and conclusions; we easily get caught up in insanity, "doing the same things over and over, but expecting different results."

5. Establish accountability; too often people fall short by confusing intent with action.

    Raymond P. Gleason
    Executive Coach
    Building Champions, Inc.

A LOOK AT THE DIFFERENCES

Coaching in mainstream business is relatively new, just a decade old. So even though it has grown in popularity in the last ten years, a fair amount of confusion still exists as to what it is. To help dispel some of that confusion, it might help to contrast coaching with several other activities that often get mistaken for it.

Is *coach* just another term for *counselor*? Is a coach a teacher? A trainer? A consultant? A mentor? Or is there something that distinguishes a coach from all these other roles? Let's take a brief look.

Counselor. A counselor can be helpful when someone is struggling with some current or past event that prevents him from functioning in the healthiest possible way. To help illustrate this, I often draw a visual.

Imagine someone trapped below the waterline about to drown. It's dark under the surface, and that person needs to get his head above water to breathe and to see things clearly. Anyone stuck like this can't help but focus on himself or on his immediate circumstances, and all that is holding him back from moving ahead. A counselor can come in to help him breathe once more. The counselor throws him the life jacket he needs.

A coach may at times do some simple counseling, but the two roles are very different from one another: one does it as a means to an end (as one step in an overall plan), the other as the end in itself.

Teacher. Teachers have an assigned curriculum; their job is to help students learn that curriculum. So they teach the curriculum and give tests on it, intending that their students gain the head knowledge that will enable them to accomplish some specific task by using the presented content.

Coaches often teach, but their role encompasses much more. They help you to learn from yourself, your past, your gifts, your environment, and their experiences.

Trainer. A trainer helps someone to learn new behaviors. If a person wants to learn a methodology, a system, or a skill, a trainer may be just the ticket. A seasoned trainer can help others learn and practice a specific skill or methodology so that they can become more effective in one or several areas of business or life.

Sometimes a coach must act as a trainer to help move someone along in a certain area of his life, but the two roles are not identical—the coach always has the "big picture" and its implementation in mind.

Consultant. A consultant comes into an organization to determine where the most significant challenges or opportunities for improvement might be and then makes specific recommendations to overcome those challenges or implement those improvements. Then the consultant leaves behind a report or a list of action items for which specific members of the organization are responsible, on their own, to implement.

A coach may often wear the hat of a consultant, but his or her focus is to get you to create the majority of your solutions.

Mentor. A mentor shares what he or she knows with someone less experienced. The mentor's past can illuminate the other person's steps. A mentor has succeeded in certain aspects of business or life. By imparting what he or she has learned, the mentor helps others to avoid pitfalls or shorten learning curves.

Many coaches find mentoring to be a useful tool in their coaching role, but again, the two are not the same thing.

Coach. So what is a coach? A coach helps others to assess their situation and then improve their skills, disciplines, and knowledge so that they can make the necessary big picture changes (usually head and heart changes). This enables the teammates to align their steps and behaviors in order to accomplish and be more.

Those who solicit a coach are already ascending the mountain; their eyes are focused upward so that they can see the mountaintop. They already glimpse the opportunity to improve. They have good skills and disciplines. They've been taught, trained, and mentored. So they're climbing.

At that point, a coach comes in and helps them to see *even more* possibilities. A coach helps them make additional changes that will enable them to benefit even more from what they have learned already. And then, through a one-on-one relationship, the coach will ask the right questions and clarify and recall their convictions. This, in turn, will assist them to change their habits so that they can become even more successful and purposeful.

Each of these roles—counselor, teacher, trainer, consultant, mentor, coach—is unique, and a good coach needs to have some skill in each area. Sometimes a coach will be a teacher. Sometimes a mentor. Sometimes a counselor. Sometimes a trainer, but *always* a coach.

EIGHT CORE COMPETENCIES OF A COACHING LEADER

Now that we've seen what a coach is (and is not), we should ask, what makes for a *great* coach? In my experience, the best coaching leaders have mastered eight core competencies. In all eight of the following critical areas, they have demonstrated a high degree of proficiency.

Core Competency #1: Discernment

Discernment refers to the ability to see what is not visible, to understand what is not being said. A person might have all of the coveted degrees and still not have the ability to discern the motives or challenges in a team-member's current situation.

Discernment enables a coach to ask effective questions, unearthing roadblocks, fears, and doubts that keep a team member from reaching his or her goals. Once these issues are held up to the light of day, a coach can begin to help a teammate through them. A discerning coach can ask the necessary questions in a way that doesn't threaten the team member. Effective questioning requires discernment.

Discernment also helps a coach to see what outside pressures might be holding a team member back from top performance. Is it a lack of vision, belief, or courage? Is it a training issue? A discerning coach might ask, "How's everything going at home?" and then follow up on something the teammate mentioned a month earlier. Discernment gives a coach a good sense of timing: when to say or ask certain things, and when not to.

As I write, I've been out of town for about nine days. Just this morning one of my coaches called me into his office with a question. After we had exchanged the normal pleasantries, he said, "Hey, I have a client who is a very successful auto dealer. He buys and sells cars, about 150 per month, and makes about half a million dollars a year. He has recently taken this business model into real estate; his father is a licensed real estate broker and coordinates the transactions. The father and son had a great relationship.

"In times past, the father took care of all the real estate transactions without a commission. The son always felt very excited to tell the father about how much money he had been making—and then, just last week, the father suddenly said, 'On this next transaction, it's going to be full commission.' That surprised his son, who came into our coaching session and asked, 'Should I no longer share my financials with my father? Should I go out and find another real estate person in order to protect my relationship with my dad?' His father's request for commissions totally absorbed him; he just couldn't get outside of it."

My coach gave the situation great thought and ended up encouraging his client to protect the father-son relationship at all costs and to refuse to let business damage that relationship. But he still wondered whether he had handled the situation as well as he might have. He wondered if he had given his client enough direction.

I told him I thought he had shown good discernment, but I challenged him to go even further: "Did you ask him any questions to get him to reflect on what's going on in his heart? What are his motives? Why is the commission situation consuming him so? Why can't he just make a decision and move on?"

My coach replied, "What types of questions could I have asked?"

"Well," I replied, "you could have taken him through worst-case thinking. The worst case is that he finds another real estate broker to help him build his real estate practice. In that case, he'll have to pay the broker—the very thing he objected to with his father. So how would that impact his business?

"You could also ask him, 'Why are you feeling these emotions with regard to paying your father? Why *wouldn't* you pay your father? Why would you rather not see your father gain financially even as you are gaining?' Ask him questions about that, without guiding or steering."

Discerning questions try to get at the root of an issue. Most of the time, when one of our coaches asks me about how to handle a particular situation, it isn't a leadership question or a communication or vision question; it's a discernment question.

And where do you get discernment? It comes with time in the coach's seat. The more you invest in people and the more focused and intentional you become about helping people overcome obstacles, the more you will develop your discernment muscle.

In his book *Emotional Intelligence*, author Daniel Goleman explains how businesspeople can experience more success in their work by bringing the concept of "emotional intelligence" to the marketplace. He defines emotional intelligence as "the capacity for recognizing our own feelings and those of others, for motivating ourselves, and for managing emotions well in ourselves and in our relationships."[1] Goleman, a former science reporter with a doctorate in psychology from Harvard, says that emotional intelligence (also called EI or EQ) is a stronger indicator of human success than IQ, designed to measure a person's intellect (or "intelligence quotient").

Goleman also says that people who have high emotional intelligence are more likely to succeed in work and in life because they are able to love and to be loved; they are more self-aware and able to empathize with others. Finding success in life depends on these attributes. Without them, IQ won't get you far.

What Goleman calls emotional intelligence, I call discernment. People *or they respond incorrectly*

with high IQs and low EQs really struggle in life because, relationally, they don't know how to respond to others, which is what life is really all about. On the other hand, people with much lower IQs, but with high EQs, can become some of the most successful people in the world. Why? Because they understand themselves, and they understand the hearts of others.

How good are you at responding to the unmet expectations of life—the letdowns, the injustices, and the mediocrity of others—in ways that create solutions? Someone with discernment, a high EQ person, will meet these challenges by bringing salve or ointment to the wound and helping to heal it, thus improving the situation. A low EQ person will simply add fuel to the fire, increasing the damage.

Do people come to you with problems? I don't mean technical challenges, such as when someone learning a new software program repeatedly asks you for application advice. That doesn't mean you have discernment; that just means you have mentor experience or teacher experience.

On the other hand, if they come to you with struggles about how to deal with their workload or how to deal with other departments or how to handle things outside of the office, that's a different story. They crave your perspective. Should they buy a second home? Should they get married? How could they deal with this marital conflict? How might they help someone on their team who is continually struggling with a tough challenge? If these kinds of conversations seem normal for you, then you can be pretty sure that people come to you because they believe you have discernment.

On the other hand, if these questions don't come up often, and you'd like them to, then let me suggest a little exercise to improve your discernment.

Sit down with each of your direct reports and find out what really motivates them. Ask them to describe their three-year, five-year, and ten-year goals. Ask them about when they were kids, what they wanted to be when they grew up. Ask them what they would change in their current life if they were given five million dollars. Ask them about what causes them professional fear. Get to know them. Get to know the *inside* of your people.

I talk to leaders all the time who have no clue as to what motivates their people. They have no idea what the ultimate dream vacation for a teammate's family might look like. They have never asked about a teammate's outside interests. They may be vaguely aware that one is an avid skier, but not that he has a deep-down desire to own a ski chalet or a ski shop by the time he reaches age fifty.

Get to know your people. And the more you get to know them, the more you'll connect with your people at a heart level. When you really understand what motivates your colleagues, you'll start to see what causes them to behave the way they do. You'll start to see under the surface, and that will jumpstart the development of discernment.

And, of course, any great coaching leader has taken the time to answer the questions outlined above before taking them to his or her teammates.

I know this sounds like more work and time than you might be used to investing into a teammate, but there is no checklist for discernment and no class to take. Discernment involves understanding the *heart* of a team member. Of the eight core competencies, discernment is the most difficult for task-oriented, project-oriented, execution-driven leaders to acquire. And yet no coach can enjoy much success without working to improve his or her discernment.

Core Competency #2: Conviction-Driven

All good coaches believe a few essential truths, convictions for which they will fight. When you watch excellent coaches communicate with their teams on the sports field, or when you watch coaching leaders in the office environment or on the job site, you quickly see that they have deep convictions about the way things should be. Some things are right, others are wrong. These clear convictions make it easier to behave consistently.

The more clarity you bring to your convictions, the easier you will find both living and leading. Leaders with clear convictions find it easier to make decisions. Convictions increase confidence and improve decision-making ability.

Each of my convictions acts as a kind of sieve, one layered on top of the other. When a life or business opportunity comes my way, that opportunity has to make its way through all my convictions. And once everything filters its way down, out will come a very clear, easy decision. My convictions enable me to make quicker, more consistent decisions, every day.

One conviction that all great coaches seem to share is that each person has the potential to change. You'll hear them say, "Everybody can improve. I believe it. I don't buy the notion that you're permanently stuck. I don't buy the idea that there are no solutions." Coaching leaders all agree that there is *always* a way to improve.

Great coaches also feel passionate about their own ability to help others improve. Great coaches make significant differences in the lives of their teammates regarding business skills, disciplines, and knowledge; coaches also exert great influence over their teammates' relationships and how they handle life.

Most great coaches also understand the brevity of life. They know they have only a short opportunity, a small window, to help people to improve. So they don't allow procrastination to take root in the lives of their teammates, in *any* aspect of their being.

Convictions also enable a coach to say the uncomfortable thing. You often have to question team members when it becomes obvious they are making decisions at odds with what they previously labeled as most important to them. So, for example, if a team member has put together a Life Plan in which she has identified several crucial areas—her marriage, her health, her family, her personal finances, her spiritual development—and you continually see her making decisions that endanger those areas, what do you do?

You have to have the conviction to confront her. "I need to hold up the mirror to your face," you might say, "and tell you that, while you stated this was important to you, I see you behaving in stark opposition to your own words." If you don't have the convictions to speak that bluntly, then you will not want to enter the battle. A conviction-driven leader will choose to enter the frequently uncomfortable areas of a team member's life.

Core Competency #3: Accountability

If you want a champion team, you can't ignore accountability. A coaching leader's greatest responsibility is to help people achieve what they have set out to accomplish. Most of the time big projects, big skill acquisition, and big improvements will take time. Each needs to be broken down into bite-sized pieces. Certain behaviors need to be repeated or changed over time, and accountability enables a coach to provide the necessary follow-up and encouragement.

It often sounds something like this: "This month, this is what you stated you wanted to do. How are you progressing?" Accountability means that a coach continually encourages and follows up with team members so that they gain the highest probability of accomplishing what they set out to do. A coach helps the team member keep his or her commitments. Accountability is a crucial competency to make that happen.

Core Competency #4: Uses Systems Effectively

My mind can retain only so much. The more people I coach, the more lives I have to track: projects to be aware of, skills that need to improve, and habits that need to be changed. I simply don't have the ability to lock all of those commitments and desired changes and details into my mind. And yet a great coach has a high degree of intimacy with each teammate. So what's the answer?

An effective use of systems.

A coach uses systems for accountability, for note taking, for follow-up, for encouragement, for intimacy. Good systems can make a coach's job very simple. No coach has to retain all the necessary information, so long as he or she has developed some good systems.

Such systems can be as basic as a manila file folder and as complex as a customized software application, designed specifically to help a leader become an effective coach. (I will highlight each of the main options in chapter 12.)

An effective use of systems allows you to be more consistent in your follow-up, more effective in your questioning, and more accurate in recalling where you left off from your previous coaching session. It can assist you in identifying the best way to encourage your teammates at key times. It helps you to track their progress, making it easier to encourage them, both when they are enjoying victories and when they are falling short. Without the use of such systems, at some point most coaches will fail to recall what was truly most important to each teammate, or what action plans the individual committed to complete and by when he or she wanted to complete them. Coaching leaders leverage their ability through the effective use of systems.

Core Competency #5: Communication

Some leaders believe that coaching is all about effective questioning. They rightly believe that the more effective they become at questioning, the easier it is for the teammate to draw his or her own conclusions or to discover what is holding them back or challenging them.

Without a doubt, effective questioning is a core component of effective communication. But so is listening! Having the ability to listen, to question, to envision where the teammate wants or needs to go, and then to communicate that in a linear way—clear, concise, bullet-by-bullet—will enable a coach to get more effective in helping the teammate see what changes may be necessary to break through the challenge or seize the opportunity.

Great coaches communicate both verbally and nonverbally. They use pace, voice inflection (getting calm when they need to, dogmatic and firmer when someone is not dealing with a challenge or needs to get knocked out of a rut), and a variety of communication styles. It's not always Vince Lombardi yelling at a misbehaving player. It's not always a passive psychotherapist asking questions. Good communication requires a blend and a cadence that changes, depending on the challenge facing the teammate. (We will explore this further in chapters 10 and 11.)

When a good coach finishes communicating with a teammate, that person leaves the conversation knowing what needs to be done. He has clarity and doesn't feel bewildered. The coach has instructed the person and helped him to uncover what needs to be done.

A lot of leaders assume that to be a good coach, they must be great storytellers. In reality, great storytelling can help—it never hurts to have another tool in the coaching toolbox (see chapter 10)—but it is not essential. Nor should it be a large part of the coaching interaction. Coaching is seldom about how the coach would do it or how the coach did it in the past; that's mentoring. Good coaches creatively look for ways to help the teammate identify what needs to be done to become *more*. Sometimes that means questioning. Sometimes it means repeating back what the person said in an earlier session. At other times, it involves voicing opinions. But in every case, the teammate leaves the interaction with a clear idea of what needs to be done.

Core Competency #6: Self-Discipline

Self-discipline is all about character. Since so much of how we function in business relates directly to our own self-discipline, we should expect to have our own disciplines carefully scrutinized. It's difficult for teammates to allow someone to serve as coach if they see hypocrisy or conflict in that person's life. After all, our disciplines reveal on the outside what lies on the inside. Our convictions drive our disciplines. It is not what we know but what we believe that drives what we repeatedly do.

Great coaching leaders know that self-discipline is about consistency in every aspect of life. Does this person regularly go to the gym? Does she keep an insane work schedule? Does he have regular fits of rage? Does she have destructive habits? The world gets to see discipline in a coach's life by watching outward behaviors such as these.

As a coach, do you consistently show up to meetings on time and end meetings on time? Are you disciplined with how you follow up? Are you disciplined with how you organize your own workspace? Your teammates will decide how much of themselves they'll share with you—and how much credence they will give your Action Plan help—based on how much self-discipline they see in you.

> *Success is nothing more than a few simple disciplines, practiced every day; while failure is simply a few errors in judgment, repeated every day. It is the accumulative weight of our disciplines and our judgments that leads us either to fortune or failure.*
>
> — *Jim Rohn*

Do they consider you consistent?

Self-discipline is not limited to your work. The examples I gave earlier—keeping personal commitments, such as dating your spouse or vacationing with your family or getting home at a reasonable hour—will impact your teammates' opinion of you and therefore your ability to coach them.

Core Competency #7: Vision-Oriented

The vision-oriented competency features two aspects. First, a great coach has the ability to see what a team member can become—often long before the team member does. The coach sees qualities, abilities, and experiences that will enable a person, if directed correctly, to become more than that teammate believed possible. A coach has vision for the lives of others.

Second, a coach has the ability to help teammates see that vision. A *great* coach encourages his teammates to discover their own vision: for their business, for their position, and for their life. And once they discover it, the coaching leader helps them create the plans to realize it. Then the coaching leader will help them to develop a routine for reviewing their vision and plan so that they become an anchor, something that drives habit changes, enabling them to become *more*. (We'll discuss this further in chapter 6.)

Core Competency #8: Leadership

Great coaches are leaders. People must be willing to follow you if you are going to coach them. If they don't want to follow you, then you can't coach them.

I assume that you're a leader and that people are following you. If you have been assigned to lead people—maybe your business card says "manager"—and yet you're struggling to get people to do what needs to be done, you might want to focus on the competency of your leadership.

Leadership is about helping people to work together in a way that enables them to accomplish something greater than they could accomplish separately. Leadership encompasses all the other competencies. Leaders have vision; they see something better for the team or the customer than is immediately apparent. Coaching leaders are communicators; they communicate the vision, the actions, the plans, and the decisions in ways that enable people to follow them. Leadership is about servanthood. Great leaders understand that the most effective way to help someone move forward is to stick out a hand and pull them along.

There's good leadership and there's *great* leadership. Great leadership is about opportunity and what can be, and all great coaches lead their people boldly and positively into the future.

COACH TO WIN

Only one football coach each year gets to lead his team to a Super Bowl victory. He is usually the coach who picks the athletes with the most character and talent, the coach who pushes his team a little harder during each practice, the coach who studies his competition and then works smarter than his rivals at developing winning strategies and plays. This coach leads by example and is passionate about his team winning at practice and each game. He coaches team members *one-on-one* so they know how they are to think and function as a winning team.

Are you serious about winning in life and in your career? Who is on your team? Develop your game plan, practice hard, coach with passion—and enjoy more victories

Key Benefits

What it does for your team members:

- Invites them to improve in all aspects of business and life.

- Offers them an opportunity to belong to a unique and special team.

- Lets them know they are appreciated, believed in, and valuable.

- Challenges them to grow in healthy ways.

What it does for the company:

- A coaching leader attracts great talent to his or her company.

- Coaching leaders build high performing teams that give their companies a competitive advantage.

- Coaching has a direct, bottom-line impact in minimizing turnover and enhancing performance.

What it does for you:

- Increases your value to the organization as you develop those who report to you.

- Fills your days with more purpose and meaning.

- Increases both your psychic income and W-2 income as you improve the performance of your team.

PART TWO

The Core Four
Success Puzzle®

FOUR

The Core Four:
The Foundation of
Your Coaching Strategy

Leaders usually give three reasons why they want to be coached:

- They want more time.
- They want more money.
- They want to improve how they lead.

Many coaching relationships start off with the client or teammate requesting that we immediately dive into a business issue. But it can be very risky and possibly a big waste of time if we focus too early on tactics. Too many companies have suffered as a result of adding products or services that dilute their focus, tap out their resources, and diminish their profits, all the while exhausting and frustrating their teams and their leaders. And many times the consequences reach out beyond the business and begin to encroach into the personal lives of those leading the charge.

That's why all of our coaches give the same response to this request: "It is not wise for us to spend time working on your daily priorities or disciplines until we have great clarity around your Business Plan. And we cannot have clarity on how you should align your team and resources around a plan until we know your strategy. So we must first understand what drives you, what you see as your purpose, and what you see for your organization in the future. We understand that your business or career is just one component of who you are, so we cannot effectively help you to build a business until we understand how your business life fits into your overall life. That's why we start off with helping our clients and teammates to create a Life Plan."

Enter the Core Four Success Puzzle® the foundation to our coaching system.

The Core Four Success Puzzle features four components that follow a never-deviating sequence:

1. Life Plan
2. Business Vision
3. Business Plan
4. Priority Management

We always follow this sequence; we never vary from it. Why? Because we cannot aid you in prioritizing your day or in making decisions with regard to your calendar until we can clearly see what items you believe are most important for your calendar. We cannot determine this until we can see what disciplines and behaviors will allow you to best succeed, as identified in your Business Plan. We cannot assist you with creating a meaningful Business Plan until we understand what you see as the future for your organization and what you see it accomplishing. And we cannot help you to discover and clarify your Business Vision until we can see how your career and company fit into your overall life.

THE CORE FOUR SUCCESS PUZZLE®

BUILDING CHAMPIONS

This is why we always start out with Life Planning. In this section you will get the instruction you need to work your way through (and coach your teammates through) all four components of the Core Four.

All the members of your team should have a clear idea of what is most important to them in life and how they can achieve those things; that's where the Life Plan fits in. Everyone on your team should have a clear vision for his or her position within the organization; your Business Vision provides this crucial piece. Everyone on your team should know the disciplines, improvements, and outcomes necessary to win, as expressed in a one-page document that serves as a road map for success; that's your Business Plan. And everyone on your team can improve efficiency by putting together a plan for an effective use of time; that's Priority Management. When these four components work together, you build a coaching culture in which people become highly productive—and that's how you set the stage for extraordinary growth and success.

FIVE

Your Life Plan: The Coaching Leader's Most Powerful Tool

Teach us to number our days aright, that we may gain a heart of wisdom.
— Psalm 90:12

Many people initially discount the "life planning" part of our coaching process. Like most people, they spend more time planning a vacation or holiday party than planning their lives. So they say to us, "We don't want any of that fluffy life-planning stuff." Usually they want to jump straight into the Business Plan.

Most of the time, they hire us to improve profitability or work efficiencies, the things they consider most important. But since life planning is a nonnegotiable with us, they either go forward with it or find another coaching company. Very rarely will they opt out; nearly all end up putting together a Life Plan.

Most of the time they end up telling us how glad they are that they went through the process. Immediately after completing their Life Plan, they consistently tell us that they have already received their money's worth and that the life-planning process alone was worth their investment.

MOMENTARY VICTORIES AREN'T ENOUGH

Many leaders substitute goal setting for life planning, but I think it's a bad trade-off. In my experience, goal setting can leave you feeling empty. Most of us set goals, but very few of us have enjoyed real long-term success. When we accomplish those goals, the victory is fleeting: immediately we get hit with the pressure of yet another goal. And if we follow the advice of most motivational speakers on goal setting, it's an annual deal. On December 31 we have to clean the slate and do it all over again.

I think there is a much better way.

While some good undoubtedly comes from goal setting, I much prefer life planning. When you choose life planning, you understand that every decision you make will enable you either to increase or decrease your net worth—not in dollars and cents alone, but in every part of your existence. Every decision you make incurs a cost

> *The purposes of a man's heart are deep waters, but a wise man of understanding draws them out.*
> — *Proverbs 20:5*

somewhere. Many people think that by not making a decision, they're avoiding exposure to that cost. But indecision is making a decision, with its own set of consequences—usually unexpected, and often much larger than imagined.

Putting together a Life Plan doesn't mean that your life will turn out exactly as mapped out. Rather, it means taking the time to examine the depths of your heart.

In life planning you get proactive and try to extract those plans so that you have the highest probability of becoming who you want to become—in business and in all areas of life that you consider most important. If you don't take the time to mine those gems, it's highly likely that you will live to regret it.

"What is your life?" asked one ancient leader. "You are a mist that appears for a little while and then vanishes."[1] The years go by way too fast.

Unfortunately, most companies care very little about their people accumulating net worth in all aspects of life. They generally have one overriding concern: accumulating net worth in productivity. So understand that if you choose to become a coaching leader, you'll be going seriously counterculture to most American companies.

And yet, you'll also quickly discover that the results will far more than justify any risk.

EXPOSING "THE BIG LIE"

Most high performers get so caught up in their business—they enjoy it so much and feel so passionate about their careers—that they find themselves consumed in the pursuit of the next deal or the next opportunity. They get addicted to the excitement and even to the stress, and the exhilaration of the game of business overpowers other areas of life, even the ones they consider most important. Days and months and even years pass, and one morning they suddenly wake up to a boardroom full of regrets.

In my experience, life planning is by far the single most effective exercise that can help you to avoid a life of regret. And it does so, in part, by exposing "The Big Lie."

"You know what?" whispers The Big Lie. "I'm going to run at this pace for a while, and then next week or next month or next year it'll slow down. *That's* when I'll get to the other areas of my life." I can tell you frankly that it just doesn't work out that way. I've partnered with the superstars, with the people who are making things happen in the business world, and I know one thing for sure: *It's not going to get any slower tomorrow.* It never does. You and your business will continue to grow and attract more opportunities, and all of it will only require more of you. So how will you avoid those end-of-life regrets unless you stop and take the time necessary to map out the type of life you genuinely want?

Here's the reality: you're either going to be proactive or reactive this year—and without a plan, you have a much greater probability of getting "off purpose."

Today times five will give you an on- or off-purpose week. That week times four will give you an on- or off-purpose month; and that month times twelve, an on- or off-purpose year. That year times some unknown number is going to be your life—and I know from experience how sad it can be to meet "successful" people who have the titles, the corner offices, and the bank accounts but consider them-selves bankrupt in life.

How does this happen? At one point in life, these leaders did not stop to put it all together. For weeks and months and years they rushed around in a "I'll get to it tomorrow" mode, running and gunning and putting everything they had and were into their careers . . . only to wake up at some point in their lives bankrupt in many areas of life that they considered vitally important.

Life's too short for that! A great Hebrew leader, Moses, gave us one of the greatest truths in the whole Bible: "Teach us to number our days aright, that we may gain a heart of wisdom."[2]

If we don't number our days—if we don't understand that we have a lim-ited number of Saturdays and New Year's Days, if we assume there will always be another—chances are, we are going to live in a very reactive mode. We won't seize the greatest opportunities or make the most of every aspect of our lives. And so we'll wind up with regrets. Lots of them.

Many people who come into coaching believe their greatest need is to improve their time blocking. Do you know why they struggle? Usually it's because they haven't set effective boundaries in their week. But how can they set effective boundaries without first taking the time to identify what is most important in their lives?

In essence, life planning is nothing but a process of accumulating net worth in the most important accounts in your life. This process gives you great clarity on what you must do to accumulate net worth in each of those accounts. Again, this is "net worth" not only in your financial accounts or your career account, but in your relationship accounts and health accounts and recreational accounts and spiritual accounts and whatever other accounts you consider most crucial. By going through this process, you will gain clarity on where you want to be in each of those accounts and then identify what you need to do daily in order to accumulate more net worth in each of them. And in that way, you remain on purpose and avoid a reactive life that leads to terrible regrets. Your actions become very congruent with the person you want to become.

WHAT IS A LIFE PLAN?

Life planning is all about assessing where you are in life, identifying which accounts are most important to you, and then writing out a vision for each one of those accounts. An effective Life Plan clarifies your purpose in each of those accounts and then identifies three to five strategies that will enable you to increase your net worth in each area.

Consider what someone's "spouse account" might look like in a Life Plan:

Account #1: My Relationship with My Wife, Sheri

Purpose: I have been blessed with a wife who is my most intimate and best friend. I am to treat her as the single most important person in my life. I am committed to her for better or for worse, until death parts us. She needs to know she is the number one person in my life through my actions, not just my words. I am to help her become the woman God wants her to be.

Vision: At age seventy-five, Sheri and I reflect back on our lives and celebrate what we have experienced and whom we have served. We covet our time together and have a life of purpose, love, romance, and fun. We have a very real and abundant life together. We mentor and teach others how to maximize the gift of marriage. We are one.

Actions:
- Pray with Sheri every day before going to sleep.
- Share "hot tub" dates. My time with her at the end of each day is most important. I encourage, honor, respect, support, accept, and love her each day by spending the last thirty minutes of the night communicating with her. This is eye-to-eye and ear-to-ear time with no interruptions.

- Date Sheri every week. A date can be for breakfast, lunch, or dinner during the week; or it may be a night out. The important thing is that it is just the two of us.

- Take her on two weekend getaways, the first prior to June 30 and the second prior to November 30.

By logging on to this book's Web site (www.becomingacoachingleader.com), you will find a tool designed to help you formulate your own Life Plan. Let me urge you to do a huge favor for yourself, your family, your colleagues, and your friends by taking the time necessary to design your personal Life Plan. But before you get started, read the rest of this chapter to gain some valuable tips on how to make the experience as helpful and satisfying as possible.

CREATE THE "LIFE PLAN EXPERIENCE"

Since the Life Plan is so crucial to the rest of the Core Four process, I highly recommend that you carve out a whole day to focus exclusively on the Life Plan experience. Make that day special!

Go somewhere awesome that you consider a treat. It might be to the river, to the park, to the beach, or somewhere up in the mountains. Choose a place where the setting puts you in a creative, reflective mood. Some clients book a nice suite at a hotel in their area, or they rent a secluded cabin, and when they're done, they invite their families to join them. Get creative! *This is a day to focus exclusively on how you want to live life.* It's not a day to hole up at a local Motel 6 or to try to scrimp by hanging out at a public library filled with a yapping herd of kids.

If at all possible, try to complete the exercise all in one day. If you try to put together your Life Plan by squeezing it in—maybe you do some of it Tuesday at 6:30 p.m. at the office, then do another bit Wednesday morning early before you get in, and then try to finish it Saturday afternoon between ballgames—it will lack the punch it needs to start changing how you make decisions.

So go somewhere special. Treat it as an experience, not an exercise. Remember, it's a life planning experience designed to benefit *your* life.

Before you start, have realistic expectations about the time commitment this is going to entail. At minimum, this is an eight-hour project. It will easily take a full day. So don't try to cram the whole experience into four hours. Some clients have sailed out on their yachts and spent the entire day working on their Life Plan. One of our most successful clients told me, "Daniel, I scheduled it for six hours, but it took me thirteen hours to really work through the entire thing." So don't plan for less than eight hours!

If you intend to do this outdoors, which I encourage, bring various types of clothing for different types of weather. You may want to bring running or hiking gear so that midway through your day you can take a physical break. I also suggest you pack an ice chest filled with water. Bring snacks and some healthy foods, including your lunch. Whatever you do, turn it into a really special day.

If you put this type of effort into it, you will definitely go beyond the head and hit your heart—The only way to change habits is to go beyond the head and reach heart. We all know how to live; the problem is that these crucial truths often don't move from our heads to our hearts. And the way to cement them deep down in your heart is by turning this process into a meaningful and rich experience.

Once you arrive, spend time pondering specific accounts. This year as I put together my own Life Plan, I thought deeply about my vision for my sons, Dylan and Wesley, and my daughters, Allie and Emily. They ranged in age from two to fifteen, and I contemplated what I wanted for them when they turned eighteen. I walked up and down the river thinking, and then I started writing. I didn't put down the first thing that came to mind. I mulled it over, because I knew if I didn't give a lot of thought to the question, chances are I would get off track pretty quickly.

As you complete your own Life Plan, wrestle through each of your accounts. Ponder your vision for each one, and note three to five key activities that will enable you to accumulate net worth in that account.

I'm a minimalist when it comes to life planning. Bring the tool we've created for you, a pad of paper or your journal, and something to write with—

and that's about it. That's all you need. *Do not* bring a laptop or a pager or your BlackBerry or a cell phone. Leave all that stuff behind! Remember, "the purposes of a man's heart are deep waters, but a man of understanding draws them out." That "drawing out" doesn't happen without a lot of work. It doesn't happen if you're constantly interrupted with e-mail on your Blackberry or if the alarm on your laptop keeps telling you that you're supposed to be somewhere else. Shut it all down for the day!

After you have your special day and complete the work, take all the sheets of paper you've created and type them into a single document. That document will clarify your vision, your purpose, and the specific activities that will enable you to accumulate net worth in each account. You've labored through it, and now you have a living document, something that you will use to guide your daily decisions and actions. And most important, it will help you to stay on purpose.

After teaching life planning to thousands of people just like you, I can say categorically that those who enjoy the greatest degree of success in living their Life Plan also give the most attention to it at the front end. Those who experience the most lift and impact from this process are those who treat this day as if it were one of the most special events of the year.

Coach's Corner

Writing your own Life Plan can be both a frightening and hugely rewarding experience. But until you actually commit the time to doing it, you will never fully understand the power of such an exercise or benefit from the resulting living document you create. Writing a Life Plan is nothing short of getting a bucket and lowering it deep into the well of your heart and pulling out its life-giving water.

Lewis was a typical client—a very driven and dominant leader. I was a bit anxious over the prospect of bringing up life planning with him. He seemed to be so clear about what he wanted. Initially disdainful, once he completed the exercise, it completely changed the way he saw his business, our coaching, and his own life. It was the beginning of a great journey. In the last couple of years, he has become a huge advocate for writing a Life Plan. He reads his own frequently and is even known to shed a tear or two when we read it together.

Steve Scanlon
Coach
Building Champions, Inc.

HOW DO I USE MY LIFE PLAN?

Going through this process is just the first step. The next step is to set appointments with yourself to follow through with the strategies you identified under each account.

Let's say one of your accounts is physical fitness. Next you should set appointments with yourself to go to the gym, so that physical fitness isn't merely something you *want*, it is a part of how you *live*. And so you schedule these appointments as if they were "big deals." Look at it as if it were a million-dollar business opportunity. If you don't, you'll always procrastinate. By making these appointments a priority, you will accumulate net worth in each of your specified Life Plan accounts.

Use your Life Plan to schedule your week. Your assistant should have a copy of your Life Plan so that he or she understands what is important to you. For example, if coaching your son's soccer team is important to you, something you do to add net worth to that account, tell your assistant, "Soccer practices are Tuesday and Thursday at 4:00 p.m." That way your assistant will never schedule a meeting at 3:30 p.m. on Tuesday or Thursday, because he or she knows what is important to you. Life planning helps you to identify *in writing* everything that is important to you, so that you can start making decisions to accumulate net worth in the areas of your life that are most important to you.

Once you print out your Life Plan, I recommend that you show it to those who care about you. You'll pick up momentum as you see the positive reactions of those close to you who also are part of your Life Plan.

Next, create "your perfect week" (more on this in chapter 8). Start plugging in some of your nonnegotiables from your most important accounts. Nonnegotiables are the actions that you refuse to compromise on because of their importance in your life. Drop them right into that perfect week's time block to create your model.

THE DAILY ROUTINE TIME BLOCKING SCHEDULE
BUILDING CHAMPIONS
COACHING BUSINESS AND LIFE ON PURPOSE

	Monday	Tuesday	Wednesday	Thursday	Friday	Saturday	Sunday
6:00 AM	OFF / Work Out	ON / Read	OFF / Work Out	ON / Read	OFF / Work Out	OFF	
7:00				OFF / Breakfast w. children			OFF
8:00							
9:00						OFF	CHURCH
10:00							
11:00							
Noon	WORKOUT	WORKOUT	WORKOUT	WORKOUT	OFF / Lunch date w. spouse		
1:00							
2:00							
3:00						GYM WITH FAMILY	OFF
4:00							
5:00							
6:00							
7:00			CLASS		OFF	OFF	
8:00	OFF	OFF		OFF			
9:00			OFF				ON / Review for week
10:00 PM							OFF

In your "perfect week" time block, you slot a 5:00 a.m. quiet time if that's important to you or a 5:30 p.m. family dinner if that's important to you. If you want to do your workouts at noon or at 6:00 a.m., you schedule them in. If you want self-development time for four hours every Friday from 1:00 to 5:00 p.m., then you mark it down. In this way you schedule your top priorities into your week, and then you schedule business around them. This is how all of our most successful clients make it happen. This "perfect week" time block begins to dictate how you make decisions each day with regard to business opportunities. Before you developed your Life Plan, opportunities like these crowded out life, but now you fit them into life, and in so doing, you better manage your priorities.

How Can I Maximize My Life Plan?

Once you've created your Life Plan, shown it to someone close to you, and used it to create a "perfect week" that you utilize to shape your real weeks, you're ready for a few other crucial steps in the process.

1. Review it. Commit to a daily review of your Life Plan for the first ninety days. This exercise will give you the highest probability of following through with your plan. If you start off every morning for the first ninety days by reviewing your plan, you'll have much improved results. Make sure to read every line.

By doing this the first thing in the morning, when you're fresh, you'll soon be memorizing it. By memorizing it, it will soon become a living document inside of you. The activities you have identified will start to serve as borders on your day. That way, as decisions and opportunities and challenges come your way, you'll be able to respond in accordance with your Life Plan.

If an opportunity arises for a dinner meeting, for example, you'll plug it into an appropriate spot. Maybe your Life Plan tells you that Thursday night is date night with your spouse, so you won't schedule a dinner meeting for that time. Or maybe you do, but since you understand that's normally date night, you immediately reschedule the date. You don't just blow it off. Why not? Because that date is a marker, something you have identified as a key activity that helps you to accumulate net worth in your marriage account. By reviewing your Life Plan the first thing every morning for ninety days, you begin to memorize it and make it a part of you.

After ninety days, you can reduce your reviews to every week. Remember, this is going to be a lifelong discipline. Every Sunday night or early Monday morning, commit to a thorough review. My associate and friend Greg Salciccioli, calls this the "red pen review." He goes through his plan with a red pen, looking for gaps and for areas where something needs to be shored up. He also looks for areas in his Life Plan where he is exceeding expectations.

2. Recruit help with it. It is wise to recruit an accountability partner to help you stay on track with your Life Plan. We at Building Champions serve as the accountability partners for our clients, while our licensed coaching leaders serve this role for their teammates. It is our job to help keep them on track, to remind them of the specific disciplines and the outcomes they have identified in their Life Plans.

If you're not one of our clients, then find an accountability partner, somebody who cares about you and who will not be afraid to get in your face and say, "Hey, didn't you say you were going to stop eating like that?" or "Didn't you say you were going to spend more time giving your best to your son?" or "I thought you were going to be in the gym today." A real friend is someone who will help you stay on track. With the help of your friends, you'll have more "on purpose" days.

3. Adjust it. Many people get overzealous in creating their Life Plan. They come up with eighteen accounts and ten strategies to accumulate net worth in each account. But in a month or so, they begin to realize that *no* superman or wonderwoman could keep up with such a plan.

So don't be afraid to adjust where necessary. Cross off some activities that don't make sense. Maybe it's not your season to do all eleven things you listed under Johnny's account. Or maybe it's not your season to be doing a two-and-a-half-hour workout five days a week. Maybe a thirty-minute workout three days a week works better.

Remember, this is a living document, so be prepared to write on it and mark it up. Do the red-pen review. I do quarterly reviews with a lot of my clients, making the client's Life Plan review the first topic of business. We go over it together to find out where we have accumulated great net worth or where we may have a deficit.

I can't encourage you strongly enough to get into this discipline. Do a weekly review, then a more formal review of your Life Plan every quarter. Then finish each year by doing a complete Life Plan overhaul every December. Evaluate how you did over the past year, and then adjust it for the year ahead.

This allows you to alter your plan as the seasons in your life change. As your kids enter their teen years, for example, you might want to free up some afternoons so you can connect with your daughter and add net worth to her account. Once the kids are all out of the house, you will have additional time to allocate to your business or to another key account.

You may also have to adjust your Life Plan around new priorities that surface in your career. Successful professionals like yourself often receive promotions or encounter some new opportunity. Along with new opportunities come new commitments. Adjust your Life Plan to reflect your new reality without giving up what you consider most important.

Some of my clients started out with regional influence and got promoted to positions with national responsibility. Their new responsibilities required them to travel more frequently or to be on a conference call every Monday from 10:00 a.m. until noon—and maybe that was when they used to work on personal development. Their Life Plan had to factor in all the real-life changes that take place. They don't simply stop taking self-development time; they find a new slot for it.

When you adjust your Life Plan according to the new priorities and demands that creep into your life, you're always making decisions. Is *this* more important or is *that* more important? Many people just say yes to new commitments or new opportunities without rescheduling or adjusting preexisting commitments and priorities. That can have very negative consequences.

Understand that your Life Plan *will* change. It's not a static thing that boxes you in. I've heard some object, "I don't want to get into that life planning thing, because it takes away all spontaneity." No, it doesn't. In fact, it gives you the ability to stay on track and reschedule the specific activities that remain most important to you. Because of your Life Plan, you've memorized which activities are going to help you gain the outcomes most crucial to you, and your plan gives you the power to stay on track.

4. Share it. As you live and adjust your Life Plan, share it with your partners and with your teammates. Ask them to help you live out your plan. Let them know that they will experience the "best you" if you remain on the plan. Explain that if you start to compromise, if you start to feel guilty, if you begin to feel resentful because this or that opportunity or challenge is taking you off purpose, then they will not get the best "you" as a leader or professional.

Many leaders feel nervous about sharing their Life Plan with their team. "You know," they say, "my team doesn't really care if I go to the gym at noon." But if they understand that you're going to be much more on purpose in the afternoon if you go to the gym at noon, they *will* care. You'll be able to give them your best because you'll be living at your best. That's what they want in you as a leader. So share your Life Plan with them.

5. *Teach it.* The best way to live the Life Plan is to teach the Life Plan. Coaching leaders share this experience with his or her teams. Coaching leaders teach this experience and this way of living with the people they care about. *The best way to walk it is to talk it.*

The more you bring the Life Plan into your conversations, the more you teach it and the greater accountability you'll have. When we get together at coach training summits and camps, we often talk about some of the benefits of our vocation. One of the greatest is that we are forced to live our Life Plans at higher levels because we talk about them every day. This puts good additional pressure on us to be on purpose, and every one of us appreciates it.

One assistant coach on our team has taught a modified Life Plan process to middle school kids. Her experience illustrates that the power of life planning is relevant for everybody! Another coaching leader just took an entire day to walk his leadership team through the process. And he did not stop there. The next day he took his best friends and his family members through the process. I saw him this week, and he gave me the most amazing paycheck—an envelope filled with thank-you cards and notes from those he took the time to walk through the process.

So give the power of life planning to everyone around you. Sit down one-on-one with your teammates, clients, partners, and friends. Offer life planning to those who want it. Believe me, you couldn't offer them a bigger gift.

HELP THEM GROW

A lot of Action Plans can be huge. Such plans may map out strategies to improve team building or recruiting or selling, and they can enable you to increase revenue by ten or twenty times. Those, of course, are fantastic results—and yet, they pale in comparison to helping somebody accumulate net worth in areas that were routinely neglected.

Many of our clients are so taken with the Life Plan that they reshape their entire companies to offer Life Plans to others. One of our clients gives every employee (hundreds of them) the opportunity to go through the life-planning process with the CEO or one of his senior VPs. It has become a part of the company culture.

Another client, an extremely successful salesperson, is doing quarterly workshops and seminars for business leaders in his community. He brings in key influencers who have the ability to help him grow his business, and every quarter he offers them something of significant value. He has told me that his life-planning workshop was by far the biggest hit.

WANTED: ON-PURPOSE LEADERS

The business world needs a lot more on-purpose leaders. People today are looking for business leaders who can help them to grow not just as professionals, but also as individuals. People don't follow companies; they follow successful leaders, which means succeeding in areas other than job performance. They want you to model success in all areas of life and then help them to do the same.

That may be a tall order, but the old saying remains true, "To whom much has been given, much is expected."[3] This is what distinguishes today's exceptional leaders. Whether they are CEOs, line managers, or producers, they willingly contribute to those around them in areas that transcend business. They help the people around them to become more successful in all aspects of life.

That's what life planning can do for you and your business. If you take this process to completion, the results will astound you. People will thank you for changing their lives. Already this process has radically transformed thousands of people.

There's no reason why it can't transform you, too.

Key Benefits

What a Life Plan does for your team members:

- May be the single greatest gift you give to your team.

- Helps them to make better daily life decisions, which will translate to more purposeful and fulfilled lives.

- Ensures they reduce future regrets and experience more overall health as a result of discovering what is truly most important to them.

- Shows that they are cared for in ways beyond how they perform at the office.

- Frees them from regret or guilt, which enables them to be more focused at work.

What a Life Plan does for the company:

- Improves overall team health, which translates into a productive and happy workforce.

- Helps the company become known as a "caring company."

- Improves the company's legacy.

What a Life Plan does for you:

- Improves the quality of your own life as you gain clarity and effectiveness in your own decision-making abilities.

- Increases the net worth in the areas of life that are most important to you.

- Expands your leadership influence.

- Makes you a more attractive and respected leader.

SIX

Your Business Vision: If You Can See It, You Can Build It

A few years ago I received an invitation to participate in a meeting at the corporate headquarters of Chick-fil-A in Atlanta, Georgia. Although the company is a household name in the Midwest and South, as a West Coast guy I didn't know much about the company before I made my first visit.

I quickly discovered that this fast-food giant specializes in serving up chicken in a variety of healthy ways. Its restaurants are open just six days a week; every single outlet closes on Sunday, a business practice that its founder, S. Truett Cathy, instituted from the very beginning. His original six-day-a-week work schedule has become a part of the corporation's strategic makeup.

At the airport, a warm and friendly gentleman from Chick-fil-A picked me up. He had a badge on his shirt with his name along with a note that said, "19 years."

"Do all Chick-fil-A team members to display their tenure on their name badges?" I asked as he drove me to the corporate campus.

"Yes, sir," he replied.

"Well, nineteen years is pretty impressive," I commented. "Have you spent nineteen years driving, or in what capacity have you been with the company for the last two decades?"

"Oh, I've done just about everything," he replied. "I've been with the Cathy family since the early days. It's just a joy for me to serve."

This guy seemed as excited and as proud of his company as any CEO I'd ever met. He clearly felt thrilled to belong to the Chick-fil-A family.

A few minutes later we pulled into the corporate campus, entering through a beautiful gated area surrounded by stately trees that framed a long driveway. My driver pointed over to his left at a large brick facility, built in an impressive colonial style.

"That's the daycare center for our employees' kids," he said proudly.

For a few moments more we passed lovely ponds and park areas, and then finally arrived at the main structure. Its sheer size surprised me. As I got out of the van and started walking toward the front door, I looked to my right and noticed the company's mission statement chiseled in stone on a large tablet at the front door. My hosts clearly wanted their teammates and guests to know the reason for Truett Cathy's company's existence:

> To glorify God by being a faithful steward of all that is entrusted to us, and to have a positive influence on all who come in contact with Chick-fil-A.

I walked into the building, and a professional young woman immediately greeted me by name. Her employee badge indicated that she had eleven years' tenure. Her first question revealed that she had familiarized herself with some of my personal interests.

"Would you like to see the car collection?" she asked.

She didn't have to ask twice! On our way to the meeting room, she took me through the company's car museum to see some of their classic and exotic collection as well as the original Batmobile. And then I came to the motorcycle section They had several beautiful vintage bikes that took my breath away. "Oh, my boys would love to see this," I said offhandedly. But I hadn't brought a camera.

My hostess politely excused herself and moments later returned with a little disposable camera, complete with flash. "Mr. Harkavy," she said, "what do you want pictures of?" It wasn't good enough for her to let me click off a few photos; she insisted on making it possible for me to show my boys that I had actually been there. So she directed me to stand in front of all the amazing motorcycles and cars while she started snapping off pictures. It blew me away.

Throughout the rest of the day, I had an opportunity to better understand what this unique company is all about. Just after lunchtime, no sooner than we had finished eating, the two Cathy brothers, who now run the company, entered the room to clear away our dishes. These two servant leaders lived out the words of the Chick-fil-A mission statement I saw etched in stone near the front door of the corporate headquarters.

Everyone I met at Chick-fil-A knew they were a part of something special. Employees of other fast-food chains might care about little else than flipping burgers and getting french fries out as fast as possible so they can collect a check and go home, but that is *not* the Chick-fil-A experience. Members of this unique organization understand they serve a need in the community. They firmly believe they belong to something special, and they can point to an attractive culture to prove it.

I have to admit it: after spending a day with these delightful people, I suddenly felt greatly attracted to the chicken business.

BUSINESS VISION: CREATE SOMETHING SPECIAL

Visionary leaders such as Truett Cathy have a way of inviting team members to take ownership of the unique corporate culture these leaders envision. The specific product or service simply doesn't matter; they end up creating something special as a result of their hard and intentional work.

The second component of the Core Four Puzzle is Business Vision. It comes down to this: If you can see it, you can build it. When I wrote out my first Business Vision for Building Champions in 1996, the company consisted of a team of one: me. Yet, I envisioned building a team of gifted leaders who wanted to be a part of something special, a group of men and women who desired to devote their lives to impacting influencers and leaders one person at a time.

I foresaw using a web-based system that would allow us to achieve a high degree of intimacy with all of our clients, not only throughout the United States, but also quite possibly throughout the world. I saw skilled coaches helping leaders to become more successful not only in business but also in life. I saw us developing a coach training center and creating a coach training team full of motivated individuals devoted to helping leaders become the best they could be at building their most appreciable asset, their people.

I saw us getting the opportunity to address large audiences, speaking as authorities on the topics central to our mission: life planning, developing vision, business planning, and decision making. I saw that we would achieve dominance in certain vertical business markets, where we would become the coaching company of choice. I saw that our culture would attract successful leaders from other industries who had reached a point in their careers where they wanted to devote themselves full time to helping others succeed. I saw that these leaders would bring to our organization skills that I lacked, experiences that I didn't have, and talents that we would need for building a great company.

Ten years later, I'm humbled to say that our company has become about 90 percent of my original vision.

If you want to become a coaching leader and build an even greater company, you have to nail down your Business Vision. You have to be able to communicate your vision and then learn how to utilize it as a strategic advantage. Once sharing it is part of your leadership routine, you will begin to coach your teammates to discover their own.

Coach's Corner

As a leader, it is your duty (and your pleasure!) to keep a clear vision in front of your team at all times. Continued focus on the vision makes the difference between excellence and mediocrity. It promotes discipline in the trenches, where battles are won and lost. A team well focused on the vision is better equipped to deal with daily wins and losses than a team merely headed in the general direction of some ideal place.

Any member of the team unable to articulate the vision is a weak link—and we all know that a chain is only as strong as its weakest link. It's your role as the leader to ensure that no link in your chain is weak through a failure to understand the vision.

Tim Enochs
Coach
Building Champions, Inc.

THE VISIONARY LEADER ADVANTAGE

Visionary leaders are better able to make good decisions than those who lack a clear vision. They have far more clarity on what they do or build, how they bring it to market, how they operate, and how they conduct themselves. The clarity of their vision gives them increased confidence; they seldom get confused about what to do next, and with that confidence comes a great calm. They have the ability to energetically, methodically, steadily, and coolly handle the challenges that come their way—challenges just like the ones you face.

Visionary leaders communicate their vision with excellence. They clearly convey their purpose, convictions, and direction; and their compelling style of communication draws in those around them. Their conviction and confidence causes others to want to be a part of their vision and the future at which they're grasping.

Visionary leaders are full of passion, excited about the opportunity ahead. They're passionate about what they're building or bringing to market, passionate about working with the team they've selected, and passionate about making a contribution to their community or society.

Because they know exactly who they want to become and what they want to build over the long haul, visionary leaders execute their Business Plans effectively. This clarity gives them a significant strategic advantage. Since they have a firm grip on both short- and long-term objectives, they are better than their competitors at using available resources and talent of the team in ways that enable them to execute the vision successfully.

Visionary leaders also are devoted to leadership development. Because they can see what they're going to build five, ten, or even twenty years down the road, they know what they must do to leverage the strengths and talents of their teammates. They know they need leaders to help carry the message and to help manage, oversee, and attract the talent required to accomplish what they have seen. Visionary leaders devote a good percentage of their time to leadership development.

In the end, these leaders build their own team of champions—a captivating, organization-wide environment that attracts quality people and encourages them to stay, labor, grow, stretch, risk, and take ownership of what the leader has envisioned.

How Vision Can Help

Whether your team has three people or ten thousand, developing a clear and compelling Business Vision can help you in significant ways.

A few years ago, one of our clients, a coaching leader who has several thousand employees, began to disseminate his vision and share it with all of his staff so that everyone had an opportunity to take ownership of it. Immediately his teammates turned his vision into an external marketing campaign so that desirable prospects would feel an irresistible desire to join the team. Even today, all of this company's marketing and recruiting material contains frequent references to some aspect of his original vision.

Do you struggle with implementing or business planning? Do initiatives in your organization frequently start and then stop? Have you noticed continual changes in direction? Do you struggle with the failure of your team to buy into an idea? Is turnover the norm in your culture?

If any of these problems hound you, it's probably not that you developed bad Business Plans or that you're a poor leader or manager. More times than not, the difficulty reflects a failure to effectively clarify the Business Vision. Somehow, you're not clearly communicating how your completed plans or objectives will move your organization to a new and better reality. You're not letting others see what you see for the company at some point in the future. Long-term success usually eludes the visionless leader.

To hurdle these kinds of formidable obstacles, your Business Vision absolutely must precede your Business Plan. The vast majority of problems regarding execution and planning are a direct result of the lack of a clear vision.

Vision is strategic, not tactical, strategic being much longer in nature. It sheds light on who you will become and what services or products you will create years from now, whereas the tactical is usually now, this year. Vision defines what you stand for, why you exist, and who your team will become. It is the necessary framework for future product offerings and services, and it provides the foundation for all plans. The Business Vision is an essential guidance tool used in countless ways for decision making, storytelling, recruiting, staff retention, team building, performance reviews, and so on.

Prospective teammates like hearing what they can be a part of and why you need their help. A clear and compelling Business Vision lets them know how they fit into the big picture, and workers today will leave visionless companies if they get the chance to join a leader and an organization that can clearly spell out how they're needed. They want to see how their gifts and talents and experiences, when used in synergy with other skilled teammates, will enable them to create something more powerful, successful, and special than they could create elsewhere. It's always good to tell the story of where you've come from, where you are today, and where you see the team going in the years ahead.

WHY YOU NEED VISION

I love how one of my dear friends and coaches, Steve Scanlon, explains the necessity of the vision process.

Do you remember Alice in Wonderland, that Disney-on-drugs kind of story from the nineteenth century? Alice takes a pill, grows small and then big, and has all sorts of crazy adventures. At one point she encounters the Cheshire cat. She comes to a fork in the road and sees this strange feline with a big smile looking down at her from his lofty perch high up in a tree. She's lost, so she asks the cat, "Would you tell me, please, which way I ought to walk from here?"

"That depends a good deal on where you want to get to," the grinning animal replies impertinently.

"I don't much care where," Alice admits.

"Then it doesn't matter which way you walk," the Cheshire cat answers.

Do you know Alice's problem? Since she didn't have a vision for where she wanted to go, ultimately the road she took didn't matter.

From a strategic perspective, we have to know not only the road we plan to take, but also where we want to end up. A compelling Business Vision offers both things. It will map out the road ahead and clarify for your team where you are going to end up.

A solid Business Vision reaches beyond the head and dives deep into the heart. It's both logical *and* emotional. As I said, people today want to belong to something special. Your teammates and employees want to know that their efforts and skills are contributing to something bigger than themselves. A good vision taps into that desire by inviting your teammates in and showing them what kind of role they can play to contribute to the ultimate destination you have envisioned.

How to Build Vision

It would not be fair to talk about Business Vision without giving credit to Jim Collins's and Jerry Porras's outstanding work.[1] In a 1996 issue of the *Harvard Business Review*, Collins and Porras explained their own model for how to build vision. We have been using a variation of this model ever since.

The coaching leaders I know who successfully use Business Vision all focus on three primary elements (although some add a fourth element as a "bonus"). These crucial elements are:

- Convictions *(values)*
- Purpose *(mission)*
- A Clearly Envisioned Future
- *Bonus: Mount Everest Goals*

In the past few years, business writers and experts have labeled these elements in any number of ways. I'll mention the most common terms to give you the best chance of understanding and relating to them.

CONVICTIONS

Some call this first element *core values, essential tenets* or *guiding principles.* Until a few years ago, I also used the label "core values." But then I helped write a book for pastors called *Leading Turnaround Teams,* and my co-author, Gene Wood, got me thinking about the significant difference between *values* and *convictions.* Eventually Gene helped me to see that convictions are far superior to values (core or otherwise) in helping a leader to identify what he or she stands for.

These days values seem essentially interchangeable; they don't mean what they used to. Convictions, on the other hand, suggest a much higher level of intensity. If your employer compromised your convictions, you'd quit. Deep convictions guide your worldview and help to shape your decisions, both large and small. Every coaching leader needs to bring strong convictions to his or her team or organization.

The convictions I bring to Building Champions are most likely the same ones I'd bring to any type of organization or company. Your convictions help to spell out who you are. And when you bring yourself to the company, you bring your convictions along with you.

Over time, these convictions define the infrastructure and the framework of your company. While I can't tell you what your convictions should be, I can identify some of the most common convictions we see in the successful coaching leaders we serve. The leader who adopts convictions like these will also explain how they are to be used to guide the behaviors of those in the organization.

Common Convictions of Great Coaching Leaders

- Honesty and integrity
- Teamwork
- Customer-focus
- Lifelong learning
- Continual improvement
- Never complacent
- Increasing value
- Truth Telling
- Simplicity

Our COO and the head of our executive coaching division, Dan Meub, has done considerable strategic work with large corporations to help them identify and then use their convictions. After he walks executives through the process of identifying their convictions, he helps them map out the steps required to take those convictions to the level of behavior. Without completing that step, convictions end up being little more than nice slogans or neat thoughts hanging on office walls. Dan has created many tools and processes for executive-level clients to assist them with leadership, strategy, and execution. The tool on the next page was designed to help companies identify which behaviors they must model to live out their convictions.

A coaching leader uses strong convictions to make good decisions. He or she also makes decisions faster and more consistently and communicates them more effectively so that the team knows exactly how to execute them. It's very simple, really. The clearer you are on what you and your organization stand for, the easier it will be for you to make good decisions. In my opinion, that's the single greatest benefit of identifying your top three to five convictions.

Core Conviction	Behaviors
Conviction 1 Conviction Name One Sentence Description	Behavior that best reflects Conviction 1 Behavior 2 Behavior 3 Behavior 4 Behavior 5
Conviction 2 Conviction Name One Sentence Description	Behavior that best reflects Conviction 2 Behavior 2 Behavior 3 Behavior 4 Behavior 5
Conviction 3 Conviction Name One Sentence Description	Behavior that best reflects Conviction 3 Behavior 2 Behavior 3 Behavior 4 Behavior 5
Conviction 4 Conviction Name One Sentence Description	Behavior that best reflects Conviction 4 Behavior 2 Behavior 3 Behavior 4 Behavior 5

One of our clients works in the Christian publishing field. He has established the following convictions and behaviors for himself and his team:

- *Integrity:* We do what we say we will do. We refrain from doing or saying what we tell others we will refrain from doing or saying. The ends do not justify the means. We do the Lord's work in the Lord's way. We protect client confidences.

- *Selectivity:* We are strategic about whom we agree to represent, especially author clients. We are strategic about whom we hire.

- *Relationships:* We value long-term, mutually beneficial, client-publisher relationships. We make decisions with the aim toward strengthening and preserving those relationships.

You may adopt quite different convictions from the list above, but whatever they are, they should clearly reflect who you are and what you represent. They should also inform and shape the behavior of your whole team—and that, of course, includes you.

PURPOSE

Some use the terms *core purpose, tip of the arrow,* or *mission* to describe what I call *purpose.* Purpose states in a sentence or two why you exist. It defines what you bring to the market, why you're here. Your purpose statement identifies what you and your team are all about. The following is our purpose statement at Building Champions:

> *We exist to use and build our God-given gifts to make a positive difference in the life of each person we coach, one person at a time.*

Our purpose statement helps us to create unique services and product offerings based on who we are. Our purpose statement reminds us that we are to make a positive difference in the life of each person we coach, one person at a time. This simple sentence has greatly helped us to make decisions with regard to new programs, new products, and new ventures. It helps us to remember what distinguishes our company from others.

Our understanding of our purpose directs us to value, above all else, what we call *a divine thirty-minute experience.* That phrase describes the potent half-hour interaction that occurs session after session between a coach and a client. We want to make sure that we use and develop our gifts and resources in a way that causes every thirty-minute coaching experience to be both powerful and unique. And as we look to create new products, we're constantly asking ourselves, "Do these products lead to a divine thirty-minute experience? Do they line up with our purpose statement?"

A CLEARLY ENVISIONED FUTURE

Jim Collins uses the term *clearly envisioned future* to describe this piece of a Business Vision document.[2] It includes the "vivid description" or "a clear picture."

This is the storytelling piece of the process, in which you begin identifying and crystallizing what you see in the future for your team five, ten, even twenty years from now.

How is your team going to operate? What systems will you use? What will the company experience be like for team members, for customers, for vendors, and for partners? What will your reputation be? How will it feel to be a part of your company? What will your industry say about you? What role will you play? What role will others play?

To do this right, you have to go beyond the head to reach the heart. That takes hard work. The picture you create has to entice your teammates and pull them into the greater reality you see. It has to help them to understand that what they're doing in their little cubicle is connected to a bigger picture, and understand how that bigger picture will help untold numbers of individuals throughout your community or the world.

When I have an opportunity to speak to an audience, I like to ask what line of work everyone is in. Then I help them to connect their position or industry or career to some greater meaning. Most don't naturally do this. But you *have* to do it, whether you're in the lending industry, the auto business, the copier trade, or the medical profession—the specific job simply doesn't matter. As a coaching leader, you need to figure out how your product or service connects to some larger contribution. How does it help people to gain a higher quality of life? How does it enable them to operate more efficiently, contribute to their health, improve their outlook, or enrich their relationships? Regardless of your business, you must identify what need you're serving that helps to improve this world.

When we see our clients' first attempt at this part of the document, we often get back a sentence such as, "We offer great service and our people are the most talented." You need to go deeper than that! Ask questions such as, "What technology are we using? What are the people saying? What are our clients saying? What does the office look like?"

I won't mislead you: this is a very difficult exercise. Most of us don't feel the freedom to dream in the way I'm recommending. But when you start to define *in vivid color* what a day will look like for you, you'll experience a moment of transcendent power. Your energy and that of your team will shoot through the roof when you're all able to *see* what you're shooting for. Naturally, there will be gaps. You're not trying to define what your business looks like today; you're trying to dream what it will look like ten to twenty years from now.

Coach's Corner

Whether you're a Fortune 500 CEO or in business for yourself, you should always think of yourself as an aligner. As I coach leaders through Business Vision and then into Business Planning, I remind them that developing a compelling vision is at best 10 percent of what is required to build a great business. The other 90 percent is in execution, and it must be directed by a business plan that aligns your highest priority near term deliverables with the big picture vision.

- First, you must **align** your Business Vision with a brutally honest view of your current situation so you have the best chance of building an annual plan that provides the shortest, most predictable path to accomplishing that vision.

- Then, you must **align** next year's plan with what needs to be done next quarter, next month, next week, and in some cases, the next day.

- You also must **align** your company plan with what each department must accomplish along with what is expected from each individual within those departments.

- And you must provide a self-correcting process to regularly review and learn what worked and what didn't so you can **re-align** future plans based on that learning.

- Finally, you must **align** your own leadership development to the ongoing growth of the company so you continue to provide the kind of leadership required.

It may not sound glamorous, but great leaders see themselves as Master Translators constantly aligning the short-term tactical details with the long-term Business Vision. And the Business Plan is that alignment tool.

Dan Meub
COO and Executive Coach
Building Champions, Inc.

Whatever you do, don't try to make your Business Vision a "perfect" document. I have yet to see a first-pass, clearly envisioned future that made me say, "Okay, we're done. Let's carve it in marble." Like your Life Plan, this is a living document. It changes as your vision changes. Rather than asking, "Is it perfect?" ask yourself, "Am I excited to see this?" If it doesn't raise the hair on the back of your neck, it probably won't raise the hair on the back of anyone else's neck. You want your team to get *excited* about this future!

I remember the first time a client really nailed this component of his vision. I remember really being drawn in to what he wanted to create, and I was not a team member or one he was attempting to hire. I can still remember the description he gave ten years ago. He told me of the experience every visitor to his ideal office would have. As I walked through the glass doors, I would notice their company logo and name above the receptionist's circular front desk. She would greet me by name, letting me know that I was expected. I would notice the finely decorated office with its rich blues and browns. She would hand me an extensive beverage menu with coffee drinks, sodas, and wines, asking which she could provide. The manager would greet me and voice his appreciation for choosing his company. Moments later the consultant holding the appointment would greet me.

Going back to the conference room, I would notice the words "Hall of Champions" written in raised bronze letters over the hallway entrance. The walls would have rich black-and-white portraits of all of the team members. Under the photos I would notice their names, positions, tenure dates, and awards. Beside the photos would be several framed business magazine and newspaper articles about the organization. I would pass by the area where all of the mortgage consultants, along with their assistants, were located, each with his or her well-decorated and organized office. Teammates would be engaged in conversations and working energetically, peacefully, and effectively throughout the office. I would feel the energy, and the thought, *This is a seasoned and very professional looking group of people,* would enter my mind. I would then be escorted into the conference room, where I would experience thorough interview and a financial plan would be created to assist me with the largest investment of my life.

When my client created this, his surroundings were chaotic, his team and office space an unorganized maze and mess. At the time, the company was growing quickly, working in several disconnected suites with mismatched furniture and people spread out in very inefficient ways. But then I had the wonderful joy of visiting his office in person a few years after he wrote his vision. Guess what? He had done it! He had nailed this aspect of his plan, and I remember feeling with all senses the realization of what I had read just two years earlier. He worked diligently to paint the picture, tell the story, and work the plan to create the environment where the best of the best would want to work.

I see many struggle when they write their Business Vision or they limit their focus to just the economics. Remember, the money earned cannot be central. It is just one of the many grades on the report card. Aim to compel people, to reach their hearts. The best way to do that is to work over your own clearly envisioned future until it compels your own heart. Then you will be able to start compelling the hearts of everyone on your team.

BONUS: MOUNT EVEREST GOALS

In many great vision documents, we'll see what Jim Collins calls "big, hairy, audacious goals." These are what we call Mount Everest goals, aggressive targets that are so big and so far out, that accomplishing them is going to require your team to stretch and work harder and smarter than they have ever worked before.

Usually these goals cannot be accomplished in a single year but require more long-term planning. To achieve these future realities of greatness, your team must unite in an uncommon manner, and your teammates must contribute in uncommon ways.

A Mount Everest goal might sound like this: "We will have number-one market share in all the markets we serve within five years." If your market share is currently number fifty-four, that's clearly a Mount Everest goal. At our company, one of our Mount Everest goals calls us for us to own a coach retreat center in an ideal location, perhaps somewhere in central Oregon.

How big is "Mount Everest"? In my experience, most leaders don't make their goals big enough. We live in a practical world where we immediately want to get down on the ground, so dreaming big may seem counterproductive. Developing an effective Business Vision document is about rising above the norm and saying, "Where can we go?"

In fact, if people from the outside don't respond to your Mount Everest goal with comments like, "Yeah, right, whatever," then most likely it wasn't big or audacious enough. Most of the time, outsiders will respond to a good Mount Everest goal with objections, such as, "You're not going to do a hundred million dollars in a year," or "You're not going to write that many units," or "You're not going to touch that many people." Know this: If you get this kind of skeptical response, you probably did something right. A good Mount Everest goal tends to make people who don't know your heart doubt that it can be done.

WRITE IT, REVIEW IT, AND REPEAT IT

Vision is not a one-time exercise for coaching leaders. It's not a one-and-done assignment they complete in order to tell others how they "did the vision thing" back in '02. Vision is a vital part of who every coaching leader is.

Another CEO client I first began coaching back in the '90s taught me two critical lessons about my Business Vision: (1) the importance of regularly reviewing it and (2) the advantage of continually repeating it to others.

By religiously following these two practices, he has gained a tremendous capacity to recruit the right people. His company flourishes today largely because of his commitment to regularly reviewing his Business Vision and to continually repeating it to his team members. Both the reviewing and the repeating are essential to becoming a coaching leader who attracts talent and causes it to blossom.

To these two important principles, I added another one that precedes the first two: Put it on paper. This makes the original two lessons much easier to accomplish and your Business Vision easier to maximize. If you skip or overlook any of the three, it won't live up to its full capability. Once you have developed your Business Vision, you must:

1. *Put it on paper.* An effective and useful Business Vision has to be in written form, concise and clear enough so that everyone in the organization grasps it, accepts it, and acts on it. It must be an easily accessible document.

"You know," some of our clients say, "I don't know if I need to write this down; it's all very clear in my head." But if it's only in your head, then people will find it very hard to follow you. They don't have easy access to your head, but they can quickly get to a readily available document.

Don't worry that you're not an author or a writer. If you want people to follow you, then make it easy for them to do so by writing down where you want them to go. Remember, this is one of the most important and strategic tools you'll ever create, so don't settle for "It's in my head."

2. *Review it continually.* Because your Business Vision is extraordinarily strategic, you need to constantly review it on your own. Ponder it enough so that it goes from your head to your heart. Know it by heart and let it imprint your soul. Make sure the contents of this vital tool live and breathe in your mind.

3. *Repeat it continually* to team members and to other interested individuals. Make your Business Vision more than just a nicely worded sentence suitable for framing. Let its words be spoken frequently and enthusiastically all around the office. People should know that it is a document that shapes every aspect of your business.

I love the following story from Michael Gerber's book, *The E-Myth Revisited:*

Why Most Small Businesses Don't Work and What to Do About It.[3] When Tom Watson, the founder of IBM, was asked to explain the phenomenal success of IBM, he is said to have answered:

> IBM is what it is today for three special reasons. The first reason is that, at the very beginning, I had a very clear picture of what the company would look like when it was finally done. You might say I had a model in my mind of what it would look like when the dream—my vision—was in place.
>
> The second reason was that once I had that picture, I then asked myself how a company that looked like that would have to act. I then created a picture of how IBM would act when it was finally done.
>
> The third reason IBM has been so successful was that, once I had a picture of how IBM would look when the dream was in place and how such a company would have to act, I then realized that, unless we began to act that way from the very beginning, we would never get there.
>
> In other words, I realized that for IBM to become a great company, it would have to act like a great company long before it ever became one.
>
> From the very outset, IBM was fashioned after the template of my vision. And each and every day we attempted to model the company after that template. At the end of each day, we asked ourselves how well we did, discovered the disparity between where we were and where we had committed ourselves to be, and, at the start of the following day, set out to make up the difference.
>
> Every day at IBM was the day devoted to business development, not doing business. We didn't *do* business at IBM; we *built* one.[3]

COACHING OTHERS THROUGH THE PROCESS

Create your Business Vision first for yourself as a coaching leader; after that, create one for your team. How is it done for your team? There are a couple of primary ways.

First, as you develop your Business Vision and share it with your teammates, they receive it and take ownership of it. And second, a coaching leader helps his or her key leaders—the individuals he or she is coaching, whether they're key producers, managers, or others, to go through the same process to develop their own Business Vision (compatible and in step with the leader's vision).

A lot of leaders stop at this point and say, "Why isn't one Business Vision document enough? Shouldn't my teammates just adopt the vision I've created? Shouldn't they take ownership of it?"

Well, yes and no.

Certainly your teammates should be in step with the Business Vision you've created. It should fire them up, motivate them, and get them moving in the direction you've set. You want their vision for the future of the organization to be congruent with your own. If it is not, then you'll have problems down the line, and you want to know about any such stumbling block as soon as possible.

On the other hand, every person you're coaching should have his or her own personal Business Vision, congruent with your own and uniquely tailored for their own positions. Maybe these teammates head up operations or accounting or systems and technology. Or maybe it's your assistant. Each has to clearly identify the core purpose for the division they run or the unit they manage. And you should know what they see for themselves in the future. What are *they* stretching for?

My partner and friend, Barry Engelman, believes in the vision I have for Building Champions, but he has also created his own vision. As the head of coach development for Building Champions, his role is to develop and train our team of coaches. Some time ago I said I wanted to create a coach development center, and Barry ran with it.

Barry has written out a vision for the project and is building a coach development team that will enable us to scale up and train several coaches per month in the years ahead. The vision he is creating has enabled our leadership team to invest in the resources needed to build what he sees. My vision wasn't enough for him; he needed his own. And that's just how it should be. Take a look at some of what he envisions.

Vision for Building Champions
Training Center

Original: February 2001
Revised: March 2004

A clearer picture of what is to come . . .
The BCI Coach Development and Training Center

The training center is located on a 500-acre working horse and cattle ranch. (It's a dream, right?) The primary purpose of this property is to provide a place for Champion Coaches to receive initial coach training, plus ongoing training and replenishment. The training facility will be state of the art.

The Central Facility will include a main training room in addition to separate training rooms for smaller groups and breakout groups. Each training room will be outfitted with the latest technological advances necessary to provide the optimum training and learning experience. The main training room will be multifunctional and can be used as a movie theater, for live music performances, and as an alternate venue for events (normally held in the outdoor amphitheater).

The Central Facility will include training studios that can be used for practice coaching sessions, as well as watching and listening to sample coaching sessions. The Executive and Training Team's offices are also located in the Central Facility.

The "Kitchen of the Mind" Retreat Center, adjacent to the Central Facility, will house a library, reading room, A/V room for watching and listening to training resources, and a coffee/espresso bar. The offices of the Learning Team, Writing Team, and Research Analysts will be located in this building. The Coach Library and the Coach Tool Box are located here as well.

The BCI Coach Training and Development Center is designed for families to experience life together. Champions Summits are family events. Some families will make it a semivacation. Families will be housed in duplexes throughout the property. The center will be able to accommodate twenty-four coaches and their families. The duplexes will be nicely decorated in a Western theme, in keeping with the nature of the property/ranch.

While coaches are learning, other family members can be as active as they choose to be, engaged in a variety of activities: cattle drives, fly fishing, horseback riding, hiking, canoeing, swimming, snow skiing, cross-country skiing, whitewater rafting, and so on. For those who want to slow down a bit, there will be "quiet zones" on the property. This will provide wonderful opportunities to spend time in meditation and reflection. Every Sunday there will be a church service held in the open-air amphitheater (weather permitting).

All of our coaches buy into my overarching vision, but each has his or her own vision as well. As a result, they have created new products and new offerings that greatly enhance our company.

What makes or breaks a company is its talent, its people and their ability to create products of value. These talented people shouldn't have to rely solely on what happens in the leadership conference room for new ideas. This "room to grow" is what enables good companies to become great. So if you're relying only on the six people at the top to create products for tomorrow, you're going to miss *a lot* of opportunities.

Business Vision, developed and clarified and publicized at the front line, enables teammates to create new opportunities, products, and services that will enable the company to enjoy a very leveraged effect. There's a huge difference when your company has forty people with vision rather than just three!

FIND OUT FOR YOURSELF

Convictions, purpose, a clearly envisioned future, and Mount Everest goals—these are the four pieces you need in order to develop and clarify your Business Vision. Remember, long-term strategy is most effective when it captures all of one's mind and heart. Most of our clients feel powerfully moved once they have completed this piece of the Core Four puzzle.

And I have little doubt that you will, too.

Key Benefits

What Business Vision does for your team members:

- Lets them know what their company stands for.

- Empowers them to make decisions that can radically impact the company, because they know what is important.

- Enables them to see what opportunities might be present, and then to act on them.

- Prompts them to be more committed to their work and encourages them to build on the company vision.

- Connects their role to a greater purpose.

What Business Vision does for the company:

- Gives clarity to business planning, and enables leaders to see whom to recruit.

- Allows leaders to create big goals and establish landmarks.

- Moves a company from the tactical to the strategic.

- Acts as the catalyst for creating a culture of execution.

- Decreases turnover.

- Defines the company's direction.

What Business Vision does for you:

- Gives you confidence, increases your clarity, and deepens your convictions.

- Helps you to see the Big Picture rather than just the immediate.

- Helps you to appreciate the significance of what you are building.

- Helps you to stay focused, energized, and on track.

- Helps you make better decisions.

SEVEN

Your Business Plan: To Execute, It Must Be Clear

Gather a group of professionals and bring up the topic of business planning, and you're certain to get a wide array of responses.

Many leaders of large organizations feel instant anxiety the moment the topic gets mentioned. Their corporate cultures mandate an arduous process for business planning, requiring them to spend countless hours building a comprehensive document that accounts for every detail within their department or sphere of influence, including detailed budgets. They agonize over these plans, and yet they know that key personnel often will not follow up on them. In fact, sometimes team members adjust them erratically or ignore them altogether. And that causes these managers or leaders to feel deeply frustrated by the business planning process.

Other managers and department heads have a very different experience. They love the process. They, too, go to great lengths of detail and planning, but they are given the authority and the resources to execute on their plans. Team members actually use them daily. For these leaders, the process feels very

99

rewarding because they know exactly what they want to accomplish, how they're going to accomplish it, and when they'll have it done.

Leaders of smaller organizations, managers of midsize companies, and independent entrepreneurs likewise have widely different reactions to the idea of business planning. Many of these leaders enjoy the freedom of being able to respond to unforeseen market trends. For this reason, some don't want to feel boxed in by a specific plan. They call themselves "opportunity seizers" and want to maintain the flexibility they need to take quick advantage of new, unexpected prospects.

Without an adequate plan, however, the entrepreneurial leader often ends up doing frequent stops and starts, making abrupt changes of direction as opportunities or challenges come across the bow. As a result, this leader's team can start to feel great frustration and even hopelessness because they don't clearly see where they're going. They might begin to fear that, yet again, the project over which they have been laboring for ninety days will get tossed as soon as a "new and improved" opportunity comes along. Unfortunately, I can speak with experience here. During the early years of running my own company, I took my poor team on just such a ride.

I really enjoy reading books that help me to improve in areas I consider most important. Leadership is one such topic. In 2001 I had the opportunity to join marketing forces with one of my favorite writers and speakers, with the goal of educating the business world about our company's existence. I felt certain this would take our little team into the big leagues almost overnight. I saw thousands of leaders clamoring for our coaching services as a result of this venture.

So I pounced. I did not bother to match it up to our vision. I told the team what I saw: We could *quadruple* our business in just months! Of course, since our current systems and infrastructure could not support such radical growth, we needed a more powerful database, we had to add new skill sets to our leadership team, and we needed to invest all our resources into making some of these new speaking events the best they could be. My awesome team loyally followed my erratic lead and built the new systems, deployed the insanely expensive new CRM, wooed the new talent, and got ready to go.

Then came the first major event, and instead of returning to our office with 2,400 leads, we had less than 200.

This "opportunity" just about did us in. For months we had lost our focus and wandered from our purpose. Our service levels dropped, our cash position dropped, our income dropped, and most important, morale dropped.

Fortune smiled upon me during this season of crisis. Despite the fiasco, my team did not lose faith in my leadership. I apologized to them and returned to our original vision and plan. Today, five years later, I lead a healthy, plan-following team and business.

The Five Most Common Reasons Why Leaders Don't Create and Follow a Business Plan

1. They don't know how.
2. They failed at it before.
3. They fear being held accountable for executing it.
4. They lack the time to plan.
5. They believe it will be a waste of time.

As their organization grows to a certain size, many entrepreneurs recognize that they'll soon hit a ceiling without the kind of framework that a Business Plan provides. They know they will start to miss opportunities because they won't be able to align resources and talents quickly enough, nor will they have the necessary systems, efficiencies, and benchmarks in place to replicate or scale their growing business.

Some entrepreneurs who enjoy the best of both worlds choose to put together small and very simple business plans that are little more than a statement of annual goals. They might say, "Our plan this year calls for us to grow our company from eight million dollars in revenue to ten million. And we're going to accomplish this by picking up two new corporate accounts." Such a plan, however, offers little in the way of strategy or tactics regarding *how* to reach the stated goal. It doesn't stipulate enough detail concerning the disciplines or the improvements needed to achieve the goal, so the plan doesn't offer much direction to team members responsible for the company's growth.

A GOOD TOOL FOR IMPROVEMENT

While you might guess that I'm all for good business planning, you might be surprised to learn that I never tell anyone they can't succeed without a well-developed Business Plan. The truth is, I've seen *many* leaders succeed without the benefit of effective business planning. You may be one such leader. You may have achieved real success, even if your leadership has not included business planning as a key discipline.

So why bother with a Business Plan? Here's why: if you were to make business planning a regular practice and use the plan for decision making, allocating resources, and managing your own time, you could enjoy even greater levels of success—and so could your team.

A Business Plan can be a tremendous tool for coaching your teammates in the areas most critical for their success. You can use it to encourage them, guide them, remind them, hold them accountable, and challenge them. It's a wonderful coaching tool.

As a successful leader, you have a lot in common with a gifted athlete. All on your own, you can jump over barriers of five, six, even seven feet. Not many people can do that! And you've been rewarded accordingly. But what if someone could put a pole in your hands, teach you how to use it, and suddenly you were vaulting over bars more than twice that high?

> *While your Business Vision answers the questions "what" and "why," your Business Plan weighs in on the "how" and "when."*

In the context of business, the plan is your "pole." Business planning can take your natural athleticism and help you jump up to the next level.

THE NUTS AND BOLTS OF BUSINESS PLANNING

So what makes for an effective Business Plan? Now that we're halfway into the book, you know that I like simple tools and simple processes. The same is true of my perspective on business planning. For it to be both useful and used, it has to be easy to follow, easy to execute, and easy to utilize. And it absolutely must fit hand in glove with your Business Vision.

Your Business Vision identifies where you want to go over the long haul, what you stand for, and your primary purpose. Your Business Plan tells you how you're going to accomplish the goals you've set. A good Business Plan, in other words, leads to the fulfillment of your Business Vision. Your plan is the execution part of your vision, outlining the specific tactics you'll use to achieve your overall strategy.

And what does such a plan look like? As I said, I'm a simple guy who likes simple tools and systems. Therefore, the Business Plan I recommend for all my coaching leaders has just three primary characteristics: it's *simple, measurable,* and *meaningful.*

A SIMPLE PLAN

A good Business Plan tells you

- *what* you will accomplish,
- *where* you need to make improvements or adjustments in order to reach your stated goals,
- *how* you will behave in order to accomplish those goals, and
- *when* designated aspects of the plan need to be completed.

The most useful Business Plans take adequate time to create, are simple to use, and simple to refer back to. They provide very clear direction for both the coaching leader and the team.

Contrary to popular belief, a good Business Plan does not have to be long and complicated. In fact, the key to business planning is clarity and simplicity. The Business Plan that actually gets executed is the one that is clear, brief, and easy to understand.

A forty-seven-page Business Plan that takes two weeks to write might impress the board, but it isn't useful as a coaching instrument. Many times no one looks at it a second time after it is created, apart from the occasional comment. It simply gets filed away, where it doesn't see the light of day until a year later, when someone pulls it out for grading purposes on a performance review.

By stark contrast, a good Business Plan is a living, breathing document that is usually no more than a few pages long. Keep it simple!

About eight years ago, Barry Engelman, SVP of Coach Development at Building Champions, walked into my office. He took a look at the whiteboard in my office, sat down and studied it in silence for several minutes. Finally he said to me, "Daniel, is this your Business Plan?" What he observed was a model taught to me by my friend and business associate, Todd Duncan, that organized and streamlined preparation for speaking and writing.

"No," I responded, "it's not. Those are my goals for the year, the disciplines I must adhere to, and the projects I must complete."

Barry soon got up and left without saying much more about it, but I could tell his mind had begun to travel down a particular road of thought. When I studied the board once again, it occurred to me that Barry might really be on to something. The more I thought about it, the more I realized that what I had scribbled on the board really *was* my Business Plan, in its entirety.

On the top left side of the board, I had noted the number of people I wanted us to impact in the year ahead; that was my goal. Next to it I had drawn a big circle with spokes radiating from it; these indicated the key disciplines I needed to focus on to effectively play out my role in the company. If I were to do those six things I had written on the board, I would have the highest probability of leading my organization in a way that would enable us to serve the designated number of people. On the right-hand side of the board, I had written down five projects, complete with target dates and prioritized in order of importance.

And that, in its entirety, was my Business Plan.

A couple of hours later, Barry returned to my office with a Word document that mirrored what I had drawn on my board. We tweaked it a little, took a step back, and then congratulated ourselves on a job well done. Here's what it looked like:

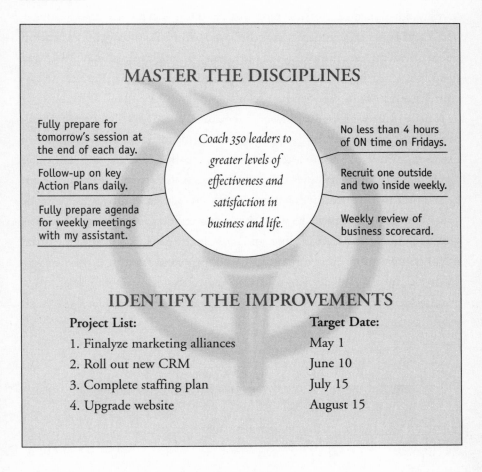

MASTER THE DISCIPLINES

Coach 350 leaders to greater levels of effectiveness and satisfaction in business and life.

Fully prepare for tomorrow's session at the end of each day.

Follow-up on key Action Plans daily.

Fully prepare agenda for weekly meetings with my assistant.

No less than 4 hours of ON time on Fridays.

Recruit one outside and two inside weekly.

Weekly review of business scorecard.

IDENTIFY THE IMPROVEMENTS

Project List:	Target Date:
1. Finalize marketing alliances	May 1
2. Roll out new CRM	June 10
3. Complete staffing plan	July 15
4. Upgrade website	August 15

And that is how we created our first, most basic business-planning tool. Simple! At that time, with a business of our size, it really didn't need to be much more than that.

In a similar way, all the hard work you put into your own Business Plan should lead to a one-page summary document.

A MEASURABLE PLAN

A good, solid Business Plan is *measurable*. What you measure in your business will differ from what others measure in their businesses, but we all measure something.

A good plan measures the most important *something* for your business, whether it be revenue, income, units built or sold, market share, people served, hours billed, or something else. All plans must identify a specific number that you plan to reach. That number is the goal or the objective that you set for your organization in the year ahead.

The best plans break down what is measured into increasingly smaller periods of time. Most plans have an annual measurement. Better plans break down that annual objective into quarterly objectives. Coaching leaders who really have a grasp on their opportunities break it down even further into monthly numbers; some further narrow it down into weekly, daily, even hourly measurements.

The better the grip you have on that key number, to be accomplished in a specified, measurable unit of time, and appropriate to your business, the easier it will be for you to make any necessary adjustments. Keeping a good handle on this key number allows you to change the course of marketing, sales, manufacturing, or whatever it may be, depending on what your results show you.

SMART: Specific Measurable Attainable Results-Oriented Time-Sensitive					
Strategic Initiative		*Systematic Marketing Database*			
Revision Date:			(List next 5 months, one above each column)		**Nov**
		11/05/05	Owner	Due Date	% Complete
Goal 1:		Create a killer marketing system	Jan	12/31/05	30%
Objective 1:		Create a lead follow-up system	Pete	12/10/05	50%
	Task 1:	Define lead types (A,B,C)	Pete	12/1/05	45%
	Task 2:	Define "touches" to be made to each	Jerry	12/3/05	60%
	Task 3:	Create an automated report to track	Jerry	12/8/05	60%
	Task 4:	Create an activity series for each	Jerry	12/9/05	30%
	Task 5:	Write scripts, letters, or e-mail	Jerry	12/7/05	0%
	Task 6:	Train/execute usage no later than	Mary	12/28/05	35%
Objective 2:		Create an "in process" CRM	John	12/15/05	25%
	Task 1:	Call Cindy Douglas for input	John	12/5/05	100%
	Task 2:	Create the letters and e-mails	John	12/7/05	45%
	Task 3:	Create policies and procedures for	John	12/15/05	0%
	Task 4:	Determine role definition among	John	12/15/05	0%
	Task 5:	Write scripts, letters, or e-mail	Jerry	12/7/05	0%
	Task 6:				
Objective 3:		Create a post closing CRM system	Pete	12/23/05	0%
	Task 1:	Write scripts, letters, or e-mail	Jerry	12/7/05	0%
	Task 2:	Create policies and procedures for	John	12/15/05	0%
	Task 3:	Create time line for sending post	Pat	12/10/05	0%

A MEANINGFUL PLAN

Does your plan give you the ability to bring your vision to reality? That is what I mean by a "meaningful" plan. It doesn't exist merely for its own sake. It exists to help you to take specific, meaningful actions that will enable you to reach your stated goals.

A good Business Plan identifies the outcomes you want, tells you whether you're on track, and guides the decisions you're making, especially with regard to how you're managing your time. You use it and refer to it on a regular, on-going basis.

Any good plan details the outcomes, disciplines, and improvements your business needs to adopt to reach your stated objectives. You need to identify all three to enjoy success as a coaching leader, and the teammates you coach also need to identify all three in their own areas of responsibility. A good Business Plan also identifies them in that specific order.

- *Step One: The Outcomes.* This is what you will measure. It may be revenue, numbers, units, clients, or something else. A solid plan will state very clearly and unambiguously what you're measuring.

- *Step Two: The Disciplines.* We call them "the Disciplines of a Champion." What three to five disciplines must you, as a leader, do on a daily, weekly, and monthly basis? These disciplines are for you as a manager or a leader, as distinguished from the disciplines as a coach that we'll discuss later in the book. These are the three to five activities that need to permeate your calendar for your department or company (or for you as a leader) to experience the most success. (I will further describe them in the next chapter on Priority Management.)

  An example might be a weekly review of key reports or leadership team meetings that you facilitate. It could be five calls to your most valuable clients every week. It could be three recruiting appointments per week. It could be five handwritten notes every day. It could be walking the floor two times a day to greet your team and to check in with them. It could be leading one training event every other week. These are the routines that only you need to master and adhere to for your organization or your department to accomplish the outcomes that you identified in Step One.

- *Step Three: The Improvements.* The improvements refer to the three to five projects that are truly most important for you to execute in the year ahead. If you have three to five projects that need to be completed every quarter, you can do this by quarter. But most leaders of small to midsize companies, or leaders who manage departments in larger organizations, have three to five main initiatives or projects that they need to lead and to execute annually for the company or the department to improve. These improvements are prioritized, with the time required to complete each step identified. Target dates are then scheduled and resources enlisted. Finally, every step is described to all of the essential stakeholders. Every essential team member must know what is required to build this improvement.

This summarizes our most basic business-planning process at Building Champions. A useful, simple, straightforward Business Plan identifies the outcomes, disciplines, and improvements needed to achieve the plan's stated goals.

In addition, we have created an "executive track" that goes into much greater depth. It includes strategic initiatives, scorecards, metrics, critical processes, and a host of other details. This can be very appropriate for business leaders with extensive responsibilities and who oversee an executive team. But for the purposes of becoming a coaching leader, you must first master the art of creating a Business Plan. Use it regularly as a guiding document, then learn how to coach others on your team to do the same.

USING YOUR PLAN

How do you use this plan once you've created it? Below are a few suggestions.

- *Review it weekly to help manage your priorities.* At the beginning of the week, review your plan. Then, as you make decisions about your schedule—which meetings seem most important, where you need to spend time in preparation, what you need to cut out of your week or day—use your Business Plan as a road map to help you make good decisions.

- *Use it to guide you in smaller decisions.* While your Business Vision helps you with the bigger picture (decisions on business challenges, crises, etc.), your Business Plan helps you to make smaller, tactical decisions throughout the week.

- *Use it to help you organize and orchestrate time and resources* so that you can hit your annual or quarterly objectives.

- *Use it to give you direction* on scheduling your development time and your project management time. It helps you to say no and to appropriately delegate, delay, or drop certain opportunities or projects.

- *Use it for team development.* Make sure your team members get a copy of it, then use it to review what is most important to the organization or the department.

- *Use your Business Plan to track everything* that you consider critical or important to your business. It will identify where you and your teammates need additional training. And it will help you to see what skills need improvement and where more knowledge is required. It is also helpful for repeated reviewing, to ensure that you remain on track throughout the year.

The more clarity your Business Plan provides for you, the more clarity your team will have in reaching your stated objectives. A clear Business Plan makes it much easier to set out benchmarks, goals, or objectives that everyone on your team can strive for.

A PLAN FOR EVERYONE

One Business Plan for the entire company is great for the CEO, COO, and president, but individuals within the company also need their own individual plans to succeed in their own corner of the company or organization.

A coaching leader brings business planning to his or her team so that all members of the team know the specific outcomes required of them in a calendar year. What three to five routines are most important for each position? What routines can make each teammate into a champion?

Make sure your teammates know what they must do *every day* to succeed. Over what specific things can they take ownership in the year ahead so that those improvements, coupled with the routines, will enable them to achieve the stated objectives?

This means that the VP of sales has a Business Plan. The marketing director has a Business Plan. The head of IT has a Business Plan, as does each salesperson under him or her. And the Business Plans they all have are very simple and very clear.

Make certain that everyone's individual Business Plan aligns with your Business Vision. You should be able to look at a teammate's Business Plan and see how the routines and improvements it highlights feed right into the Business Plan you created for the whole company, group, or organization. You should never see a plan to launch a new training division or new product, for example, that doesn't mesh with your Business Vision. Companies that chase good opportunities outside of their guiding strategy tend to go out of business.

When you take the business-planning process to those you coach, a new level of ownership takes place. When those you're coaching go through the process, they'll accumulate the same kinds of gains you did when you went through it.

All of us want our teammates to improve their performance so they can contribute to the company at the highest levels. Once you lead your team members through business planning, you will have a powerful tool for coaching them. You will be able to help them nail the routines they have identified as critical for their success. You can help them with project management, because under their improvements they will have identified the three to five areas in which they want to develop, whether that be in system improvements, projects that need to be finished, marketing collateral, or whatever.

You'll also use their completed Business Plan for regular reviews to help them stay on track. Use it to celebrate the milestones and the victories as they reach their quarterly numbers or as they complete major projects. When they find themselves off track, whether due to a problem or to an opportunity, you can bring them back to the Business Plan and say, "Where does that fit into what you're already committed to?" A good Business Plan can serve as a sturdy anchor to bring them back to what is most important.

And by the way, don't wait until the beginning of the calendar year to lead your teammates through this exercise. Business planning doesn't always need to be done between October and November. It's great if you can begin utilizing it in the first quarter, but it's not essential. As a coaching leader, you can begin coaching your teammates through this process regardless of where you are in the year. The main thing is to get started and then to follow through.

One Page Later

So there you have it—a good Business Plan covers all of your essential business categories and should be summarized on a single page. It doesn't have to be huge, and it doesn't have to cover every eventuality in the known universe.

Many years ago, during his business school days, one of our coaches had to write a Business Plan to fulfill the requirements of a college term project. He put his heart and soul into the assignment; weeks later he wound up with a massive document bulging out of a thick, three-ring binder festooned with tabs, dividers, appendices, and a lengthy table of contents.

To this day this coach remains proud of his creation, remembering it fondly as an impressive document chock-full of great information. "It was a beautiful thing," he recalls. But he also quickly admits it could *never* serve as a useful, practical, or legitimate business tool.

In reality, every useful, effective, and tactical Business Plan must answer just three basic questions:

1. *What* specifically is going to be done?
2. *How* is it going to be done?
3. *When* will it be done?

So leave the fat, three-ring binders at home. A good Business Plan needs to be concise, specific, and user-friendly. Do you know the real difference between a *good* Business Plan and a *great* Business Plan? Execution! It's not the number of pages or amount of detail that goes into your Business Plan; it's how well you *follow* it.

Don't overthink this exercise. Refuse to make your plan more complicated than it needs to be. Instead, focus your time and energy into its implementation and execution. That's the way to greater success, and that's the road to deeper satisfaction.

Key Benefits

What a Business Plan does for your team members:

- Gives clarity on what is expected of them and what is important to you.

- Allows them to take ownership of what is expected of them and how they are to contribute to the overall plan as they complete their own plans.

- Helps them to improve their performance.

- Helps them to focus.

- Gives them confidence and peace of mind.

What a Business Plan does for the company:

- Improves predictability, accountability, and strategic execution.

- Creates the foundation for the budgeting process.

- Improves corporate culture as all members operate within the same framework.

- Improves accountability.

What a Business Plan does for you:

- Increases peace of mind and power in decision making.

- Improves your ability to manage priorities.

- Reduces stress as you lead others to the plans they create and own.

- Greatly enhances your leadership influence.

EIGHT

Priority Management:
How Do I Fit It All In?

"I can't do it all. I can't be it all. I'm crazed!" How often do you hear people saying things like this? It has become the mantra of this generation. Most of us feel overwhelmed. There's just so much to do! Over and over again comes the same frustrated question: "How do I fit it all in?"

"Fitting it all in" is a function of Priority Management. And managing your priorities is really all about decision management. In fact, it's less about managing your calendar than it is about managing your decisions. By learning to do this well, you'll have a leg up on most of your competitors because you'll be putting onto your calendar what is truly most important to you.

Unfortunately, while most people have thoughts, hunches, and ideas about what is important, they rarely transfer those ideas to their calendars. And that is why it so quickly fills up with reactive stuff:

"Oh, I need to be in *that* meeting?"

"Oh, there's *this* crisis?"

"Oh, I haven't got *that* done?"

"Oh, I have to take *this* call?"

Leaders who talk like this get to what in saner times they label "important" only after reacting to the crisis stuff. And I'm not talking theory here; we see it every day.

PRIORITY MANAGEMENT: WHERE TO BEGIN?

When Building Champions takes a call from a prospective client, nine times out of ten the caller wants our help with ordering his or her day. The leader on the phone wants to begin our coaching relationship with emergency assistance on filling a calendar with the right activities.

But as I've explained already, we never deviate from our Core Four model, and Priority Management is the fourth piece of that model. It's the final item that a leader needs to address to make the changes that may be required to perform at improved levels.

Coach's Corner

As a working mom, finding a way to "fit it all in" isn't just important, it's a personal mission. Several years ago I attended a marriage and family seminar and had a lightening-bolt moment: I realized my main identity had become my role as a worker. I was all about success but had left out a significant part of who I was. My priorities were all out of whack, and I needed to change—*now.* I left the meeting in tears, fled to my room, and vowed to do whatever it took to get back on the right track.

Shortly after this major revelation, I developed a Life Plan. Eventually I found I could shave fifteen hours from my workweek and still maintain a heavy client load. Sticking militantly to a time block—to this day—has allowed me to be all I want to be as a businesswoman, leader, mentor, friend, and home manager. I am a living testimony that reflection is worth the effort. Fitting it *all* in is impossible—but designing a plan to do what matters most is very possible!

Tammy London
Coach
Building Champions, Inc.

The Priority Management piece of the puzzle brings order to the key elements of your Core Four. That's why we can't start out with Priority Management. If we try to help you manage your daily routine without first knowing what is most important to you, then more than likely we'll fill your calendar with the wrong activities. How can we offer help with time blocks or schedules until we truly understand what you most want to accomplish?

Until you've completed your Business Vision, we can't help you to create an effective Business Plan. Running a business without vision is much like building a puzzle without having the picture on the box. Too many leaders forget this and build plans that do not lead to the results they expected. Therefore, they ditch the plan as soon as a crisis hits or an opportunity comes knocking. They see the Business Plan as a stand-alone thing, not as a crucial component to their long-term strategy. That long-term strategizing gets done in the Business Vision process.

Of course, we can't help you develop an effective Business Vision until you understand what you really want out of life or your career. Who do you want to be five, ten, even twenty years down the road? That's the question the Life Plan is designed to answer.

So, once more you should see why we start off with the Life Plan, and then move to Business Vision, then work on your Business Plan, and only then end with Priority Management. It just doesn't work well any other way.

SCHEDULE YOUR DAY . . . OR THEY WILL

You need to understand a basic premise regarding Priority Management: *if you don't schedule your priorities, everyone and everything else around you will.* If you don't take charge of your schedule, teammates, vendors, solicitors, managers, golf buddies, relatives, and whoever or whatever else will fill your days for you. If you don't identify your top priorities and schedule your day around them, at the end of the day you'll always find yourself using leftover space to cram in what you consider important. And you know the worst thing? That's usually exhaustion time.

If you find yourself in that regrettable situation, there's only one thing to do: get out of the backseat and drive to success.

Imagine that it's 7:00 a.m. Monday and you're looking forward to a productive day. *This* will be the week that you finally do "it." No excuses!

As you walk out the front door, there sits your four-door sedan. The sight of it reminds you that you now have a decision to make: Are you going to drive your day or hop in the back and let someone else drive you? You hear your cell phone ringing, and instinctively you choose to climb into the backseat and go for a ride.

The caller is your new assistant; he becomes the first driver of the day. He says that Mr. Johnson needs you to deliver numbers to one of your key clients for a deal that has been in the works for three months. You listen patiently as he takes you down this road for approximately twenty minutes.

When he hangs up, the next driver enters, the head of IT. He has a problem with the primary e-mail server and needs to make a $20,000 decision on equipment *right now.* You sense his urgency, so you help him work through the problem and make the requested decision instead of working on "it."

It's now 9:15 a.m. and you're sitting at your desk in the office, hurriedly going through weekend mail and memos. You are halfway done when the next driver arrives on the scene. It's Joanne from your sales department, and she needs some information to close the ABC deal to make this month's quota. She takes you down her road for about ten minutes, then scoots over and hands the wheel to the next individual in line, your newest hire. She gets in, slams the door, and takes you across town for a very long forty-five minutes.

You hardly have time to lament the neighborhood you're driving through, however, because one of your mediocre clients (who always wants more from you at a cheaper price) wants to drive your car during lunch. So you lurch across town, arriving fifteen minutes late, and then listen to his theories on driving until you agree to throw him the keys once or twice a month. He leaves, and you look at your watch. It's now 2:00 p.m. and you're *way* behind—not even close to the destination you really wanted to reach today. In fact, the "it" looks farther away than it ever has.

Does this story sound ridiculous? Don't laugh, because so many managers and leaders make the decision *every day* to give the controls of their day—and with it, their success—to anyone and everyone who asks. How does this happen? They don't make and stick to a daily plan. Because they lack a road map for today's success, they don't get into the driver's seat and control the route and outcome of their day. And so they miss "it."

What is your "it"?

Setting up your new team development plan?

Observing your sales team making calls?

Working on this quarter's MBOs?

Spending time with your spouse, your kids, or a friend?

Going to the gym or having a daily quiet time?

Whatever "it" is, you know that getting it done will enable you to be more focused, productive, profitable, and successful.

And a whole lot happier.

Know Your Hourly Wage

As a leader, you probably have some control over your income; if you increase profits, no doubt some sort of profit sharing kicks in. If you increase revenue and net income, you probably earn a bonus, MBO, or larger distribution. If you run a successful sales team, you likely get a commission or an override. If your team continually performs, you will likely receive salary increases.

If you really want to improve your productivity and help those around you to increase their own, then spend some time thinking about your hourly wage.

Understanding what an hour of your time is worth will allow you to delegate and schedule with greater conviction.

To calculate your hourly wage, divide your *desired annual income* by 2,080 (the number of working hours in a year, assuming a forty-hour work week). If you want to make $100,000 a year, that's about $50 an hour. If you want to make $200,000 a year, that's about $100 an hour. If you want to make $500,000, that's $250 an hour; a million a year, $500 an hour.

Once you know your hourly wage, it becomes much easier to ask the cru-cial question: "Is what I'm doing right now really worth $100 an hour, or should someone else on the team be doing this so that I can handle the organization's money more responsibly? Does it make sense for me to perform a $20-per-hour activity when I see several $100-per-hour activities on my desk going undone?"

> *$160,000 ÷ 2080 (hours in a 40 hour work week) ≈ $80.00 per hour*

Most people just don't think this way.

I have interviewed thousands of leaders who have no idea what their hourly wage is. But if you don't know your hourly wage, it's easy to make foolish deci-sions and so mishandle the company's money. Maybe you spend big chunks of your day responding to lower-level needs, playing firefighter to the urgent or managing everything instead of delegating to others. You're stuck in a rut, not as aware and focused as you could be. If you don't have a good concept of your hourly wage and you don't know which activities truly warrant that wage and which don't, you will be far less effective than you could be.

So, what's *your* hourly wage? Figure it out before you go any further.

IDENTIFY YOUR HIGH-PAYOFF ACTIVITIES

A champion leader who knows his or her hourly wage can distinguish with absolute clarity between high-payoff and low-payoff activities. This is one discipline that you simply can't do without.

High-payoff activities are the things you do that bring the greatest value to your organization, team, or customer. They are the three to five activities that lie in your "sweet spot." You do them with excellence. They are your unique disciplines or distinctive skills, abilities that distinguish you from other team members.

Common high-payoff activities for CEOs might include sharing vision, recruiting key talent, or networking. For COOs, high-payoff activities might include budget reviews, coaching managers, or executing the strategic plan. If you're a production head or are in charge of a sales team, your high-payoff activities might include recruiting, training, and observing sales calls.

Knowing what your high-payoff activities are and actually doing them, however, are two very different things. Many surveys over the past several years have shown that the average American worker spends only 50 to 60 percent of the workday on activities specified in his or her position description. That means that workers waste 40 to 50 percent of their time on low-payoff activities, tackling things that others with less skill or training should be doing.

What are your high-payoff activities? The more time you spend doing those things, the more value you will bring to your team, organization, and customers. By disciplining yourself to clearly identify your high-payoff activities, and then by filling your calendar with those things and appropriately delegating, delaying, or dropping the low-payoff activities, you can go from being a good coaching leader to becoming a great coaching leader.

Once you identify your own high- and low-payoff activities, you can help the teammates you coach to do the same thing. By helping your people to fill their days with what they're truly best at you can significantly improve team and corporate effectiveness.

TIME TRACK YOUR WEEK

Once you've figured out your hourly wage and identified your high-payoff activities, it's wise to do some time tracking. For at least five days straight, write down everything you do, in fifteen-minute increments, from the time you start working until the time you go home. Although this may seem like a hassle, it's vitally important for you to become very clear on how you actually spend your time.

Once you've time tracked for five days, mark anything that's a high-payoff with a green highlighter and all the low-payoff activities with a pink highlighter. At the end of every time-tracked day, tally the total hours you spent in high-payoff versus low-payoff activities. Soon you'll gain a clear picture of how you're actually spending your time and whether you have room to fill your calendar with the activities that will truly add the most value to you and your organization.

Consider the following example:

Time	Activity	High/Low Priority
7:00–7:15	Exercise	
7:15–7:30	"	
7:30–7:45	"	
7:45–8:00	Clean up and eat breakfast	
8:00–8:15	"	
8:15–8:30	Drive to office	
8:30–8:45	Walk the floor	H
8:45–9:00	Unpack briefcase	L
9:00–9:15	E-mail	L
9:15–9:30	"	
9:30–9:45	"	
9:45–10:00	Kramer call (partner)	H
10:00–10:15	Marketing meeting	H
10:15–10:30	"	L (too long)
10:30–10:45	Call from banker	L
10:45–11:00	Call from Jones (VP of sales, crisis)	H
11:00–11:15	"	
11:15–11:30	Prep for IT meeting	H
11:30–11:45	Drive to lunch	
11:45–12:00	Lunch meeting with ABC (key client)	H
12:00–12:15	"	
12:15–12:30	"	
12:30–12:45	"	
12:45–1:00	"	
1:00–1:15	Drive back to office (phone call to spouse)	H
1:15–1:30	Quick review of Wall Street Journal	H
1:30–1:45	E-mail	L
1:45–2:00	Return voice mail messages (vendor)	L
2:00–2:15	Return voice mail messages (marketing partner)	H

2:15–2:30	Return voice mail messages (accountant)	L
2:30–2:45	Read pricing memo	L
2:45–3:00	Respond to memo	L
3:00–3:15	Leadership team meeting	H
3:15–3:30	"	
3:30–3:45	"	
3:45–4:00	"	
4:00–4:15	"	
4:15–4:30	E-mail	H
4:30–4:45	" (could be delegated)	L
4:45–5:00	"	
5:00–5:15	Take call from Green (top sales rep; should have called VP)	L
5:15–5:30	"	
5:30–5:45	Write agenda for Carlson meeting (delegate to VP of marketing)	L
5:45–6:00	Look at calendar for tomorrow and organize files to prepare (Delegate to assistant)	L

Total in High: 4:45 Hours   **Total in Low: 4 Hours**

Once you complete this process, take your teammates through the same exercise. Ask them, "What are the three to five activities that are most important for you to accomplish every week?" Once they know these, they can become more effective at delegating or dropping activities they shouldn't be doing so that they'll have more time to do what they should be doing.

TIME TO TIME BLOCK

As a coach, I continually hear from leaders who struggle with their day. They lament how often time seems to get away from them. They may have tried time blocking before, but they got thrown off track the first time a crisis hit.

But blocking times in your day in which to focus on high-payoff activities is a must if you are to become a more effective leader. Remember, you can give away only what you possess—and if you live primarily in "react mode," your well will quickly run dry.

Now it's time to create your "perfect week," which is nothing more than a model plan for how you want to spend your time Monday through Friday. For some, the perfect week also includes weekends.

To create this perfect week, take the key disciplines from your Life Plan and the key dscipline from your Business Plan and start plugging them into your ideal week.

If going to the gym at 6:00 a.m. every Monday, Wednesday, and Friday is one of your key Life Plan activities, it should show up in your perfect week time block. If you want to have leadership meetings every Monday at 9:30 a.m., you plug them in. If you want time with your sales department Thursday afternoons from 1:00 to 3:00 p.m., plug that in. If you want e-mail correspondence time twice a day and your Business Plan shows that one of your routines is to handle all correspondence within twenty-four hours, then you'll schedule two slots in your time block just for responding to all inbound inquiries. Maybe you'll plug in one time block from 11:00 to 11:45 a.m. and another from 3:00 to 4:00 p.m., just so you're not nibbling at it throughout the day.

If one of your Life Plan activities highlights your son's soccer practice every Friday at 2:30 p.m., then plug it in. If you have lunch dates with your spouse on Tuesdays, plug that in. Again, the idea is to take the key items from your Life Plan and your Business Plan and build a schedule around *your* priorities instead of around someone else's crises. If you live that schedule, you'll experience the most success at work, at home, and in life.

The challenge, of course, comes in changing from your current reality to your ideal reality, as reflected in your perfect week. Our typical clients admit to spending 40 to 50 percent of their time on their priorities; the challenge is to begin spending 80 to 90 percent of their time there. That's what the perfect week exercise is designed to help you accomplish.

THE DAILY ROUTINE

About ten years ago, I created the Daily Routine. It is nothing more than a model to be used for time planning. It has provided immense help for many of our clients. The Action Plan takes all of your activities and associates them with one of the following headings:

- **Growth**

- **In**

- **On**

- **Off**

THE DAILY ROUTINE
TIME BLOCKING SCHEDULE

BUILDING CHAMPIONS
COACHING BUSINESS AND LIFE ON PURPOSE

	Monday	Tuesday	Wednesday	Thursday	Friday	Saturday	Sunday
6:00 AM	OFF Work Out	ON Read	OFF Work Out	ON Read	OFF Work Out		
7:00	PREP & COMMUTE	PREP & COMMUTE	PREP & COMMUTE	OFF Breakfast w. children	PREP & COMMUTE		OFF
8:00	GROWTH Walk the floor	GROWTH Walk the floor	GROWTH Walk the floor		GROWTH Walk the floor		
9:00	IN	IN 1-on-1 w. VP Sales	IN 1-on-1 w. VP IT	IN Email/ Calls	ON		
10:00	Leadership Team Meeting	EMAIL/CALLS	IN 1-on-1 w. Controller		BP Review Plan Implement	OFF	CHURCH
11:00		CLIENT MEETINGS	EMAIL/CALLS				
Noon	GROWTH - IN	GROWTH - IN	ON	FREE	OFF		
1:00	With client or team member	With client or team member	Read Industry Magazines		Lunch date w. spouse		
2:00	IN	CLIENT MEETINGS	FREE		IN Email/Calls		
3:00		CLIENT MEETINGS	IN Email/ Calls	IN	ON Plan for tomorrow	GYM WITH FAMILY	OFF
4:00	Email/ Calls	IN Email/ Calls		Email/ Calls			
5:00	ON Plan for tomorrow	ON Plan for tomorrow	ON	ON Plan for tomorrow			
6:00			Implement				
7:00					OFF		
8:00	OFF	OFF		OFF		OFF	
9:00							ON Review for week
10:00 PM		OFF	OFF				OFF

Growth time is the selling part of your job. It includes prospecting, net-working, interviewing, meeting with prospective recruits, and adding value to prospective big clients. It enables your department or your company to grow and helps you and your team to bring value to the rest of the organization or to the marketplace.

In time is administration time. Imagine your company as a conveyor belt. The front door is the beginning of the belt; it starts up every time you throw a prospect there. Depending on your profession, it takes some time for that relationship to work its way down the conveyor belt until it drops off and the relationship or transaction is sealed. Your job *in* the business is to work along-side of that belt, troubleshooting and making sure that everyone working on the product or the service is handling the prospective client with excellence. By doing the "in" functions with excellence, your conveyor belt takes care of today's clients in a way that causes them to become tomorrow's sales force.

On time happens when you remove yourself from the daily excitement of running your business. Here you look down, as if you were in a helicopter. You observe the activities, the growth, your time spent *in* the business, and you begin working *on* it, improving your productivity and profitability. This includes your self-development plan. This is when you're reading, planning, strategizing, thinking. This is when you're implementing and executing.

Off time is when you set all your work aside. This is time for you to focus on your Life Plan. *Off* time for you may fall in the middle of the week, in the middle of the day, at your gym time, at lunch, or when you coach your son's soccer team in the afternoon. It can also be on Saturday when you are read-ing a good book on the beach with your family. This is time for you to get recharged.

It's very important for you to get comfortable putting all your activities into these four buckets. Give each bucket a top-priority commitment, and make sure no one interrupts you when you're spending time in each of these areas. This means you may need to change your voice mail and e-mail or give your recep-tionist and your assistant the necessary script so that they can let all would-be interrupters know when you'll be returning calls and getting back to them.

With this Action Plan, every day you must block out time for all four criti-cal functions. Begin by committing only a portion of your day to them. I rec-ommend you begin by blocking out 50 percent of your week and managing your calendar to this for a month. Then increase your blocks to 60 and 70 per-cent. Plan your days in accordance with this time plan at least one day in advance, and then stick to the plan for ninety days. This will allow you to experience consistent growth with more balance and less chaos. Give it a try and take the driver's seat of your business and your life.

OPT FOR THEMATIC TIME BLOCKING

A second method for managing your priorities is called *Thematic Time Blocking*. This method works well for those who truly know their high-payoff activities. If your high-payoff activities are sharing vision, recruiting, reviewing the pipeline, and coaching, you can begin to schedule your week around those four activities.

You might leave Monday as an *In* day, a day to react and respond, with no specific theme other than catching up and taking care of all your "in the business" type stuff.

Tuesday can be your Recruiting Day. Fill it with as many recruiting appointments or opportunities or activities as you can profitably handle.

Wednesday can be your Team Day, when you coach your direct reports and conduct your internal meetings.

Thursday can be your Sales Day. Fill it with appointments, with outside potential clients, vendors, and anyone who has the ability to help you further your department or your company.

You get the idea. Pick a theme for a few days in the week, then fill your day with activities around that theme. This method works well for individuals who struggle with the daily routine, with switching throughout the day from *Growth* time to *In* time to *On* time to *Off* time. They may feel more comfortable designating Fridays as their *On* time, for example, when they work *on* their business, *on* projects, and *on* themselves.

SCHEDULE NONAPPOINTMENT APPOINTMENTS

Another key to taking control of your calendar is to schedule appointments for nonappointment type activities. Coaching leaders who excel at accomplishing their goals tend to fill their calendars with appointments with themselves.

This is where we see so many leaders fail. They just pick a deadline that appears convenient for the company or for someone else, and eventually it becomes a little like cramming for a final. If a project has to be done because a presentation is scheduled for April 1, they may say they'll have it done by March 31. Unfortunately, they won't give much thought to how many hours they actually need to complete the task—and when March 31 rolls around, it's Cram City.

The key to your success, and to the success of your teammates, is the excellent completion of Action Plans. The only way you (and they) will improve as executors is if you master the process of completing Action Plans. You need

> *When you identify an Action Plan you need to complete, make sure you schedule time in your calendar to do it.*

to start seeing the Action Plans you create as some of the most valuable appointments you have in your week. And the same is true of the team members you coach.

As the coaching leader, make sure that a teammate commits to an Action Plan. For example, to create a marketing calendar for the remainder of the year you help him to identify how much time will be required to complete that calendar, as well as what resources he'll need. Clarify the total amount of hours necessary, not only from the team member with the assignment, but also from any of *his* team members. That way the team member can schedule it appropriately and nail the deadline.

Maybe your marketing VP tells you that creating the marketing calendar should take no more than eight hours. With that in mind, have her schedule appointments with herself, maybe in two to four hour blocks, to make sure she gets that Action Plan done. That's a key to changing your culture and to helping people become better executors. Teach those you coach to schedule appointments for their high-payoff activities and to schedule time to work on their Action Plans. And again, make sure you're leading by example.

USE YOUR SYSTEMS

In chapter 12 we'll discuss systems in more detail, but I assume you're already using some form of a day planner, anything from a pad of paper to Outlook to a PDA.

If you are using an electronic calendaring program, use the alarm feature in your planning system to schedule recurring weekly activities for the remainder of the year (once you've laid out your perfect week time block). So if you want to spend every Monday from 9:30–10:30 a.m. at a sales meeting, then use the recurring feature to help you make it happen.

At the same time, train your assistant to keep you on track. Share your perfect week with him or her. You may even ask your assistant to help you create it, so that he or she can take ownership of keeping you on track. Let your assistant understand the value, not only to him or her, but also to the organization, if you live it. Strongly encourage your assistant to help you live that time block.

At Building Champions, we share and synchronize our time plans. If you choose a method and then plan around your joint commitments, you will experience a huge lift with reducing reschedules. And you won't find yourself skipping other important commitments you had already booked.

DON'T FORGET MARGIN

Several years ago Dr. Richard A. Swenson wrote a great book called *Margin: Restoring Emotional, Physical, Financial, and Time Reserves to Overloaded Lives.* Coaching leaders would do well to listen to his counsel. "The conditions of modern-day living devour margin," he wrote. "If you are homeless, we direct you to a shelter. If you are penniless, we offer you food stamps. If you are breathless, we connect the oxygen. But if you are marginless, we give you yet one more thing to do."[1]

And we all have a lot of things to do, don't we? When our minds drift in this direction, we typically think of the high-stress activities our jobs require of us. But that's only part of the story. We're busy all the time, in countless ways. Did you know that in a typical life span, the average American spends

- six months sitting at traffic lights,
- one year searching through desk clutter,
- eight months opening junk mail,

- two years trying to call people who aren't in or whose line is busy,
- five years waiting in lines,
- three years in meetings, and
- fifteen years watching television.

In addition, we

- learn how to operate twenty thousand pieces of equipment, from pop machines to can openers to digital cameras;
- commute forty-five minutes every day; and
- are interrupted seventy-three times every day (the average manager is interrupted every eight minutes).

With all the time demands on you, both from life and from work, how can you really fit it all in? Technology doesn't provide any final answers; many times the "time-saving devices" we create just end up gobbling more of our time. As Dr. Swenson remarked, "Progress builds by using the tools of economics, education and technology. But what are the tools of the relational life? Are they not the social, my relationship to others; the emotional, my relationship to myself; and the spiritual, my relationship to God? None of the tools of progress have helped build the relational foundation a society requires."[2]

The truth is, you really can't fit it "all" in, and neither can I. Those who try to do so destroy all margins in their lives and wind up failing anyway. You can't do it all but you really can do the most important things. And a key to pulling this off is to pair margin with balance.

"Life is a constant struggle for balance," writes Bobb Biehl. "Balance is a result of one word: schedule. Typically, you determine your own schedule. Therefore, you schedule your own balance or imbalance."[3]

I found great help in scheduling my own balance by acting on the wisdom of a memorable analogy. If life is very much like a juggling act, as many think, then the key to living well is understanding that some of the balls we juggle are made of crystal, while others are made of rubber. Unexpected crises or opportunities will storm into our lives, forcing us to drop some balls. We can't do everything! But those who know what's most important to them also know which balls they can drop. They'll allow the rubber balls to drop but not the ones made of crystal.

What are the balls of crystal in your life? They probably include your relationships, your spouse, your kids, your health, and your faith. You don't want to drop any of those! You don't want to wake up one day to realize you've been spending most of your time on things of lesser importance. If you drop the balls of crystal, you can sometimes still pick them up but you can't easily repair their cracks. Rubber balls, on the other hand—your career, your finances, your possessions—can drop, and when they hit the ground, they can bounce back.

What are you juggling right now? Do any of the balls flying through the air look as though they might drop? And if they did, are the ones in danger made of crystal or of rubber?

MAKE YOUR LIFE COUNT

In his book *The On-Purpose Person*, author Kevin McCarthy describes the difference between efficiency and effectiveness: "Efficiency is doing things right; effectiveness is doing the right things."[4]

In essence, that's what Priority Management is all about. It's about doing the right things at the right time. It's about moving from *reactive* to *proactive*, from *unfocused* to *focused*, from *unclear* to *clarity*, from living out someone else's priorities to living out your own, and from being driven by circumstances to being directed by purpose.

Priority Management has everything to do with your convictions and passions. What's most important to you in your personal life and in your business? How can you be intentional about making those things happen?

Everybody wants to live a life that counts, both at work and personally. I do, and so do you. But to do that, you need to stay in the driver's seat of your business and of your life. You simply can't spend most of your time letting others drive you wherever they think you ought to be going.

By managing your priorities, you can begin to create a very intentional and purpose-filled week for yourself. Doing this can move you from the backseat of your day to the driver's seat. It can help you to say, "I am not going to be kicked around by my circumstances anymore. I refuse to be driven by whatever comes across my desk or whatever the phone brings. I want to make sure I'm doing what I really want to do."

When you begin to live your life in an intentional and on-purpose way, you start to benefit many others tremendously. You also begin to experience something you may not have felt in a long, long time: a genuine sense of control and freedom—as will those you coach through this process.

Key Benefits

What Priority Management does for your team members:

- Improves clarity and decision making.
- Increases productivity.
- Improves effectiveness.
- Improves team communication.
- Forces higher dollar-generating activities.
- Aligns their convictions with their actions.

What Priority Management does for the company:

- Improves productivity.
- Increases profitability.
- Improves morale.
- Improves efficiency.

What Priority Management does for you:

- Improves focus.
- Improves your effectiveness.
- Forces higher dollar-generating activities.
- Aligns your convictions with your actions.

PART THREE

How Will
This Change You and Your
Organization?

NINE

The Knowledge
of a Coaching Leader:
The Critical Content

For the last five years, I have had the privilege of doing some work with one of my favorite leadership mentors, John Maxwell. Building Champions has coached many executive team members from John's various companies, and he and I have periodically shared the teaching stage in front of thousands of leaders. I have compiled countless pages of notes filled with insights and gems from John, and his best-selling books on life and leadership have sold more than 12 million copies.

How does he go about amassing such comprehensive and useful knowledge? It simply is not possible to collect and communicate such a huge volume of lessons and insights without having a successful strategy for acquiring knowledge. So what's his magic?

"I read, I write, and I file every day," he says. John has created a few simple disciplines that, practiced over time, have enabled him to possess, use, and communicate great wisdom on the topic of leadership. And so he makes the difficult simple.

Two years ago, I had the opportunity to spend some time in his home office. There I saw plenty of evidence of how John Maxwell walks his talk. I observed countless files on a vast menu of topics, filled with stories, facts, articles, and anything else that might pertain to the discussion. John has amassed this knowledge so that he might give it away to millions of leaders like you and me—but of course, you can give away only what you already possess.

Coaching leaders must have levels of knowledge above and beyond that of most managers and leaders. They have toolboxes, repositories for storing all their learning, filled with varied resources specific to their company, industry, and team. And they frequently use the contents of these toolboxes to give their teammates the best possible chance of achieving real success.

BUILD YOUR PERSONAL KNOWLEDGE

Champion coaches are lifelong students and learners. They are continually reading, studying, attending seminars, or going to workshops to become increasingly effective at managing their processes, products, and companies.

They don't learn so they can boast; they learn so they can continually give away the knowledge they are gathering to help others improve. The more they learn, the more they can give away.

That's why pursuing knowledge as a coach is so vital. You can give away only what you possess. And the more knowledge you have regarding your own industry, the specific roles within your organization, its distinct functions and processes, your competition, current trends, and any nuances taking place with competing products or services, the more effective you can be as a leader.

So what kinds of personal knowledge should you gain to become a more effective coaching leader? Let me suggest a few primary areas of knowledge.

1. A thoughtful self-development plan. Effective coaching leaders have and follow a self-development plan. At the beginning of the year, many coaching leaders devote time to mapping out how they intend to amass even more useful knowledge in the year ahead. They list the books they're going to read, the seminars they're going to attend, the workshops or courses they're going to take. They embrace learning as a regular discipline. As a result, their lifelong learning enables them to give away knowledge to those around them, which increases their value to their teammates.

Champion coaches have a multidimensional self-development plan. Many coaching leaders map out these planned learning experiences on their annual calendar so they can proactively see where and how they will grow in the year ahead. Further details regarding these self-development plans are found in their Life Plans.

Coaching Leaders also study leadership. They have a plan to build a library on leadership, which they share with their team. Since you're reading this book, I assume you have a passion to become the best leader you can. That's why you study leadership.

To become more effective as a coach, you must design a self-development plan that will help you to become a better leader, and then some. All leaders should have a thoughtful self-development plan—but coaching leaders will want to kick their program up a notch or two.

The following is an example.

Personal Growth Plan[1]

I will seek wisdom in all areas of importance to me by following the plan below.

Reading Plan

- 30 minutes per day of Scripture time
- 30 minutes per day reading on business and leadership
- Google News daily
- Read *HBR* and *Fast Company* monthly
- Read twelve books on business and leadership this year
- Read four books on life topics—marriage, parenting, finances, etc.
- Work with my coach monthly

Reading List:

Business and Leadership

1. *The Five Dysfunctions of a Team*
2. *The 360 Degree Leader*
3. *Time Traps*

---

4. *The Tipping Point*

5. *The Fred Factor*

6. *Think Big, Act Small*

7. *Little Giants*

8. *Now Discover Your Strengths*

9. *Management Challenges for the 21st Century*

10. TBD

11. TBD

12. TBD

Life

1. *Heaven*

2. *Sacred Marriage*

3. *Rich Dad, Poor Dad*

4. TBD

Classes, Seminars, and Workshops

- Attend two seminars on leadership, the first being "Achieving Leadership Excellence" in July

- The second to be determined

- Participate in CBS Executive Development Program June 5–17

PEOPLE DEVELOPMENT

A coaching leader wants to know more about people development. You should want to know how other motivators have managed to bring out the best in their teammates.

The knowledge you gain here not only will have an impact on the content of your conversations and what you can give away to your teammates, it will do something even greater: it will raise your own level of confidence. And the more confident you feel in developing people, the more confident you will be in your industry and the more attractive you will be to key teammates.

Knowledgeable leaders tend to possess a level of confidence that enables them to feel comfortable in almost all business settings. If they have what they feel to be an acceptable level of knowledge, they can enter into almost any business opportunity or challenge and believe that they can provide something of value to the team. And as a result of sharing what they know, they can further help the team to seize an opportunity or reach a tough but crucial decision.

A LEARNING JOURNAL

Most of the great coaching leaders I know keep a learning journal with them at all times. In that journal, they write down key lessons or actions that they want to act on, come back to, file, or share with teammates. Since it's always with them, they can record whatever they need to at any moment. By constantly keeping a learning journal with you, you can systematically record all key lessons, thoughts, or actions needed, regardless of your location.

This journal becomes your main repository of daily lessons learned. As you read a book on leadership, for example, you write down in your learning journal the key lessons you gained. When you're in a meeting and you identify an important need or opportunity, you mark it down in your journal. If you have a conversation that you want to follow up on, you record it in your journal. You also use it to note all of your Action Plans. In this way, it becomes an extension of your brain.

The key to using a learning journal is to regularly do something with its content. Once you put information into it, you must have a system for getting that information out so that it goes where it needs to go. I assign ideas and actions to the appropriate people on my team. I write down their name in front of the idea or action for easy referencing. We encourage our clients to regularly review the journal with their assistants, making sure that the information finds its way "home." Your assistant can help you to direct your instructions, questions, or insights to appropriate team members. Or maybe you will file some of your thoughts away for your next sales meeting, shareholder meeting, or board meeting. Having a simple, usable system to extract and use information from the journal is vital for any effective coaching leader.

What kind of journal should you use? That is completely up to you and your personal preferences. Many coaching leaders effectively use a simple, five-by-eight inch lined journal. I use a nice Raika leather journal. Others like more technological approaches, such as Trios or BlackBerrys. You should choose whatever tool you're most likely to use consistently.

Coach's Corner

As the curriculum development manager for Building Champions' Coach Training and Equipping Team, I have the opportunity to work with a great number of individuals who come through our coach training program. I see attributes of continuous learners in these leaders who come to learn how to lead with a coaching style.

- They utilize some system that they "own" for topically depositing and retrieving content to help them be better leaders. For example, it could be hard-copy file folders, or software such as Microsoft One Note. During coaching sessions, they are able to recall or access a great number of resources they have read and digested.

- They view others as "10s" as they interact with them in honoring and respectful ways. They believe that they can learn something from every person they come in contact with, and that others can add value to their own lives. Haughtiness and pride are not seen or felt by those they interact with.

- They have regular "think-tank time." They understand the importance of allowing themselves time to get their creative juices flowing. Additionally, they have come to recognize their optimal environment and time for brainstorming and planning.

- They have intentionally and purposefully developed a think-tank friendship with another person. In this relationship they have created and maintained an atmosphere of safety where they regularly share their best authentic ideas—usually in an informal friendship. Both parties show a willingness to invest in furthering, improving, or refining the ideas of the other.

- Coaches recognize and commit to learning through self-reflection. They practice regular honesty in evaluating and assessing their own behavior and thoughts. They commit to regular time for self-reflection. They have also developed their own process for maximizing personal growth during their self-reflection. They may journal, capture key thoughts, or create personal Action Plans. They make an investment in developing their intrapersonal intelligence—through seeking to understand what is going on behind their own eyeballs.

- They also exercise their commitment to improving their interpersonal intelligence as they seek to effectively understand and communicate with others.

Heidi Scott
Coach and Curriculum
Development Manager
Building Champions, Inc.

INCREASE YOUR KNOWLEDGE OF PERFORMANCE

Champion coaching leaders know how to do effective performance reviews. Frankly, I have been surprised by the number of leaders in publicly held firms that don't even do performance reviews. Others do them because HR mandates them, but their reviews seldom describe areas of needed improvement, nor do they build on the teammate's strengths. Coaching leaders, on the other hand, use performance reviews as an opportunity to provide helpful input and speak with specific direction into the lives of their team members.

While I didn't write this book to take you through Management 101, I do want to make sure that you grasp the basics of doing effective performance reviews. There are three basic types of reviews:

- Regularly scheduled performance reviews

- As-needed reviews

- 360-degree reviews

Let's take a brief look at each one.

1. Regular, predetermined, and set performance reviews. In my experience, most managers and leaders rate their own ability to do regular reviews at a C level, at best. Since these leaders lack clarity on why the review needs to be done in the first place, most of their reviews are not intentional, nor are they regularly scheduled.

Why should you do regular performance reviews? Many business reviews and studies suggest that a high percentage of teammates who leave an organization do so because they don't feel appreciated, nor do they know what level of contribution they're making to the group. Most employees readily admit they don't have a clear idea of how they're doing. The discipline of regular reviews gives them the feedback they need to perform at the highest levels. And if you develop a culture where employees regularly receive feedback, you'll create a much healthier culture, something that new teammates can sense almost immediately.

If you don't feel competent in this area, a huge number of great books and workshops exist to show you how to improve. You can learn how to conduct the review in a way that gives your team members good, honest input. From my own coaching experience, I'd also like to offer a few tips to help you more effectively coach your teammates before, during, and after the review.

- *Get the team member's perspective before you give yours.*

How does the team member think he is doing in the position? How does he think he is doing with specified job responsibilities or functions? Many coaching leaders begin by having a teammate fill out a company review form. The leader fills out the same form separately, then they compare their conclusions. However you choose to do it, always get the team member's perspective first. The truth is, you may not know everything he is doing with regard to a specific function or task.

- *Make sure the review is truthful.*

Reviews that hedge on the truth or dance around problem areas are not helpful; they often cause substantial damage. Coaching leaders uniformly desire to build a culture or environment of trust in which teammates can hear the truth about where they're excelling, where they're performing acceptably, and where they need to improve.

- *Always start out with the positive.*

Start off your review by affirming the individual. What has he or she done right? How does this teammate add value to the team? In what ways has the individual encouraged you or others in the company? As you go through the review, you can move to the areas where the teammate needs improvement.

- *Help teammates to create their own Action Plans.*

A review can serve as a great coaching opportunity. End your review by helping teammates to clearly outline specific, measurable, attainable, realistic, and time-sensitive Action Plans. Make sure they create them and therefore own them. That way, the next time you meet, they will have a much higher probability of having achieved the required improvements.

- *Clearly communicate follow-up dates, rewards for success and growth, and consequences for failure to improve.*

By the time you leave the session, your teammate should know several things with absolute clarity. First, he should know exactly when you plan to follow up with him to see how he is doing on the items you discussed. You never say, "Let's check in again in a month or two." Nothing that vague! Instead, you say something like, "Okay, let's plan to meet again on April 10. How does 10:30 a.m. look?" Second, your teammate will know exactly what will transpire if he should succeed on the items discussed; he will have a clear idea of the rewards for success. Third, he will know exactly what will happen if he does not make the stipulated improvements. He will not have to guess about the consequences for failure; you will have already clearly outlined them.

- *As the review ends, have the teammate restate the highlights of the review—the good and the bad—including specific Action Plans and target dates.*

To make sure the teammate has heard what you intended, have him repeat what you said. Get him to practice active listening in his own review. He will tell you, "This is where I'm really doing well and where I'm performing best. Here are areas where I'm mediocre; I have room for improvement. And here are areas where I'm holding the team back, where you really want to see me improve. You and I agree that I'm going to do this and this, you're going to help me with this, and we're going to get this done by this date. If I accomplish these things, this is what takes place. If not, then these will be the next action steps." Have him repeat everything to ensure that he has heard and understood your words as well as the intent behind the review.

- *Put it all in writing.*

To ensure that you don't merely leave your conclusions ringing in your teammate's ears, put the whole thing in writing. Let him take it with him, and instruct him to review it on a regular basis.

- *Schedule your follow-up dates, and do not miss them.*

A lot of leaders fall down here. If you agree to a follow-up date ninety or a hundred days from the review, then enter that date into your system and schedule the appointment right then and there. There is nothing wrong with scheduling appointments that far in advance. I strongly encourage you to do so. And if something comes up and the date needs to be moved, you now have a placeholder for it; just move the appointment to a day before or a day after. But don't risk missing it.

- *Follow up often, and make sure you're encouraging your teammates.*

Do everything you possibly can as a coaching leader to help your teammates succeed. Look for opportunities to "unofficially" inquire about their progress, and make sure it doesn't sound like nagging. Encourage them, keep it upbeat, see if there is anything you can do to assist them. Remember, your job as a coach is to help your teammates succeed.

Don't think of reviews merely as opportunities to correct mediocre performance; you can also use reviews to encourage a teammate who is really excelling and exceeding expectations. An upward review can increase the confidence of a top producer and lay out a possible increase of responsibility, authority, compensation, or whatever it may be.

2. As-needed reviews. If someone is underperforming, you can schedule a performance review as needed. Such a review will look much like the one just outlined, but I would put more emphasis on clearly communicating the necessary Action Plans that will enable the teammate to succeed. I'd also make sure that the consequences for failure are clearly identified. Allow no ambiguity here.

If you see chronic underperformance in a teammate, don't assume that a brief conversation or three or four verbal warnings will be the most effective way to bring about improvement. An effective coaching leader will sit down with the person, go through all the necessary paperwork, make sure he or she understands what you think may lie behind the mediocre performance, and then help the individual to identify specific and realistic Action Plans—to be taken in short order—to help bridge the gap.

3. 360-degree reviews. While it is very easy to gauge your success based on what your fans think of you, many people on your team often won't tell you where you're letting them down or where they think you have weaknesses. They don't have a natural vehicle or platform to give you such sensitive feedback. You need a tool to bring out those comments, to expose your blind spots, and that's the role of a 360.

A coaching leader understands that a 360 is an effective way to see how she is doing in the eyes of those around her. For that reason, 360s have become very common in the business world.

Every coaching leader should have a 360 done on themselves, as well as on key team members, every year. We use a 360 that measures eighteen main leadership disciplines. Such a tool allows you to get feedback from your leaders, your boss, your peers, and your subordinates, so that you can best see how others believe you are performing in certain primary business disciplines. Once you have the 360, you can begin to tackle what specific improvements you might need to pursue.

It's also really good to have such objective data when coaching one of your teammates, because objective data is very difficult to dispute or discount. Data is data, and these kinds of numbers don't lie. Perception is reality, and when you solicit input from everyone around an individual, it becomes clearer how that person might improve in areas of weakness or leverage areas of strength.

BROADEN YOUR COMMUNICATION KNOWLEDGE

A coaching leader has knowledge of many tools that enable teammates to communicate more effectively. Some of these tools are designed to give the coaching leader as much accurate and realistic data as needed to continue to make decisions that lead to success. By using these tools, outlined below, you and your team can communicate in more creative ways and ask better questions so that you can better help your teammates succeed.

1. Keep-Start-Stop. The keep-start-stop is nothing more than asking a specific team member (or an entire department or company) to suggest what behaviors or practices currently in the organization need to be continued, started, or stopped.

The "keep" element asks, "What are the behaviors that we as a company (or I as a leader) need to keep doing to have the greatest level of success? What do we need to continue doing to best move ahead? What do I need to keep doing to best help you succeed?"

The "start" element asks, "What do I need to start doing that I haven't been doing? As a company, what do we need to begin doing to have the highest probability of success? What behaviors do you need to start doing to succeed?"

Finally, the "stop" element asks, "What do we need to stop doing that's hindering you from succeeding? What do I need to discontinue so that you can enjoy more success? What is keeping you from being all you can be, that needs to stop?"

The keep-start-stop is an incredibly effective tool for every coaching leader. It's a great communication tactic that can be effectively used by an entire team, a department, an office, or one-on-one. By keeping the questions in this order, you will usually find a list heavy on the "keep" side and very light on the "stop" side, making this a great process for team building or to facilitate collaborative meetings.

2. Behavioral languages. Most coaches and coaching companies have become students of the behavioral languages. At the root of most behavioral assessments lies the DISC language—an effective, easy-to-learn and easy-to-utilize communication tool.

All current versions of DISC (and there are many) descend from the work of Harvard professor Dr. William Moulton Marston and his book *Emotions of Normal People.* Bill Bonnstetter, founder and CEO of Target Training International, later refined and enhanced Marston's research, yielding DISC as we know it today.

The DISC Behavioral Report we use consists of twenty-four questions and can graph more than nineteen thousand individual responses, resulting in 384 different behavioral styles. Most DISC assessments can be completed in only twenty minutes and will reveal your *natural* behavioral style (how you intrinsically operate) and your *adapted* behavioral style (how you respond to the demands of various environments). They suggest how individuals of a particular behavioral style tend to act, communicate, and respond emotionally. DISC can also help you to understand how you, as a coaching leader, can best communicate with people on your team, regardless of their behavioral style.

Building Champions is a certified DISC organization. We use an assessment to profile all of our clients so that we know how to best communicate with them right out of the chute. In what follows, I'd like to give you a basic, working knowledge of DISC.

D stands for dominance; it measures how you handle or respond to problems or challenges. High *D* individuals bring vision and execution to an organization. They're very task oriented and are great at executing and implementing. Under extreme pressure a High *D* tends to come across as arrogant, cocky, abrupt, and self-focused, with a default emotion of anger.

I stands for influence; it describes how you deal with people and or contacts. *I* types are highly relational. Usually they're the life of the party, great influencers, and terrific salespeople. Under stress they can be too trusting, overly effusive, and charismatic to a fault, with a default emotion of optimism.

S is for steadiness; it describes how one handles pace and consistency. *S* types are wonderful supporters. They're calmer and more consistent and tend to plod; they don't like fast-paced change. They're very relational and are great to have on a team. Under pressure they hold a grudge and become slow to act, with a default emotion of stoicism.

C is for compliance; it measures how one deals with processes and constraints. The *C* type is very task oriented and greatly values detail. These personalities need to have their i's dotted and t's crossed. They want to make sure everything follows policy and procedure, and that everything has its order. Under pressure, they become bound by procedures and lean on their supervisor, with a default emotion of fear.

Everyone is a combination of DISC characteristics, and a person can be some combination of any of the four. Some people are high or low on a particular segment; some are in the middle. There is no right or wrong combination. But how you score on the DISC profile greatly impacts how you interact with people, handle problems, and look at life.

It so happens that a great percentage of top performers and leaders generally score high in the *D* or *I* factors. That doesn't mean an *S* or a *C* can't be a great leader; we've seen outstanding leaders with DISC profiles across the board. The key thing is to know your own score, as well as those of your team members. The more accurately you understand the behavioral language of both yourself and your teammates, the easier it will be for you to communicate effectively with them.

If you're coaching a High *D*, for example, you need to know that you'll cause that individual high stress if you start talking about things not relevant to the conversation. If she wants to discuss a problem with you and you start asking about her weekend and describing your recent trip to Disneyland, she'll lose it. She doesn't want that; she wants to get right to the nitty-gritty of her question. So if you understand that, you can jump immediately into the facts, which she wants to see laid out in a precise and neat order. Having an agenda in advance will also help a High *D*.

If someone is a High *I*—deeply influential, warm, and personable—and you jump right into the facts as if he was a high *D*, he is going to assume that you don't care about him, that you have no heart. Doing that will cause him great difficulty, and you may even lose him. You need an icebreaker so he knows you care. High *I*s tend to have more energy, so you might talk with them at a faster pace, making sure you communicate the feeling behind the facts and the possibilities of the proposed action. First you connect with them personally; only then do you bring in the details.

When dealing with the *S*, the steady, you can't go nearly so fast. You can't charge into the facts; you need to spend more time on a personal level. If you're instituting change or asking an *S* to change, you need to help her take ownership of that change. If she can realize on her own that she needs the adjustment, you'll be better off than forcing it. Throttle back a little and allow her more time to deal with the new reality.

Since High *C*s want all the details in order and don't tend to be very trusting, any relationship with them is going to take time. You have to make sure that you have your facts in order, arranged in a nice presentation binder, because that puts their minds at ease. They need to know that you followed a process that makes sense. They're very logical. They get stressed out if you're too dominant, leading by mandating and charging. On the other hand, if you're only relational, they think it's all fluff; they want to get to the meat of the issue.

Below are the DISC profiles of Donald Trump and Tom Brokaw. Donald Trump is a classic High *D* profile, common among successful entrepreneurs; he is extremely driven and focused on results. Anyone who forgets to communicate with him in a direct and efficient manner will quickly discover the short fuse typical of a High *D* personality.

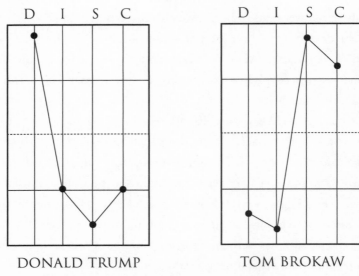

DONALD TRUMP   TOM BROKAW

Tom Brokaw, on the other hand, is a High *SC.* This combination makes for a highly analytical personal profile, very fitting of a journalist. Mr. Brokaw's High *SC* demeanor makes him persistent and willing to persevere through almost anything to reach his original goal.

We believe it is critical for a leader to know how his or her team members are naturally wired and how they prefer to communicate. It is the leader's responsibility to connect with team members, to get to their level, and then to communicate in a way that engages them and pulls them forward. It is *not* up to the team or the teammate to figure out what you're trying to say or to try to relate to your style. The leader, by definition, assumes the responsibility to connect and communicate with all teammates in a way that causes each one to achieve the highest probability of success. By knowing everyone's behavioral language, you gain a higher probability of doing just that.

Have you ever considered the mechanics of a train? Cargo trains transport goods from manufacturing plants to buyers throughout the United States. For some companies, the arrival of loaded freight cars makes possible their continued existence. They pay for the cargo to show up, not the engine. But in order for the cargo to make the trek from coast to coast, the engine must first back up to the cargo cars and connect the couplings. The lead car, the engine, backs up to ensure the freight cars get connected before pulling the whole train forward to its final destination.

In a similar way, we leaders have to take the time to "back up" if we are to create products or services worth more than what we can produce on our own. Learning this behavioral language will help you to back up, connect, and then move forward to deliver the precious cargo that your company provides.

Every coaching leader should have a good grasp of a useful behavioral language like DISC. I recommend DISC because I strongly believe it will help you to understand how each of your teammates will respond to you and to one another and how they'll deal with challenges. For more information on the DISC language or to learn how to receive an assessment on yourself or your teammates, you can learn more at www.becomingacoachingleader.com.

3. *Learning styles.* Just as there are differing behavioral languages, so are there differing learning styles. The effective coaching leader gains the knowledge to use different methods of communication for the various learning styles represented among his or her teammates.

Some people on your team are more apt to learn by experiencing the lesson *physically*. So when you're communicating with them or training them or coaching them on a specific skill, you need to make sure that at least a good part of the training includes hands-on utilization of the new system. Role playing, hands-on practice, on-the-job training—that is how they learn best.

Others are *readers*. They need to read the manual over and over again. They need to take some tests or assessments to make sure they really grasp the material.

Others like to *learn alone*. They learn best by using a software program or a tutorial in the privacy of their own station. As a coaching leader, you need to know who on your team learns this way, then look for resources that will align with their style.

Others are *synergistic*. They need to be in a group environment where the process or skill can be discussed and bantered around. They are most apt to learn the new skill or discipline in a group setting.

Others are *visual*. They need to see the information with their own eyes. For this group, videos and DVDs might be most effective, or going to an actual workshop might be the most effective method for learning a new skill set.

Others are *audible*. They do best listening to a program. They can listen to a presentation on the Internet, hear it through a CD course, or listen to you in a lecture setting. This group uses their ears to learn most effectively.

As a coaching leader, you must identify each of your teammates' unique learning styles. Ask yourself, "How does each team member learn best?" And it doesn't hurt to ask each teammate how he or she prefers to learn.

In the systems chapter (chapter 11) I'll talk about how you can take all of this information and effectively store it, systematize it, and utilize it so that you can become the best coach possible for each of your teammates.[1]

Encourage a Culture of Learning

As you increase your knowledge and share it with your teammates, you provide them with a fantastic opportunity to grow. Believe me when I say that's one of the greatest benefits of becoming a coaching leader!

Very few companies have the platform or the systems in place to help teammates get the continuing education they need to improve in their roles so that their jobs become more to them than just a way to pay the bills. A culture of learning enables teammates to become *more*. They grow as a result of being in your culture, whether you're directly coaching them or not.

Some companies sponsor learning lunches, where interested staff work their way through a book study. Other teams opt for video or audio programs on leadership, systems, or organization. In our company, we regularly do life-planning workshops, vision workshops, or teamwork workshops led by various members of our team. We also have invested in the Building Champions Management System to ensure that our methods are applied most effectively.

However and whatever you choose to learn, there's always an opportunity to grow—and that is one of the chief things observers commonly see in a thriving coaching culture led by a committed coaching leader.

Why not be one of them?

Key Benefits

What Knowledge does for your team members:

- Increases their respect for you.

- Increases their levels of knowledge and competency.

- Increases their overall value to the organization.

- Helps them to solve problems and to aid fellow teammates and clients.

- Challenges them to grow, which increases their self-worth.

What Knowledge does for the company:

- Gives you an "unfair" competitive advantage.

- Produces a more knowledgeable team that works together more effectively and profitably.

- Improves your company's reputation as a result of your team becoming better problem solvers.

What Knowledge does for you:

- Increases your influence.

- Increases your value to others.

- Increases your confidence.

- Helps you to make more right decisions.

TEN

The Skills
of a Coaching Leader:
The Necessary Abilities

Being coached will be a different experience, thought the CEO of a medium-sized, privately owned yacht dealership in San Diego, California. It was the questions that got to him.

"The questions my coach threw my way stopped me dead in my tracks," he said. "He wanted me to do more than just respond; he wanted me to reflect, assess, and really examine why I was building my company this way."

His coach didn't make it easy on him. Would his current structure allow him to use his gifts and talents to their fullest? Was he building the business in such a way that it encouraged him to live out his values? He didn't expect such questions, but they made a huge difference in his life and career.

"Uncommon questions from an uncommon coach caused me to make uncommon yet very right business decisions," he declared. "I believe these 'stop and think' type questions are helping me to build a business and life on purpose."

If you want to help your own teammates stop and think about what they're doing in their careers and in their lives, you need to learn and master a set of skills particular to a coaching leader. Coaching leaders intentionally develop some specific skills that enable them to enjoy more success in developing their team members. And in this chapter, I'll highlight a few of the skills that I consider most important.

ACTIVE LISTENING AND POWERFUL QUESTIONING

Questions have a power all their own, and the best way to show others that we care about them is to truly listen to what they say. Most leaders don't take the time to do this, nor do they really understand how to do it. And the reason is not hard to identify.

A large percentage of leaders are High *D*'s in the DISC behavioral language. They're dominant. They are thinking about what they need to say even while others are still speaking. They're reloading and preparing a response, which makes them less than great listeners. This doesn't mean they're bad people; they simply need to learn a new skill, which takes training and practice to develop.

Most of us have reached our places of leadership as a result of the advice we give, the direction we provide, and the decisions we make. So many of us, whether we own our companies or lead a department, have relied heavily on our ability to communicate in an instructional way, a very one-sided process. We'll observe a situation, think through all of the aspects of the problem, crisis, or opportunity, then inform our team members what each one needs to do, specifically.

The coaching leader must possess not only the instructional skill set, but also the active listening and powerful questioning skill set. Leaders who take on the coaching role sign up to intentionally help a teammate succeed but the coach's natural way of addressing a challenge may not be a good fit for the teammate. If coaches limit themselves to telling others how they did it, they're staying in the teacher or mentor role instead of moving into the coach role.

A coach attempts to draw out the meaning behind a team member's words, to understand the motive or the intent behind the spoken sentences. Active listening is all about asking questions that cause the player to peel back the onion, to get to the heart of performance issues, or to reveal limiting beliefs. These powerful questions, asked in many ways, will help you to best understand what's going on in the head and heart of your teammate. And after you ask these powerful questions, you acknowledge what your teammate is saying in response—that's active listening.

Suppose your teammate is telling you why she's having trouble learning a new skill, or why she's struggling with expanding her territory, or why she just can't get the hang of a new system. Every few sentences, you want to acknowledge that you're hearing what she's saying by repeating back what you believe you've heard. You don't parrot or repeat her words verbatim; it's more like summarizing the essential content of her statements.

Last night I had a dinner meeting with a gentleman who is interviewing to join our company. As I asked this potential coach several questions about his career and about why he might want to make a transition from his position as president of a company to becoming a coach in ours, I repeated back to him what I thought he was saying just to make sure I truly understood him. I didn't want to take anything for granted.

After he spoke for a couple of minutes, I said, "Okay, what I hear you saying is that one of the main reasons you want to become a coach is because there's nothing that brings you more joy or energy than developing people in a one-on-one relationship. Is that right?"

"Yes, that's what I said," he replied.

"You also stated," I continued, "that you've discussed it with your wife and kids, and as a family you are open to making a move to Portland. You've worked through this already, is that correct?"

He nodded his head.

"Okay, great," I responded. "I also understand that you've already mapped out a transition plan, both financially and professionally. You have built it already. Is that correct?"

"Yes, Daniel," he said, "you are hearing me."

As a coach, you want to make sure you understand the main nuggets in the conversation. When you're coaching a teammate, your whole objective is to make sure you grasp exactly what he's going through, where he feels bound up, where he is having success. You want that coaching session to end with the person taking ownership of a specific Action Plan that will enable him or her to continue moving forward and enjoying success. So if you don't understand exactly what he's going through, if you don't grasp the meaning and the heart behind his words, there's a good chance you're going to help create Action

Plans that will frustrate him and not lead him to the success he had hoped for.

Powerful questioning enables you to go from head to heart. Habits change only when convictions change or are clarified. Most people will not change their habits simply because they have the necessary knowledge. *They won't make a change until they have hurt enough, heard enough, or had enough—all heart-level experiences.* Powerful questioning enables you to probe a little deeper to help your teammates identify roadblocks, what's holding them back, or to suggest specific strategies or actions that will enable them to become more professionally and personally successful.

> *You can tell a man is clever by his answers. You can tell a man is wise by his questions.*
> — *Naguib Mahfouz*

The skill set of asking powerful questions enables you to ask a team member many questions around a specific issue. You seldom take a first response at face value. So if teammates are having difficulty in closing a transaction or a deal, for example, and the reason given is that they don't have access to the decision maker, you'll want to ask several questions about what they have done to approach the decision maker.

You can ask all sorts of great questions to get your teammates to think and to probe and to stop in their tracks so they can break through any barriers holding them back. When a teammate continually misses deadlines, for example, instead of saying, "Hey, when are you going to get that project done?" you might ask a powerful question: "Tell me, what do you think are the two or three greatest hindrances to your getting this done? What are the two or three specific things that we need to change in order for you to have success here?" Get the teammate to identify what, specifically, seems to be holding him or her back.

Understanding the heart of a team member takes work. When you become a coaching leader, you take a special interest in understanding what motivates and inspires your team members, as well as what might hold them back. You have no choice but to take the time to ask powerful questions and then to spend more time listening carefully to their answers.

At Building Champions, we tend to use numbers in our questioning. We try to get specific by asking a client to identify "the top three to five," "the top one to three," or "the top two" reasons behind some challenge. We want to force the individual to think hard about what is motivating him or holding her back. The more succinct the questions, the easier it is for the teammate to take ownership of the problem. And when the individual takes ownership of the problem, it's usually easier to take ownership of the Action Plans that lead to success. So we often ask questions such as the following:

- "What are the top three regrets you have today with regard to your personal and professional life?"

- "If money were no object, how would you spend the next ten years?"

- "If you could go back to school to learn a new skill or trade, what would it be?"

- "What would you say are the top two to three greatest limiting factors in your career or your life?"

> We coach most effectively when we do no more than 30 percent of the talking. I recommend a 70/30 model—the player talks 70 percent of the time; we talk the rest of the time. When our teammates discover their barriers and create their solutions, we are truly unleashing the power of the player.

Don't let the possibility of discomfort keep you from making an even greater difference. When coaches move from session to session, day in and day out, the greatest danger they have is that their relationship with their clients might get too comfortable—but a coaching session simply can't feel like any other meeting. It has to remain distinct, focused, and special.

Therefore, start off your coaching sessions by letting your teammate know that this time together is special and unique. You don't ask about the weather, the family, or the weekend. Get right to the heart of the matter. Ask questions with regard to areas of needed improvement previously identified by the teammate.

So instead of asking, "Hey Steve, how've you been? What's going on? How's your daughter?" you immediately let him know that you'll be jumping into the Action Plans or the projects he said he wanted to tackle since your last meeting. So if Steve wanted to learn about how best to utilize the company's database, you might walk into his office and say, "Steve, today the main thing we want to accomplish is to make sure you're making the progress you said that you wanted to make with the CRM." Before you get to pleasantries, before you get to any of the "normal" things that friends and colleagues usually talk about, let Steve know that you want to hear about the successes or challenges he has encountered with the CRM since you last met. Such an approach immediately lets Steve know that this session is about him growing and mastering whatever it is that he said he wanted to master.

As a coaching leader, you have to set the tone for your coaching sessions first, then make sure that you understand not only what is being said, but also the meaning behind the words. You do that through active listening and powerful questioning.

LEARN HOW TO TAKE GOOD NOTES

You will master active listening and powerful questioning more quickly if you learn to write down, or to enter into your system, all key points that you discuss during a coaching session. You do this not only to create a historical record that you can review from time to time, to make sure you're still on track with your player, but also to help you focus on what your team member says during the session. This is much easier to do if you conduct your coaching sessions with your teammates over the phone; it seems to be much more of a challenge to conduct these sessions face-to-face. It can be done, of course, but not as easily.

During some sessions, your mind may wander off to thoughts of e-mails piling up, or you may find yourself preparing what you want to say next. By writing down all the key points your teammate is communicating, you ensure that you're hearing not only the individual's words, but also the meaning behind those words. That helps you to actively listen.

I'm not talking here about writing down paragraphs or about taking down everything the team member is saying verbatim. Look for the nuggets, the core concerns, and the bullet points. Enter those into your system or write them down on a piece of paper that you'll keep in your player folder for future sessions (There's more to come in chapter 12 on the teammate folder). This skill isn't hard to master, but it's crucial.

GIVE CLEAR, APPROPRIATE, AND CONCISE DIRECTION

A good coach gives his or her team members a road map, a direction, so that if they can't figure out what they need to do next, the coach communicates in a linear fashion: "Do this first; let's figure out together how long it would take. Then next you do this." The coach helps them develop a game plan so that they can see what's required for them to improve.

This kind of communication can (and should) take various forms, because your teammates think and relate in different ways. The DISC model reminds you that you can't speak to all of your teammates in an identical manner.

Some of your team members will be more visionary, while others will be more linear. Visionary or artistic teammates tend to see the big picture with ease; they have little difficulty seeing things in a conceptual way. Those who are more linear will often have difficulty seeing the abstract. They don't easily picture how all the pieces come together; instead, they see things in a very systematic way and understand how, by connecting the dots, things get done.

Wise coaching leaders will know how each of their team members prefer to think and how they look at and tackle projects or problems. They then use this knowledge to help them shape how they communicate to best aid their teammates.

To the abstract or visionary team member, a coaching leader will give direction in a confident, clear, and concise way. Visionaries quickly grasp how some proposal might impact their performance or the organization, but they struggle with figuring out the steps required to execute that vision. As a coaching leader, you need to be able to communicate with your visionaries in a way that helps them to identify sequential, concrete steps that lead to success. Practice breaking down projects into five to ten specific steps so that you can show your visionaries how it might be done. This kind of help enables visionaries to execute a project, a new discipline, or a new skill.

Speaking to your linear teammates in a linear way, on the other hand, might be a waste of time. They "get it"; that's not where they need help. They need help in understanding the big pic-

> *Vision + execution*
> *= success*

ture. So a coaching leader will help them to think more in the abstract and get them to see how this project, when completed, will impact their department or their specific role. You have to take them up to thirty-five-thousand feet and talk about how this project will enable teams to improve communication, reduce turnover, increase job satisfaction, or expand system flow. You need to connect to their hearts so they can begin to take risks, break the old patterns, and begin to adopt new ones.

Coaching leaders see the immense value that both kinds of teammates bring to the table. Without individuals of both types on my team, our company would be nowhere near the organization it is.

Dave Anderson heads up our sales force and is a dear friend. He is an absolute visionary. He has the ability to conceptualize new products, new offerings, and new coaching experiences. This is what gets him most energized. He can think of how a product needs to be built and how that product or service needs to be delivered to the customer. He sees the big picture with ease.

But if I were to ask him to execute on his idea, the project would stall in three or four days. His strengths do not apply to the task of breaking down a project and allocating specific resources to get it done. His mind doesn't click with the details as it does with "big picture" things. His value to the organization is in his ideas, not in the implementation of them. He's great with relationships, both with our partners and our sales team. Without him, we would have maybe half the products and offerings we have today.

So if I'm coaching him to work through a problem or a challenge, I will ask, "This sounds like a great idea. What I need for you to do is to map out the five or ten basic steps that you think are required to get it done." He might make it sound as if we could just wave our magic wand and the project will be completed and offered to our customers within thirty days. "I want to make sure we do it with excellence," I might reply, "so you can help me by identifying what you think are the ten mission-critical steps for us to go from this concept today to execution."

As I coach, I'm always trying to encourage him to identify specific steps and specific time frames. Once he identifies the steps, I'm going to ask, "How much time do you think it will realistically take to get each of the steps finished? And do you or those on your team have the hours to get it done?"

I want to ask questions that will get him to think about all of the specific details, all of the functions, all of the man-hours, all of the resources. As a coaching leader, I want him to develop in this area. I don't need him to become excellent at it, but I want to help him so he becomes a more successful project manager or executor.

Another individual on our team heads our systems and technology department. Clayton Greer is very linear and easily masters the specifics; that's what makes him a great project manager. It's no problem for him to break projects into bite-sized pieces. The skill he brings to our organization is his ability to execute, to enlist all the right resources, and to get everyone to understand how many full-time man-hours are required and what kind of budget we need, and then to rally the team to execute the project.

He most often gets hemmed up in communicating with the rest of the team. So when I coach him, it's usually around relationships. Since my goal is to help him succeed, I have coached him on how to better communicate with teammates of different behavioral profiles. In a coaching session I might say, "Hey, you have to develop your friendship with so-and-so in another department. If that doesn't happen, you will greatly hinder your ability to get the project off the ground."

I have spent time working with him on "soft" skills, things that are more abstract and more difficult for him to get his arms around. He doesn't see those blind spots. So I work with him on how he presents, on how he casts vision for completing a project. I want to make sure that he's building into the people resources required to succeed.

I also want to make sure that when I'm speaking with a teammate about a topic, we're both talking about the same thing. When I say "chair," for example, what do you think of? You may think, *a place to sit*. I think of a specific blue rocking chair; even now I can see it. A single topic may generate a host of images.

Earlier this week, for example, two of my coaches and I were on a conference call with two business partners, owners of a very successful, multibillion dollar firm. We are helping them to work through a transition plan as they come into a season of five-year growth. As we talked about their roles and titles, I asked them to take five minutes to write down what they saw as the top three to five functions for a CEO, a CFO, and a COO. Through that exercise, I made sure that we were talking about the same thing. I knew what my two coaches and I were talking about, but I didn't feel so sure about my clients. To make progress, I knew we had to get on the same page.

To give clear, concise, and appropriate direction, a coaching leader needs to help both parties gain clarity around the specific topic of discussion.

Help Others to Create Concise Action Plans

Every coaching interaction should include the creation of new Action Plans, as well as follow up on existing Action Plans. Those plans should move your teammate closer to fulfilling his or her long-term strategy or goal. The Action Plans you help create should be so clear and specific that your teammate knows exactly what he needs to do, when he needs to do it, and how he's going to get it done.

Don't overload your teammate with too many Action Plans, and try not to leave coaching sessions without forming any Action Plans. We find that teammates execute best when they have three to five open Action Plans. When their list grows beyond seven, they become easily distracted and unfocused.

We have found a few keys to creating compelling Action Plans. Great coaches will ask a teammate at the appropriate time, "What specific action do you think you need to take to seize this opportunity?"

The team member might say, "I need to write five handwritten notes a day for the next ninety days," or, "I need to call every warm prospect in the database between now and next week." Help your teammates create specific, measurable,

> *The coaching relationship is all about helping your player improve. So Action Plans are going to be the essential ingredients; they're going to be what makes things happen.*

attainable, realistic Action Plans. You've probably heard the acronym, SMART:

Specific
Measurable
Attainable
Realistic
Time-sensitive

SMART Goal

Solidify one new contract that generates $100,000 in revenue in the fourth quarter. Our top three prospects to work with to make this happen by September are ABC, J & J and XYZ.

Not SMART Goal

Solidify as many contracts as it takes to increase revenue this year.

Every one of those traits is essential to creating compelling Action Plans. That means that every time you end a coaching session, you do so with the teammate describing the Action Plan just discussed. Team members should also report on any outstanding Action Plans—when they're going to get them done and how they're going to complete them.

You judge the success of a session by how well a teammate articulates the Action Plan just discussed. If a team member leaves the session able to articulate the Action Plan—including how she is going to get it done and when she is going to get it done—you know she has the highest probability of actually doing it. Then, at your next session, you immediately start off by following up on that Action Plan.

Tell the Truth & Value Accountability

A great coach knows how to address an individual's misconceptions and possible blind spots in a way that will highlight the problem without crushing the person.

To do this takes courage and a trust-based relationship, in which teammates know you have their best interests at heart. In effect, they're granting you permission to tell them the truth and to show them where they may need to smooth over some rough edges. Just by agreeing to have you as their coaching leader means they're welcoming this type of input.

When a blind spot holds back a teammate, you can help not only by pointing out the weakness but also by explaining how fixing it can bring great improvement. Nine times out of ten, this has to do with a "soft" skill, with people relationships, with communication habits, with how the person gels with the team. If we tell the truth in a hurtful way, however, the teammate will not welcome our coaching.

Because of the strong relationships you've built with teammates, they feel confident you're telling them the hard thing only because you want them to succeed. A coaching leader has the ability to tell team members what they may not want to hear so that they might become everything they'd always hoped to be.

Great leaders do not shrink from describing what they really see. They're not afraid to call someone on the mat. They do not hesitate to tell you when your behaviors are incongruent with the convictions or the values you identified earlier.

Get comfortable with the idea that accountability is a good thing. These days, many people get anxious when the topic of accountability comes up. And in fact, accountability seldom feels comfortable. Accountability means that some outside individual is asking you hard questions about your actions, making sure you're doing the things you said you wanted to do. Many leaders shy away from this. But while accountability in a coaching relationship can be uncomfortable, it yields terrific results. Accountability is often *exactly* the thing that helps someone to achieve his or her stated goals.

In his book *The Five Dysfunctions of a Team*, my friend and client Pat Lencioni lists the absence of conflict as one of the most critical dysfunctions of a team. Many leaders avoid conflict at all costs—but not a coaching leader. Coaching leaders don't enjoy conflict, but they understand that their teammates seriously desire to improve; that has already been discussed and agreed to. So entering into a relationship of accountability does not mean agreeing to bad conflict. All you're doing is making sure that your teammates do what they said they wanted to do, when they said they wanted to do it, in a way that brings them success.

According to Jim Rohn, business philosopher, author, and speaker, the ultimate sign of maturity is taking responsibility for one's own actions.

> *Accountability is the friend of top performers.*

That's what accountability helps your teammates do. So get comfortable with the idea that by holding them accountable, you help them to improve in their business and in their lives.

Building Champions has a program we call the Master's Coach. We get together every quarter with about forty of our highest performing clients. In our last quarterly meeting, we taught a lesson on how every champion has a way of preparing for the game. He has certain disciplines that he incorporates into his schedule on a daily, weekly, monthly, quarterly, and yearly basis to get mentally prepared for the battle of business. We call this "the Champion's Way."

In preparing for the lesson, I identified forty-three disciplines that I attempt to do on a daily, weekly, monthly, quarterly, and annual basis. I can't lead my team unless I lead myself. These forty-three disciplines enable me to have the highest probability of leading with success. They help me to be in the right spiritual, mental, physical, and emotional state to best impact those around me. They help me to be my best *me*.

At this quarterly retreat, we challenged participants to a team accountability contest. We asked everyone to identify three to five new disciplines (or existing disciplines they had yet to master), and then we created a contest. We invited the seven teams, each composed of about five members, to compete for ninety days to see who could best master these disciplines.

The response floored me. Despite the massive peer-to-peer accountability required, these professionals accepted the challenge with great excitement. They eagerly wanted to grow—and today we're seeing impressive results. The results have been so good, in fact, we're tracking and posting each team's performance on a website for the benefit of participating team members.

Here's the point: *They all stepped up when they learned there was going to be another form of accountability.* They understood it wouldn't be just us coaches holding them accountable; they would be holding each other accountable. And they responded with great enthusiasm.

Certain players on your team hunger for more accountability. They know they're not performing at top levels in business or in life, and they want you to play a greater role as a coaching leader by holding them accountable and by telling them the truth when it needs to be told. In that way you'll help them to stay on track and have the highest probability of accomplishing what they want to accomplish and becoming who they want to become.

BECOME PROFICIENT AT STORYTELLING

Seasoned coaching leaders will tell stories, use word pictures, and employ different styles of creative communication to help teammates understand what needs to be done.

With linear thinkers, you might need to tell stories to connect with their hearts. They're so analytical that grasping the abstract or the big picture can be a real struggle for them. So a coaching leader tells stories to help linear teammates hear not only with their heads but also with their hearts. Well-chosen stories enable them to gain a better understanding of why they might need to change their perspective on a situation or why they might need to take a bit more risk with a relationship.

Word pictures, verbal descriptions that bring a concrete picture to mind, can accomplish the same thing. Often when team members seem stuck or in a rut, the limiting factor is their perspective. They don't lack the necessary knowledge or skills or competencies; it's their beliefs that hold them back. They've strayed so deep into the forest that they can't see beyond the trees (that's a word picture, by the way). So you let them see what you see. By using word pictures, you try to pull them out of the forest so that they gain a better picture of what's possible for them.

Many successful coaches use storytelling and word pictures when they want to help someone adopt a new discipline. These coaching leaders tell stories or use a movie clip to help teammates see the new discipline as a good thing.

In the past few years, we've gotten a lot of mileage out of the movie *Miracle*, in which Kurt Russell plays a U.S. Olympic hockey coach. He takes a group of individual hockey players and turns them into a gold medal team. In one especially potent scene, Russell has his players working hard on the ice, running sprint drills. Even though the team had just lost a game, the players all display a lax and casual attitude. Their hard-nosed coach will not accept such a loser's mentality and has them repeat the drill over and over to the point of exhaustion. The players keep at it for probably ten minutes. Just when they think they're done, the coach blows his whistle once more and says, "Again. Again. Again." The weary players nearly get sick—and only then do they finally grasp a crucial lesson about the importance of teamwork.

For some time our coaching leaders have been showing this movie clip to their clients to highlight the necessity of working together, practicing, and perfecting what they do. Words might not get to certain team members, but a story often works wonders.

"But I'm not a natural storyteller," you say. "How can I use this skill?"

It helps to be a natural storyteller, of course, but you can learn to use the power of stories and word pictures even if this skill doesn't come naturally to you. When I first started my coaching company, I had to find a way to make sure I was connecting with my clients on the life-planning process. I needed something that could reach their hearts, not merely their heads. So I began to use a story called "The Station," out of the best-selling book, *Sixth Bowl of Chicken Soup for the Soul.* I read the story countless times to help my clients understand the brevity of life.

"The Station" compares life to a train trip. As we travel from one side of the country to the other, we look out the windows and see passing neighborhoods, city skylines, village halls, mountains, and oceans. But uppermost in our minds remains the station. We curse the minutes, anxious to reach the station. We expect that when we arrive, everything will be perfect and all will fall into place.

The author, Robert Hastings, says the station is nothing but a dream that consistently eludes us. The twin thieves, Regret and Fear, rob us of today. He reminds us that we'll get to the station sooner or later; what's important is how we take the trip.[1]

What is that station for you? Is it a new Mercedes? Is it retiring? Is it getting your kids off to college? Is it paying off your mortgage? Of what is it that you think, *When* that *happens, I'll really begin living*?

Time after time I read that story verbatim. I used someone else's creative story to help prove a point and connect with the heart. In fact, I continued to use that story until I developed the right life-planning story of my own.

A highschool friend of mine died of cancer at the age of thirty-eight. He and I spent the last year of his life together, all the way up to his last breath. Through this experience I learned to have a great appreciation for the brevity of life. I learned not to take for granted the big hand on the clock. I have no guarantee that I will live to see tomorrow. This story gave me the ability to speak with conviction about life planning. And I found that this story, all by itself, often would move people from intellectual acceptance of the idea to an emotion-packed decision to move ahead.

Until we take emotional ownership of a problem, a project, or an opportunity, most of us will not execute it wholeheartedly. But if every bit of us—both head and heart—feels consumed with getting something done or becoming something more than we are today, we'll gain a much higher probability of success.

Coaching leaders work not only to develop their own stories, but welcome the idea of using the potent stories of others. Does it get the lesson from the head to the heart? That's the ultimate goal.

STAY ON TRACK AND ON TIME

If you want to kill a coaching relationship, just arrive tardy to the session or fail to end it on time. In short order you'll tell your teammate, "You know, you don't really matter to me at all."

If you're going to follow our model, with sessions lasting from thirty to forty-five minutes, make sure you end on time. In that way you'll demonstrate good time management, efficiency, and respect for your teammate. You'll demonstrate that you are effectively controlling the content of the dialog, the pace of the meeting, and the outcome of your time together.

Great coaching leaders honor their teammates by sticking to agreed-upon time frames and by avoiding the temptation to be late, either at the beginning or at the end of the session. And by so doing they declare, loudly and clearly, "You're important to me. You matter. And I want to do all I can to help you succeed."

COMMUNICATION:
THE BIG DIFFERENCE MAKER

Coaching is communicating. Great relationships depend on many factors, but all of them funnel through the skill of communication. How we communicate impacts everyone and everything around us, all the time. That's why I maintain that good communication is one of the most essential life skills any coaching leader can master.

You probably know many people who have great brains and terrific hearts but suffer from relational mediocrity. What accounts for their dilemma? In my experience, most of them do not understand the power of personal communication. They think excellent communication is about what *I* say, but this is only partially true. In fact, it is not only what *I* say; rather, it is what I understand *before* I say.

What separates a coaching leader from a leader? It comes down to how they communicate. Coaching leaders listen carefully to their teammates and then speak careful words that instill belief and confidence, enabling those they coach to make better decisions and improve their performance. By mastering the skills we just outlined, you will position yourself to add value to everyone around you—and not merely from nine to five.

Key Benefits

What the Necessary Abilities do for your team members:

- Help them to discover what is holding them back.

- Get them to confront reality.

- Hold them to higher levels of accountability.

- Give them a higher probability of success.

- Show them what they need to do in order to improve.

What the Necessary Abilities do for the company:

- Increase overall levels of trust.

- Surface healthy conflict.

- Improve execution.

- Improve morale.

- Decrease turnover.

What the Necessary Abilities do for you:

- Help you better understand your people.

- Increase your value to your team.

- Drop your levels of anxiety as your follow-up improves.

- Help you become a more effective leader.

ELEVEN

The Disciplines
of a Coaching Leader:
The Consistent Behaviors

As I write this chapter, the XX Winter Olympic Games are in full swing. Every four years I look forward to watching these exhilarating competitions. And every time I tune in, I'm amazed at the extremely narrow gap in performance between the athletes who win gold, silver, and bronze, and the other competitors who miss the opportunity to see their countries flag's hang from behind the winners' podium.

An almost imperceptible gap—as little as a hundredth of a second—can separate those who get to hear their national anthem played over the roars of the crowd and those who can only watch the jubilant ceremony from the stands. *One one-hundredth of a second!* That just blows my mind. An athlete can be less than a blink of an eye behind a front-runner and not even place.

After each race, eager reporters swarm the medal winners for interviews. Very often you hear how the new champions submitted to grueling disciplines that were just a bit more radical, a bit more extreme, a bit more fanatical than the ones used by the great athletes they defeated. These Olympic heroes believed that such extraordinary disciplines would enable them to perform at uncommon levels. And now, for the rest of their lives, they can finger their gleaming medals and know they were exactly right.

Performing at uncommon levels is more than the goal of Olympic champions. It's also the goal of every coaching leader. More than anything, they want an uncommon leadership experience. While they loathe mediocrity, they also want more than great numbers or great earnings. They want great people to develop in great ways, and they want to be an integral part of the process. That's not common! But it is what separates coaching leaders from other fine leaders.

YOU FIRST!

Everyone on your team watches you. They really do! They take note of all your actions, all your reactions, and all your behaviors. They watch how you respond to challenges and opportunities; how you deal with vendors, customers, and suppliers. They mentally record what you identify as important, then watch to see if you live out your words.

What kinds of leaders have the most influence with their teams? My experience tells me that it's not always the most charismatic, verbally skilled, or best-educated leader who holds the most sway. Impressive résumés and a raft of MBAs simply don't guarantee influence. Most often, the most influential leaders are those who tirelessly live out their convictions. They may seem humbler and more reserved than some high flyers, but their disciplines— their financial disciplines, their planning disciplines, their health disciplines, their relational disciplines, their overall life disciplines—have enabled them to become who they are, and *that's* what their teammates find so attractive. Such obvious integrity tends to attract a very high level of respect. And influence is the natural result.

No doubt you've heard the old saying, "He walks his talk." In our company, we reverse the order to say, "He talks his walk." The two have to be congruent if our coaching is to have any effect. Nine times out of ten, it's

> *Your regular disciplines are the outward manifestation of your true convictions.*

the congruence between a leader's convictions and his or her consistent behaviors that prompts a team member to go to extraordinary lengths to grow. Most people lay it on the line for a leader of integrity who practices attractive and consistent disciplines.

Your example will demonstrate the disciplines in which you truly believe. Your walk will reveal what you really accept as true. Your regular disciplines are the outward manifestation of your true convictions.

So what does this mean for you?

By now you may have your Core Four completed. You have your Life Plan, Business Vision, Business Plan, and Priority Management piece all pre-

> *The first responsibility of a leader is to define reality. The last is to say thank you. In between, the leader is a servant.*
> — *Max DuPree*

pared. If so, you should have clarity for your life and business as never before. If you are like me (and the clients we serve), you also see some gaps, the gaps between where you are today with disciplines and what you desire for the days and years ahead.

CREATE A GAP LIST

As you compare your present schedule to your perfect week's time block, you probably see a real gap. Do not let this discourage you! You are already far ahead of the majority who never take the time to map out what they want to build professionally or personally. Imagine a contractor who specializes in remodeling homes. He must first envision the new structure before he starts demolishing the old one. He has to see the desired result before he can create and execute on plans to build a better structure.

So you must create a list of personal and professional areas of knowledge needed, systems needed, skills needed, and most important, disciplines needed. We call this "creating your Gap List." To create it you must review your Life Plan, Business Vision, and Business Plan with the purpose of identifying the most critical areas of required improvement. It may look something like the following.

Gap List

Life Plan

- Not sleeping seven hours per night
- Not drinking enough water
- Not dating weekly
- Not exercising consistently

Business Plan

- Not walking the floor daily
- Not reviewing the numbers weekly
- Infrequent and inconsistent team communication
- Not coaching teammates proactively

Once you know where the gaps are, you can focus on those areas and take steps to shore them up.

SHARE IT WITH YOUR TEAM

Now it's time to share a bit of your Core Four with your team members. Let them see where you're struggling, let them hear what you're aspiring to accomplish—and then live it out in front of them. Over time, as you gain more clarity around your Core Four, your team will start to see the positive changes in you, and they'll soon want more of what you have.

One of my clients leads a large company. He's a gifted leader with big vision. He's a High *D*, very assertive, aggressive, confident, and skilled at executing. When I first started working with him a few years ago, he had real trouble connecting with his team. That was his Achilles' heel, the biggest obstacle holding him back. Worst of all, he had no clue about any of his blind spots. And because he struggled with building strong and meaningful relationships, his team members never gave him or the company their all.

On a scale of 1 to 10, this man already was a level-8 leader. But unless he got the relational piece down, I knew he would never get to the tenth level. So he and I started working on the problem.

We began with a 360 assessment and obtained some honest feedback from his boss, peers, subordinates, and wife. I found out how he was doing, where he was helping them, and where he was hindering them from succeeding. I had the opportunity to conduct interviews with his assistant and with some of his other key team members. Soon we began working on the softer side of his leadership, developing specific disciplines to enable him to better connect with his people. He began

- walking the floor of the office first thing in the morning to greet his team;
- keeping his door open so that team members could come in and converse with him;
- arriving on time for meetings;
- starting conversations off with, "How are you?" and then waiting for a response;
- looking at those who were speaking to him instead of multitasking;
- getting home on time for dinner; and
- initiating a daily prayer time with his wife.

Since he also had some undisciplined eating habits (he was a ten-diet-soda guy every morning) and struggled with regular workouts (he disliked his appearance and continually berated himself for his lack of gym time), he soon replaced the diet soda with water and started taking a midday break to work out.

Do any of these changes seem revolutionary or earthshaking? Hardly. But even these little changes, consistently applied over a period of time, started to show his team and his family that he really did care.

Two years after our coaching relationship began, I had the opportunity to speak with his team and his wife once more. This time around, I heard a single phrase repeated consistently: "He is a changed man." Through coaching, he was learning how to live out his convictions, which enabled him to build high-trust relationships. As a result, his division now consistently performs at the top of his organization. And that's not all. He's also enjoying his job much more, even as his team members are better enjoying his leadership. Tenure, morale, and performance—they've all markedly improved.

He knew that his conviction of "people first" needed to be acted upon. When he started behaving in a way that was congruent with the convictions he'd identified in his Life Plan and Business Vision, life soon improved for everyone around him. His team members noticed that working out had become a nonnegotiable for him. Once they saw him doing something about an area in his life that he said needed improvement, their respect for him grew. And as a result, he is gaining the ability to coach others on his team.

How can you effectively coach others until you're living out what you're trying to coach? The little things, done repetitively over time, will turn you into a champion leader.

> *You can't effectively lead others until you've effectively led yourself.*

If you truly want to have the most influence possible over your team, you cannot overlook any aspect of who you are. That doesn't mean that you have to have everything mastered, of course. Nobody does. That doesn't mean that you have to be a level 10 in every aspect of life and business. It does mean, however, that you need to be consistent with the disciplines you have identified as integral to your success.

One of the greatest benefits to becoming a coaching leader is that your own disciplines—the consistent behaviors you carry out daily, weekly, monthly, and quarterly—are naturally forced to improve. As you coach others, your own game improves. It just happens.

As a champion coach, you have already completed your time block, Life Plan, Business Vision, and Business Plan. You're reviewing them regularly. You know what your three to five high-payoff activities are, as does everyone on your team. So you communicate them. You schedule them. You don't ask your team to time block or to create a perfect week until you've finished your own. You lead by example—and now I'd like to challenge you to identify one discipline in particular as a high-payoff activity: coaching. The reason is simple.

Coach's Corner

A client of mine is a coaching leader within his company and has experienced significant results in the development of his people. He is a good example of how to turn the skills of coaching into tangible gains for his company and his team. A specific example has been in the area of communication.

My client has several managers that report to him, one being a gentleman that was with the company prior to his arrival. This manager was headstrong and epitomized some of the characteristics of a Dominant behavioral style. My client was tasked with implementing a major philosophical shift in the way products were going to be sold and soon realized that he was going to need a different communication style if he was going to get this manager on board. He discovered that instead of "telling" this person what to do, he would instead "ask" him where he thought he fit in the vision and ask him where he thought he could add the most value to the vision. He also asked his opinions on how best to accomplish the vision. Soon this manager began to take ownership of the new initiative. He has become the number one salesperson leading the number one branch in his region in this new way of selling. He has also become the most outspoken advocate for the new sales process.

D. Barry Engelman
Senior Vice President, Coach
Development
Building Champions, Inc.

The best coaching leaders I know—those who effectively develop the talent around them, who have the highest performing teams, the most profitable divisions, and who boast the most tenure in the organization—are consistently those who consider people development as one of their three to five highest payoff activities. They see coaching as a primary responsibility, not as an add-on to their position. They have a deep conviction about developing their team-mates. Through coaching, they build their most appreciable asset, their people. And in the end, it pays big dividends for them.

DISCIPLINE YOUR SCHEDULE

How do I know that successful coaching leaders don't see coaching as some additional, extracurricular activity? I look at their schedules. When I do, I see that they reserve regular, consistent blocks of time for one-on-one people development time. I see they have scheduled time for reviewing the Action Plans of their teammates and for preparing for coaching sessions.

I see, in other words, that coaching has become a discipline.

As I have said throughout this book, you need to consider the scheduled coaching sessions between you and your team members as sacred. Nobody should be late or feel free to blow off a session. Treat each coaching session as if it were an appointment with one of your company's most valuable clients.

What happens if you need to reschedule with one of your company's most valuable clients? Do you give them plenty of advance notice? And you give a very solid reason for needing to reschedule. You would never say, "Hey, I just got too busy to meet with you," or "Sorry, but time just ran away from me." Only something significant would cause you to reschedule.

Train yourself to look at your coaching sessions in the same way. When you show up on time and are ready to go, the example you set encourages your teammates to do the same. Few things are more frustrating than coaching sessions that don't start on time or failure of a coach or player to show up. That is a sure-fire recipe for a coaching relationship to go sideways.

Also, make sure you follow through with your team members on all critical dates—that's a key discipline. If your team member plans to spend March 7 working on her Life Plan, for example, schedule an encouraging phone call or note to get to her the day before. Let her know that you're excited for her to go through the experience. And then schedule a follow-up with her the day after, making sure she knows you can't wait to see her plan.

The best coaching leaders encourage in advance, consistently follow up, then celebrate noteworthy accomplishments with their team members. In that way they build team momentum and the team member grows through the coaching process.

I must also admit that becoming a coaching leader has a downside. Your schedule may suffer. When you schedule coaching sessions a year in advance, as I strongly recommend, you're pretty much locking yourself into a rhythm and a routine—and that can feel a bit confining. You may initially feel as though you're getting less freedom instead of the greater freedom you had hoped for as you climbed the corporate ladder.

While I can't do much about that feeling, I can tell you it masks the real truth. For, in fact, although initially it may seem as though coaching takes away some of your freedom, you're actually creating more of it. And here's why.

If you intentionally, proactively develop your people, you'll end up spending far less time in reactive crisis mode, because your people will be growing in skill and competence. They'll know to save the real challenges for your coaching sessions, which means far fewer interruptions for you. So although you are scheduled a year in advance, your coaching sessions will so effectively set your teammates straight that you'll have more freedom to grow in other areas of your responsibility.

VALUE ACCOUNTABILITY

The topic of accountability has popped up throughout this book. Why? Because it's a key ingredient to a healthy coaching relationship. When clients come to us, one of the things they are hoping to get is more accountability. They know they need it to stretch and to reach even higher levels of performance.

Therefore, value accountability. Don't regret it or apologize for it. Treat it as a nonnegotiable discipline, and let it perform its crucial function.

This means scheduling regular checkup points on clients and teammates. I check in on my teammates on all kinds of items. I have one teammate, for example, who wants to exercise at lunch. He works out of the office, so I call. He said he wanted to be at the gym today at noon, so as I drove to an appointment, I dropped him a voice mail: "I know that right now it's lunch time, and my hope is that you followed through on your commitment to hit the gym. If not, there's tomorrow; don't beat yourself up. Get it done. And if you have, congratulations, I'm proud of you. Let me know how it went."

I may follow up with others on their commitment to make five sales calls in the afternoon. When I turn to my calendar, it directs me to follow up on how those calls went.

One of the greatest things I can do as a coach is to follow up with my teammates. Most leaders think they don't have time to follow up, but follow-up is the difference maker in building a team of champions. Your consistency and your commitment to following up—your discipline—will show your team how serious you really are about them improving. If you don't follow up, you could go through all the exercises suggested so far in this book, and it would be a gigantic waste of time. So discipline yourself to follow up. It's crucial for your success as a coaching leader.

And how should you follow up? Take your pick. You can communicate via e-mail, at meetings, one-on-one, or through phone calls or handwritten notes. The method can vary widely; the key is that you regularly follow up.

Remember, too, that different levels of accountability exist. At times you'll have to hold your team members accountable more frequently. If a team member has a difficult habit change that she wants to incorporate into her business or her life, it could be a make-it-or-break-it proposition. In that case, you might have to launch the discipline of holding her accountable every day. While this kind of high accountability isn't the norm, you'll do whatever is necessary—*if* your goal is to help your teammates improve.

BE SURE TO ENCOURAGE THEM

While all of the disciplines highlighted in this chapter are important, make sure you don't overlook one of the most critical: encouragement. If your teammates know that you genuinely care about them (and not just about increasing revenue or meeting quotas), they will respond in amazing ways. Regular encouragement can accomplish far more than frequent faultfinding.

Again, you can choose from a variety of ways to encourage your teammates. Handwritten notes, a public "well done" in front of peers, positive e-mails, upbeat voice mails—all are disciplines that a coaching leader will utilize to build a coaching culture.

OVER AND OVER AGAIN

"What I have liked most since becoming a coaching leader is how my own life has improved."

"The decisions I am making and the new disciplines that are forming are truly enabling me to enjoy even greater success at work and at home."

We hear statements like this all the time from coaching leaders we have coached and certified. Throughout this book, I have mentioned that your own quality of life improves as you coach others to ever-greater success. I have insisted that it has been the single greatest unexpected benefit of becoming a coaching leader.

I don't want to boast or to suggest that I have arrived or have it all together. I haven't and I don't! But by coaching others on my team to be congruent, to excel, to bring even more value to the marketplace, my game has improved in every aspect of my life. My quiet times, workouts, eating routine, meeting preparation, reading, learning, and dating my wife and kids—they all have improved. By coaching others, I have improved my own disciplines and, as a direct result, my overall quality of life.

So get ready for your own game to improve as you focus on helping others to improve theirs.

Key Benefits

What Consistent Behaviors do for your team members:

- Improve their effectiveness.
- Increase confidence as they better live out their convictions.
- Improve their performance.
- Aid them in following through, therefore improving how they view themselves.
- Clarify priorities.
- Increase accountability.

What Consistent Behaviors do for the company:

- Improve overall team performance.
- Improve morale.
- Minimize wasted time.
- Improve execution.

What Consistent Behaviors do for you:

- Improve your performance.
- Eliminate hypocrisy.
- Increase clarity.
- Improve the quality of your personal and professional life.

Twelve

The Systems
of a Coaching Leader:
The Organizational Tools

We could not do what we do at Building Champions without the many systems we utilize. Our foundational system is our proprietary coaching platform that enables us to achieve a high degree of intimacy with those we coach. At any given time, our full-time coaches are coaching from forty to seventy business leaders—and without systems, they would have no way to keep everything straight.

We've seen how the systems we've developed for our own coaches can tremendously benefit leaders who coach far fewer individuals. As we have trained business leaders to improve their coaching skills, many have become coaching leaders within their own organizations and use modified versions of our systems. Through these systems, one can methodically and consistently conduct coaching sessions, organize one's thoughts, and most important, follow up with team members to keep them on track.

In this chapter I want to walk you through what I consider to be a few essential and easy-to-use systems. At chapter's end I will also outline some beneficial systems that, while not essential, can definitely make your job as a coaching leader a lot easier.

Why reinvent the wheel? What follows will give you some proven, basic systems that can help you to become a better coach.

Start with the Essential Systems

The first component of an effective coaching system concerns fact-finding and information gathering. When you're about to enter into a formal coaching relationship with one of your teammates, you should clearly spell out several things from the beginning.

Any formal coaching relationship should start off with an *agreement* and a *questionnaire* that you have your teammate complete.

1. A basic coaching agreement. This agreement outlines what is expected from both the coach and the teammate, and it also lays out the specific period of engagement.

Why do you need a formal agreement? While you may continue to be someone's manager and leader for many years, you may coach the individual proactively only during certain seasons. You may be coaching the person informally right now. But I'm talking about entering into a more intentional coaching relationship, designed to help this person improve in the areas that matter most to him or her. Therefore, any such agreement should include the following items:

- *What's expected of the teammate.*

The teammate agrees to be honest and truthful in all aspects of the coaching relationship, to come to sessions prepared, and to complete the agreed-upon Action Plans on time. The individual agrees to give 100 percent to the coaching sessions, acknowledging that he or she is entering into this coaching relationship for one purpose: to improve in business and/or life.

- *What's expected of the coach.*

You agree to be honest and truthful in all aspects of the relationship, to come prepared and on time to the sessions. You agree to follow up as necessary with the teammate to keep him or her on track and to do all you can to keep him or her inspired and on purpose with regard to the areas previously identified for growth.

- *The term of the coaching engagement.*

How long does a coaching relationship last? Three months? Six months? One year? A lot of our coaching leaders choose the one-year option; this seems to be the most effective period of time.

- *The length and frequency of the coaching sessions.*

We have found thirty-minute sessions, every two weeks, to be most effective.

As you can see, this agreement is neither exhaustive nor overly formal. You simply want to lay out the basic ground rules for the coaching relationship so that both you and your teammate have a good platform from which to launch your new relationship.[1]

Remember, you coach only those teammates who want to be coached; coaching cannot become mandatory. Compulsory coaching relationships simply do not work because they lack the underlying desire for improvement that makes coaching viable. A coaching agreement, mutually agreed to, says to your teammate, "This is above and beyond what I'm doing as your boss. By signing this agreement, we both freely agree to commit ourselves to the deeper responsibilities involved in coaching. And we do so for one purpose only: to help you make the improvements in business and life that you identify as areas of need or opportunity."

2. *A basic questionnaire.* Once you have both signed the coaching agreement, have your teammate fill out a simple questionnaire that gives you all the vital information you need about him or her, personally, professionally, and financially. While some coaching leaders prefer to get this information through a casual interview, most use a written document containing twenty to thirty pertinent questions.

Our client questionnaires at Building Champions feature more than seventy questions, but you don't need anything nearly as comprehensive as that. Why not? You already know your teammates. When clients come to us, they're strangers, so we have more gaps to fill in than you do. Since it's more than likely that you already have a substantial track record with the individuals on your team, you don't need to ask a lot of the questions on our questionnaire. It would be redundant for you (and a waste of time for your teammates).

I recommend that you develop your own basic questionnaire. The goal is to find out a few key pieces of information: Where does the individual want to improve? What are his or her goals? What struggles does he or she have? What dreams or ambitions can the individual identify for you? Consider a few sample questions you may want to include:

- What does success look like for you in your current position?
- What are your personal, professional, and financial goals in the year ahead?
- What are your dreams?
- Rank yourself on a scale of 1 to 10 in the following areas: organizational skills, planning, communication, etc. (Ask questions specific to your team and your line of work. If you're running a sales department, you could ask about prospecting, client follow-up, or making presentations. If you're running an operations department, ask about project management or utilizing the company's systems. Use the 1 to 10 scale to ask questions appropriate to the product or services of your company or organization.)
- Identify your number-one need. What's the one thing you would most like to see improve in the year ahead?
- What do you consider to be your business strengths and weaknesses?
- What is your vision for yourself personally and professionally ten years from now?
- Rate your personal life on a scale from 1 to 10.

- Rate your health on a scale from 1 to 10.

- What do you expect of me as your coach in the year ahead?

Questions like these form a good basis for a helpful questionnaire. This kind of information will enable you to spend a few minutes, prior to every session, to get reacquainted with each of your teammates, to know what they consider most important, and to recognize their unique needs, strengths, and weaknesses. Getting familiar with this document and having its information at your fingertips will best prepare you to be "in the moment" with each of the teammates you coach.

Without question, you'll get to know your coached teammates more intimately than your other employees. And the more you know about who they are off the job, the better you will be able to help them to improve in the areas of business and life they identify as most important to them. I strongly suggest that you run your questions by your HR department to ensure they do not violate any laws or corporate policies.

3. Your mental helper. As mentioned previously, at Building Champions we have developed our own proprietary coaching software. We have a CRM that we use to track and report on every aspect of a coach-client relationship. This enables our coaches to achieve a high degree of intimacy with a large number of people. It works as an extension of our coaches' minds, continually reminding them of when things are due, what to discuss in future sessions, and what is most important to each client.

A lighter version of this system works very well for most coaching leaders. You can learn more about our proprietary system at www.becomingacoaching leader.com You can use anything from an off-the-shelf database system, such as ACT or Goldmine, to a simple spreadsheet or a manila file folder with lined paper inside. Back in the '80s, the very first coaching system I used was the manila file folder. It worked beautifully. I've been teaching many coaching leaders throughout the country how to build this system, and they're using it with great success.

As you already know, I'm a big believer in simplicity. The easier a system is to use, the higher the probability that you'll use it—and that is what it's all about. Therefore, for every one of your teammates with whom you are entering into a formal coaching relationship, I recommend that you create a manila file folder, a Teammate Folder with the individual's name on it. What you put inside gets stored as follows.

- *On the left-hand side of the folder*:

Fasten in about ten pages of notepaper. You'll use these pages to enter in all the key points from your coaching session conversations. You can use your notes to get your bearings later in the conversation or later in the relationship.

In the left-hand margin, write down the date of each session. At the end of that session, draw a line under your notes, then write down whatever specific Action Plans you both have developed. Each session might have from three to five Action Plans, with a due date written in the right-hand margin. Cross off each Action Plan as it is completed. In that way you can easily see any Action Plans that are outstanding or that have had their due dates modified.

Four or five months into a coaching relationship, you might note the left-hand side of the folder and see that certain Action Plans have yet to be done. You'll see the dates that the individual committed to, recommitted to, then recommitted to again. Every time an Action Plan completion date gets bumped, write down the reason under that Action Plan. What happened? Why is the individual struggling with it? And what's the new date?

Under the note pages on the left inside of the folder, keep your coaching schedule. We advise our coaching leaders to have a printout of the entire year's coaching sessions on one document so that both parties have it.

Also on the left-hand side, use a different color of paper to track the key goals and areas for which the person most wants accountability. Key goals, broken down into realistic time frames, could be anything from production numbers to market share to certain efficiencies within the organization. Or they may be financial goals, personal goals, health goals, reading goals, or the like. Track *anything* that is important to the person.

- *On the right-hand side of the folder:*

Here you'll keep the coaching agreement that both you and your teammate have signed, as well as the completed questionnaire. On top of these two documents you'll fasten all the completed tools the individual will send you as he or she completes Action Plans related to the Core Four.

It's very easy to pull out this file folder, look at any open Action Plans, scan the questionnaire, and review the Core Four so you can get centered on the things the person wanted to accomplish. You can look at the disciplines listed in the Business Plan. You can study the Life Plan activities the individual highlighted or scan the elements of the Business Vision. It's all there on the right-hand side, in one easy place.

And that's it. It's not complex. And yet, for the last twenty years or so, this has served as a very effective system for countless coaching leaders across the country. This simple system enables you to immediately pick up where you left off last session. It also gives you a great tool for scheduling appropriate follow-up.

If you're more technologically advanced, you can design your own software application; some of our coaching leaders have done exactly this in programs like Excel or Word. Others use our proprietary Coachbuilder System™. They keep an electronic file folder in Outlook or some other application that tracks it all. If you are gifted in this way or you have someone on your team who can assist you with it, fantastic. Others use our proprietary Coachbuilder™ System. But that doesn't mean you have a leg up or you're a better coach than the one using the paper system. Again, use whatever works best for you, especially taking into consideration whether you're a mobile leader who's constantly moving from office to office and covering a large territory, or whether you're always in a single geographic location.

4. A basic coaching routine. Set up your scheduling system to help you most effectively coach your teammates. From experience, I can categorically state that quarterly sessions don't work. Monthly is probably right for many coaching leaders, but I think bimonthly sessions are usually the most effective.

Sometimes the best thing you can do at the beginning of a coaching session is to immediately focus on a troubled Action Plan. This usually involves some issue the person has consistently said he wants to improve upon or a project he wants to complete, but you see persistent procrastination or some stubborn hurdle. So start off the session by jumping into that Action Plan, perhaps something like the following:

"Rick, before we get into any new business and before we discuss anything that's taken place since our last conversation, I want to dive into the Action Plan that we created seven months ago, back in June. You originally wanted to have it done by the end of August, then by the end of October, then by year's end—yet here we are in February, and it's still not done. I am concerned. Let's spend some time figuring out whether this is really important to you. Let's talk about the benefits of getting it done and the consequences of not getting it done so that I'm not continually hounding you on something that may not be all that important."

> *What leaders consistently pay attention to, reward, control, and react to emotionally communicates most clearly what their own priorities, goals, and assumptions are.*
> —*E. H. Schein* [2]

Starting off the dialog like this differs markedly from how a manager might start off a dialog on a similar problem. It's a unique style of communication that we highlighted in chapter 10, "The Skills of a Coaching Leader."

To get an even clearer idea of how effective systems can help you, the following "Thirty-Minute Coaching Session Guide" may offer you some valuable assistance.

Action	Description	Suggested Timeline
Welcome; Opening Question	Tie in the last session	1-3 minutes
Provide direction to this session	Get Team Member agreement; identify #1 need for today's session	1-2 minutes

Action Plan review	Review status on Action Plans completed since last call or still outstanding	2-3 minutes
#1 Need	Begin dialogue and coaching on team member's #1 need	13-16 minutes
Establish Action Plans	1. Determine APs 2. Ask Team Member what success of APs will look like (and perceived benefit) 3. Have them repeat APs with commitment dates	5 minutes
Close and end call	Encouragement and closure	30 seconds
Coaching wrap-up	Fill in topic or ideas for next call in system for follow-up	1 minute

CONSIDER SOME BENEFICIAL SYSTEMS

In addition to what we have just discussed, you'll probably want to build a reservoir of information designed to help you improve as a coach and to encourage growth in those you coach. Most coaching leaders begin to file stories, testimonials, examples, studies, and tools for all key areas that repeatedly seem to come up in coaching contexts.

This reservoir of information becomes your key resource tool. Many coaches like to create filing systems that include:

- A Life Plan folder featuring great examples of Life Plans (or components of Life Plans), taking out names to ensure confidentiality. It may also include great stories that help clarify the need for Life Planning.

- A Business Vision folder that collects great examples of these completed documents and affirms the benefits of having completed such a document.

- A Business Plan folder that collects great examples of this third element of the Core Four. It may also include your favorite articles on how to most effectively build and utilize a Business Plan.

- A Priority Management folder that features time-management articles and tools others have developed to help them better manage their time and schedules.

- Inspirational stories, quotes, poems, and cartoons.

- Articles or studies on how employees become more productive and fulfilled when working in environments where they feel their life matters.

- Articles that explain why it is important to live a more balanced life.

- Materials on effective teamwork.

- Materials on improving communication in the workplace.

Many of the best leaders I've coached have developed filing systems for all sorts of resources they use to effectively lead their people. The foregoing topics merely suggest some of the categories you may want to create for your own files. Start off slow, and wherever you see continual need, create a file for it. Then add to it as you see fit.

CONFINED OR FREE?

> *Systems and procedures can formalize the process of "paying attention" and thus reinforce the message that the leader really cares about certain things.*
> —*E. H. Schein*[3]

Many visionary and entrepreneurial leaders believe that systems tend to confine or limit them. They believe their success depends upon their ability to react and respond to each opportunity or challenge in a unique way. I have found the opposite to be true.

While I am not naturally a guy who likes to systematize my days or activities, I have come to realize (as have many of our clients) that one can find real freedom by creating and then following systems designed to improve performance. Such systems allow you to operate with much more efficiency and effectiveness, resulting in even more freedom to do what you consider most valuable to you and your organization.

And isn't that the point?

Key Benefits

What the Organizational Tools do for your team members:

- Makes them feel more listened to and cared for.

- Prepares them for your undivided attention.

- Forces them to be even more accountable, increasing the likelihood they will make the changes they desire.

- Gives them a better coaching experience.

What the Organizational Tools do for the company:

- Improves the overall quality of the team.

- Creates a leader who excels at follow-up and people development.

- Improves the culture of execution and accountability.

What the Organizational Tools do for you:

- Gives you confidence and peace of mind because nothing slips between the cracks.

- Keeps you on track and better organized.

- Prevents you from neglecting any teammate, because you're intentionally with each one every two weeks.

- Makes you more credible and better at accountability and follow-through, skills that help you to succeed.

EPILOGUE

The Champion Challenge

I just returned from a five-day Todd Duncan conference called Achieving Leadership Excellence. Todd, a group of our Building Champions coaches, and author Tim Sanders worked with a group of about seventy-five participants to identify the best practices of excellent leaders. You can learn more about Todd's masterful training offerings at www.toddduncan.com

One specific leadership attribute seemed to consistently rise to the top. Can you guess what it was? I've boxed it here.

As I've said already many times in this book, coaching leaders feel driven to make a positive difference in the lives of those around them. So here's the key question: Do *you* have a deep conviction about making a positive difference in the lives of others? That's what it will take to become an outstanding coaching leader.

> *Excellent leaders have deep convictions about serving their teams and their clients in uncommon ways.*

Although by now you have been equipped with many of our proven philosophies, strategies, processes, and skills, be aware that all sorts of obstacles will confront you as you launch into your new role as a coaching leader. Your opponents will use many masks—busyness, company policy, doubt, fear, packed schedules, and a host of others—to disguise themselves. Don't let them discourage you!

I challenge you to step out of the business norm. I challenge you to re-invent yourself as a leader who chooses to add "coach" to your resume. Take what will work for you from this book and use it to make an even greater difference in the lives of the men and women on your team.

I'm confident that you will find, just as thousands of others already have, that your decision to coach will have hugely beneficial ramifications far beyond what happens in your office from nine to five. Your new skills will aid you tremendously as a spouse, parent, and friend. Count on it!

Remember, life and work are not slowing down; in fact, the pace continues to increase. Work no longer has boundaries that stop at the office walls. As a result, your teammates can often feel overwhelmed—and that's why they are seeking out honest, passionate, difference-making leaders as never before.

So what does this mean for you? It means you will have to fight the reactive "busyness machine" with all of your strength if you are to fully embrace what you have learned in these pages.

Coach, develop those around you so that they can live and work with more passion, focus, and skill. In the end, I believe that's what becoming a coaching leader is all about. It's about living a life—and equipping others to live a life—full of

Fulfillment,

Purpose,

Intentionality, and

Effectiveness.

As you endeavor to become a coaching leader, I know you will enjoy heightened levels of satisfaction and performance. So, Coach, change your ways, change your title, and enjoy serving as a catalyst that changes lives. My team and I are here to help you in any way we can.

ACKNOWLEDGMENTS

This book is dedicated to my mom and dad.

Thank you for always believing in me.

No book project is the result of just one individual. I am incredibly grateful to those who directly and indirectly helped me to document our leadership model.

First off is my bride Sheri. You are my strong beauty. Thank you for all of your insights, coaching, and for your belief in me. I love you.

Thank you to my awesome kiddos, Allie, Dylan, Wesley, and Emily for being there to eat and hang with me when I needed my midday breaks from writing. I love you guys so very much!

Thanks to my awesome teams at Building Champions and Ministry Coaching International. I am grateful to all of you for believing in our vision, making it a reality, and for all you do to make BCI and MCI special places to work. I must mention the special contributions of Katie Hoffman, Jessica Traffas, Raymond Gleason, Steve Scanlon, Kate Wilson, Heidi Scott, Tim Enochs, Dan Meub, Barry Engelman, Tammy London and Greg Harkavy. Your help was invaluable!

Thanks to Beth Hegde for helping me to launch this project and to my writing coach and collaborator, Steve Halliday for really bringing this project home. You caught my voice, Steve.

Thanks to Todd Duncan for writing books first and showing me that it could be done. More importantly, for believing in me and the Building Champions team. I so appreciate you and all you have done for us.

Thanks to Gene Wood, my coauthor of Leading Turnaround Teams. Thanks for inviting me into the book writing process and for the role you played in my life.

To Mike Hyatt for turning the tables in a coaching session or two and challenging me to write this book.

To Michael Van Skaik for being the catalyst for BACL with his company. You caught the vision Coach.

To Pat Lencioni and Amy Hiett for volunteering to help me. Your insights have been so greatly appreciated.

To my B.O.B. Thanks for walking by my side.

And finally to the Lord. I am so very grateful!

A Road Map
for Implementation

What good would a book on coaching be without a road map for implementation? I have done my best to give you a proven plan, complete with time frames, that I feel confident will give you the best chance at success. Still, I believe you will be most successful if you go through the book one more time to identify which chapters cause you the most trouble. Once you know that, tackle the troublesome chapters in the order in which they appear in the book.

If, for example, you are already clear on your Life Plan and are utilizing it as stated in chapter 5, but have struggled to implement the ideas in chapter 6, "Your Business Vision," then make the latter your first Action Plan.

Below you will find a fourteen-week schedule to fully execute your coaching leader plan (I assume you will create or revise each plan you may be using).

14-WEEK PLAN TO BECOMING
A COACHING LEADER

Action Plan	Time Required to Complete	Week
Reread the book	3 hours to review	1
Create your implementation plan	1 hour	1
Schedule ON Time for each step below	1 hour	1

Life Plan	8 hours (without interruption)	2
Business Vision	8 hours (without interruption)	4
Business Plan	6 to 12 hours (in 2 to 3 sittings)	6
Perfect Week Time Block	2 hours	7
The Knowledge of a Coaching Leader		
• Self Development Plan	2 hours	7
The Systems of a Coaching Leader		
• Create your coaching agreement	1 hour	9
• Create your coaching questionnaire	2 hours	9
• Create your coaching folders	2 hours	10
• Create your coaching schedule	2 hours	10
The Skills of a Coaching Leader		
• Active listening	Practice daily	
• Creating concise Action Plans	Review daily	
The Disciplines of a Coaching Leader		
• Create your Gap List	1 hour	11
• Schedule time to close gaps	1 hour	11
Invite your team into a coaching relationship		12
Teammates complete questionnaires and contracts		13
Conduct first sessions with your teammates		14

The key to your success in this next phase of your leadership journey is to commit to the time you need for each Action Plan, then follow through on each of your commitments. Make it happen, Coach!

We'd love to hear from you about your experience with this book. Please go to **www.thomasnelson.com/letusknow** for a quick and easy way to give us your feedback.

Love to read? Get excerpts from new books sent to you by email. Join ShelfLife, Thomas Nelson's FREE online book club. Go to **www.thomasnelson.com/shelflife**.

NOTES

Chapter Two

1. http://www.abiworld.org
2. http://www.cdc.gov/od/oc/media/pressrel/fs051028.htm
3. http://www.cdc.gov/nchs/fastats/divorce.htm
4. http://stats.bls.gov/oco/ocos056.htm
5. Claire Raines, *Connecting Generations* (Ontario: Crisp Learning, 2003)

Chapter Three

1. Daniel Goleman, *Emotional Intelligence* (New York: Bantam, 1998)

Chapter Five

1. James 4:14.
2. Psalm 90:12.
3. Luke 12:48.

Chapter Six

1. Jim Collins and Jerry Porras, "Building Your Company's Vision." *Harvard Business Review,* September/October 1996.
2. Michael E. Gerber, *The E-Myth Revisited: Why Most Small Businesses Don't Work and What to Do About It* (New York: Harper Collins, 2004), 69-70.

Chapter Eight

1. Richard A. Swenson, *Margin: Restoring Emotional, Physical, Financial, and Time Reserves to Overloaded People* (Colorado Springs: NavPress, 2004), 13.
2. Ibid.
3. Bobb Biehl, "Quick Wisdom-Balance," *Quick Wisdom E-mails,* 6 Sept. 2006. www.quickwisdom.com/Quick/WisdomEmails/7180/Balance.lsp
4. Kevin McCarthy, *The On-Purpose Person* (Colorado: Pinon Press, 2001), 59.

Chapter Nine

1. At Building Champions we have developed another set of tools designed to increase the knowledge of a coaching leader. If you'd like to access those tools, go to our Web site at (www.becomingacoachingleader.com).

Chapter Ten

1. Jack Canfield, *Sixth Bowl of Chicken Soup for the Soul* (Deerfield Beach, FL.: HCI, 1999), 341.

Chapter Twelve

1. If you'd like to see a sample agreement, check out our Web site at www.buildingchampions.com/becomingacoachingleader.

2. E. H. Schein, *Organizational Culture and Leadership*, 2nd ed. (San Francisco: Jossey-Bass, 1992), 254.

3. Ibid., 265.

BUILDING CHAMPIONS™

COACHING BUSINESS AND LIFE ON PURPOSE

Since 1996 we have been equipping leaders with the skills, knowledge and disciplines needed to succeed in business and in life. Contact us today to learn how we can help you move from idea to implementation.

PROGRAMS INCLUDE:

One-On-One Executive Coaching
One-On-One Sales Coaching
Custom Onsite Coaching Workshops
Team Performance Assessments

BECOMING A COACHING LEADER™ CERTIFICATION

If you want to truly master what you have just read, this program is the answer. The Becoming a Coaching Leader™ Certification Program is a leadership development experience designed to train and equip leaders to intentionally and strategically develop their teams to their full potential. It consists of a one-year certification track that includes live and virtual training, our coaching platform, all systems and tools. Visit www.becomingacoachingleader.com to learn more.

TURNING IDEAS INTO ACTION
SINCE 1996